What People Are Saying About
Chicken Soup for the Parent's Soul . . .

"Being a parent is life's greatest privilege. *Chicken Soup for the Parent's Soul* is a joy to read. I will treasure the personal stories and share them with my children and their children. What a lovely reminder of the miracle that is family."

Dr. Caren Kaye, Ph.D.
director of Parent Education,
Los Angeles Unified School District

"Inspirational storytelling has been a part of the human experience since the earliest cave drawings. *Chicken Soup for the Parent's Soul* provides a wonderful visionary guide, full of hope, wisdom and encouragement, to help anyone through the peaks and valleys of parenthood. A must-read."

Larry Shaw, Ph.D.
director of Family Counseling, Hollywood YMCA

"Whether you're thinking of becoming a parent, new at parenting or your children have left the nest, *Chicken Soup for the Parent's Soul* is for you. These stories are witty, funny, comforting, inspirational and helpful. There is something here for everyone."

Jennifer Chikato

"*Chicken Soup for the Parent's Soul* offers a kind of 'kitchen-table wisdom' for mothers, fathers, grandparents and stepparents alike. It heals, consoles, nurtures, teaches and reminds us of what parenting is all about."

Terri Festa

P9-DHN-029

"Take an hour out of your busy life and sit down and read *Chicken Soup for the Parent's Soul*. These stories are full of heart, life and love—they will nourish you and revive your spirit! I couldn't put it down!"

Sue Harvey

"The stories in *Chicken Soup for the Parent's Soul* show, again and again, that even when we are attending to the often mundane details of our children's lives—whether it is a spinning plate, a Barney video or a pickle jar—the Big Love we have for them shines through in rainbows of color. It seems both beauty and love reside in the details. Throughout this book you will laugh and cry; you will reminisce and daydream; but most important, you will always feel at home."

Mike Riera
author of *Field Guide to the American Teenager*
and *Uncommon Sense for Parents with Teenagers*

CHICKEN SOUP
FOR THE
PARENT'S SOUL

Stories of Loving,
Learning and Parenting

Jack Canfield
Mark Victor Hansen
Kimberly Kirberger
Raymond Aaron

Health Communications, Inc.
Deerfield Beach, Florida

www.hci-online.com
www.chickensoup.com

We would like to acknowledge the following publishers and individuals for permission to reprint the following material. (Note: The stories that were in the public domain, or that were written by Jack Canfield, Mark Victor Hansen, Kimberly Kirberger and Raymond Aaron, are not included in this listing.)

The Pickle Jar. Reprinted by permission of A. W. Cobb. ©1999 A. W. Cobb.

Geraniums of Love. Reprinted by permission of Harriet Xanthakos. ©1999 Harriet Xanthakos.

The Tooth Fairy. Reprinted by permission of Elaine Decker. ©1999 Elaine Decker.

The Good Stuff. Excerpted from *It Was on Fire When I Lay Down on It.* ©1988, 1989 Robert Fulghum. Reprinted by permission of Villard Books, a division of Random House, Inc.

Let's Go Fly a Kite and *My Ray of Hope.* Reprinted by permission of Robert Dixon and Zan Gaudioso. ©1999 Robert Dixon and Zan Gaudioso.

My Second Birth. Excerpted from *Expecting Adam* by Martha Beck. ©1999 Martha Beck. Reprinted by permission of Sanford J. Greenburger Associates, Inc.

(Continued on page 359)

Library of Congress Cataloging-in-Publication Data

Chicken soup for the parents soul : stories of loving, learning, and parenting / [compiled by] Jack Canfield ... [et al.].
   p.   cm.
   ISBN 1-55874-748-6 (hardcover) — ISBN 1-55874-747-8 (trade paper)
   1. Parenting—anecdotes.   2. Parent and child—Anecdotes.

HQ755.8.C447 2000
649'.1—dc21   00-040699

©2000 Jack Canfield and Mark Victor Hansen

ISBN 1-55874-747-8 (trade paper) — ISBN 1-55874-748-6 (hardcover)

Publisher: Health Communications, Inc.
          3201 S.W. 15th Street
          Deerfield Beach, FL 33442-8190

Cover redesign by Andrea Perrine Brower
Inside book typesetting by Lawna Patterson Oldfield

From our hearts to yours,
we dedicate this book to all the parents of the world
who have taken on the demanding, yet extremely
rewarding, role of parenthood.
We deeply acknowledge your commitment,
love and perseverance.

And to our own parents,
whose love, understanding and support
we are forever grateful for.

Contents

3. A FATHER'S LOVE

4. SPECIAL CONNECTIONS

5. SPECIAL MOMENTS

6. INSIGHTS AND LESSONS

7. OVERCOMING OBSTACLES

8. SURVIVING LOSS

9. LETTING GO

10. ACROSS THE GENERATIONS

Acknowledgments

Chicken Soup for the Parent's Soul has taken over two and a half years to write, compile and edit. It has been a real labor of love that has grown into a passion. Special acknowledgment is due to certain people whose contributions were central to the success of this book. It is our privilege to honor them.

First and foremost, we want to thank our parents and our children. Our families are our blessings, and the love we have for our parents and our children is the love we bring to this book.

We would also like to give special thanks to the following people:

Janet Matthews, who threw herself into the daunting task of dedicating more than two years of her life to this project so that millions of lives could be uplifted for years to come. We know Janet would dedicate this book to her parents, Norm and Eleanor. Her mom slowly died from acute leukemia during the first year of this project, but no matter what pain she was suffering, she always listened with love.

Mitch Claspy, who works so hard and whose dedication is inspiring. Mitch was involved in each and every aspect of this book. His commitment to doing things the right way has made this is a great book.

Darlene Montgomery, Raymond's publicist and dear friend, who somehow managed to keep the flow of stories coming in, while keeping our desks clear at the same time.

Tasha Boucher, one of the most focused people we know. When she has a goal, you better not be standing in the way! It is that kind of focus that she brought to this book and we couldn't be more grateful.

Nina Palais, for her never-ending support, and being the mom and nurturer in Kim's office.

Kelly Harrington, for being resourceful and instrumental in so many areas.

Lisa Wood-Vasquez, Kim's assistant, for being so gracious, and for her continuous support and hard work.

The amazing staff at Raymond's office—Liz Ventrella, Wendy Kuchar, Geoff Taylor, Sue Lacher, Chris Johnson, Sue Higgins and Patty Sibolibane—for their tireless help and support of this project.

Debbie Holmes, who picked up the pieces during the last months of Janet's mom's illness and kept the project moving.

Gillian Clinton, a researcher, who uncovered some stories we would never have found.

Patty Aubery, for always being there in the crucial stages, as well as being a great friend and amazing person. We can't say enough good things about you. We love you!

Nancy Mitchell Autio, for her tremendous ability to come through with a signed permission agreement just when we thought we had to eliminate the story. We appreciate all your hard work and expertise.

Heather McNamara, for her meticulous and insightful editing, and her amazing ability to always produce the final manuscript with perfection. You are awesome!

Leslie Riskin, for her consistent, top-notch performance and for making the permission process go smoothly.

Deborah Hatchell, for being so thorough and accomplishing a million things at once!

D'ette Corona, Veronica Romero, Robin Yerian, Teresa Esparza and Cindy Holland, for your commitment, dedication, professionalism and making sure Jack's office runs smoothly.

Zan Gaudioso and Rebecca Hart, for your expert feedback and your ability to always come through when asked to edit stories.

Bob Land, Erica Orloff and Rebecca Sykes, for their brilliant edits and input on these stories.

Christine Belleris, Lisa Drucker, Allison Janse and Susan Tobias, our editors at Health Communications, Inc., for their combined hard work in editing this book with such expertise and dedication.

Kim Weiss, for being such a great publicist at Health Communications, Inc., and always a pleasure to work with.

Larry Getlen, Kimberley Denney and Maria Konicki, Health Communications, Inc.'s brilliant publicity team, whose publicity efforts continue to keep our books on the bestseller lists.

Randee Feldman, *Chicken Soup for the Soul* product manager at Health Communications, Inc., for her masterful coordination and support of all the *Chicken Soup* projects.

Terry Burke and Kelly Maragni, at Health Communications, Inc., for their wonderful sales and marketing efforts.

Andrea Perrine Brower, at Health Communications, Inc., for her inspiring and cooperative efforts to complete the cover design of this book.

Those dedicated souls who read and reread our proposed stories and made so many valuable contributions and suggestions—Beth Kalisz, Bridget Ubochi, Sherri Zeifman, Michelle, Mary and Darlene Montgomery, Wendy Kuchar, Rose Veltheer, Nancy Lee and Dale Doige, Jane Pulkys, Elsa Aabo, Mark and Sue Higgens, Liz Ventrella, Diane Parent, Compton Drayton, Melinda Upshur, Christine Culbert, Sharon Boucher, Wendy

Woolf, Nina Palais, Bruce Fisher, Jessica Lamden, Jamie Claspy and Carla Garland.

We deeply appreciate all the *Chicken Soup for the Soul* coauthors, who make it a joy to be part of this *Chicken Soup* family: Patty and Jeff Aubery, Nancy Mitchell Autio, Marty Becker, Ron Camacho, Barbara Russell Chesser, Dan Clark, Tim Clauss, Barbara De Angelis, Mark and Chrissy Donnelly, Irene Dunlap, Bud Gardner, Patty Hansen, Jennifer Read Hawthorne, Carol Kline, Hanoch and Meladee McCarty, Heather McNamara, Paul J. Meyer, Maida Rogerson, Martin Rutte, Amy Seeger, Marci Shimoff, Barry Spilchuk and Diana von Welanetz Wentworth.

Larry and Linda Price, who, in addition to keeping Jack's Foundation for Self-Esteem operating smoothly, continue to administer the Soup Kitchens for the Soul project, which distributes thousands of *Chicken Soup for the Soul* books free each year to prisoners, halfway houses, homeless shelters, battered women's shelters and inner-city schools.

Claude Choquette and Tom Sand, who manage year after year to get each of our books translated into over twenty languages around the world.

Steve Magee and Dave Corrigan of the Harbourfront Canoe and Kayak School in Toronto, for their patience, tolerance, flexibility, encouragement, love and compassion.

Dan Sullivan, teacher and mentor, who has given so much, and Frank VanderSloot, whose high integrity and family values have been an inspiration.

Because of the immensity of this project, we may have left out the names of some people who helped us along the way. If so, please accept our apologies, and know that you are appreciated.

We are deeply grateful for the many caring hands and hearts that have made this book possible. We love you all!!

Introduction

The relationship between parent and child is the deepest, most intense and richest in all our human experience. As we watch our children grow from babyhood to adulthood, we experience the full spectrum of emotions, from the heights of total elation to the depths of sorrow. Parenthood is complex and the experiences we have raising our children can be a mixed bag, both good and bad. Our goal in creating *Chicken Soup for the Parent's Soul* is to inspire, uplift and honor parents everywhere—to allow them to feel good about being parents and to help them know that during the difficult times, they are not alone.

Over the past two and a half years, we read more than five thousand stories to find the ones we present to you now. We were so amazed and touched by the depth of feelings and the range of experiences that people shared with us. We read stories about the joys of giving birth, the awe of being a new parent, and the struggles and complexities associated with being a family. People told us of their deep grief at the loss of a beloved child, and shared with us how they found the strength and courage to move on.

We were moved by the touching stories about the struggles and triumphs of being a parent of a "special needs" child, as well as the stories where parents and children were separated because of war, divorce or adoption, then miraculously and exultantly found each other again.

We received stories from parents of new babies, toddlers, teenagers, young and aging adults, as well as stories from young parents, old parents, married parents, single parents, stepparents, foster parents and widowed parents.

Through our contact with some of these writers we realize they came to some kind of personal closure or resolution as a result of writing their story. We hope that as you read these stories you are able to capture something special from them and apply it to your own life. May you experience the miracles of love and inspiration when you read this book. May it touch your heart and move your spirit, as it has done for us.

And so, from our hearts to yours, we offer you *Chicken Soup for the Parent's Soul*. This book is our gift to you, the parents of the world.

Share with Us

We would love to hear your reactions to the stories in this book. Please let us know what your favorite stories were and how they affected you.

We also invite you to send us stories you would like to see published in future editions of *Chicken Soup for the Parent's Soul*. You can send us either stories you have written or stories written by others you have liked.

Send submissions to:

Chicken Soup for the Parent's Soul
P.O. Box 30880-P
Santa Barbara, CA 93130
Fax: 805-563-2945
Web site: *www.chickensoup.com*

You can also visit the *Chicken Soup for the Soul* site on America Online at keyword: chickensoup.

We hope you enjoy reading this book as much as we enjoyed compiling, editing and writing it.

1

THE JOYS OF PARENTING

What gift has Providence bestowed on man that is so dear to him as his children?

Cicero

The Pickle Jar

*His heritage to his children wasn't words or pos-
sessions, but an unspoken treasure, the treasure
of his example as a man and a father.*

Will Rogers

As far back as I can remember, the large pickle jar sat on
the floor beside the dresser in my parents' bedroom.
When Dad got ready for bed, he would empty his pockets
and toss his coins into the jar. As a small boy I was always
fascinated at the sounds the coins made as they were
dropped into the jar. They landed with a merry jingle
when the jar was almost empty. Then the tones gradually
muted to a dull thud as the jar was filled. I used to squat
on the floor in front of the jar and admire the copper and
silver circles that glinted like a pirate's treasure when the
sun poured through the bedroom window.

When the jar was filled, Dad would sit at the kitchen
table and roll the coins before taking them to the bank.
Taking the coins to the bank was always a big production.
Stacked neatly in a small cardboard box, the coins were
placed between Dad and me on the seat of his old truck.

Each and every time, as we drove to the bank, Dad would look at me hopefully. "Those coins are going to keep you out of the textile mill, son. You're going to do better than me. This old mill town's not going to hold you back." Also, each and every time, as he slid the box of rolled coins across the counter at the bank toward the cashier, he would grin proudly. "These are for my son's college fund. He'll never work at the mill all his life like me."

We would always celebrate each deposit by stopping for an ice cream cone. I always had chocolate. Dad always had vanilla. When the clerk at the ice cream parlor handed Dad his change, he would show me the few coins nestled in his palm. "When we get home, we'll start filling the jar again."

He always let me drop the first coins into the empty jar. As they rattled around with a brief, happy jingle, we grinned at each other. "You'll get to college on pennies, nickels, dimes and quarters," he said. "But you'll get there. I'll see to that."

The years passed, and I finished college and took a job in another town. Once, while visiting my parents, I used the phone in their bedroom and noticed that the pickle jar was gone. It had served its purpose and had been removed. A lump rose in my throat as I stared at the spot beside the dresser where the jar had always stood. My dad was a man of few words, and he never lectured me on the values of determination, perseverance and faith. The pickle jar had taught me all these virtues far more eloquently than the most flowery of words could have done.

When I married, I told my wife Susan about the significant part the lowly pickle jar had played in my life. In my mind, it defined, more than anything else, how much my dad had loved me. No matter how rough things got at home, Dad continued to doggedly drop his coins into the jar. Even the summer when Dad got laid off from the mill, and Mama had to serve dried beans several times a week, not a single dime was taken from the jar. To the contrary, as Dad looked across the table at me, pouring catsup over my beans to make them more palatable, he became more determined than ever to make a way out for me. "When you finish college, son," he told me, his eyes glistening, "you'll never have to eat beans again unless you want to."

The first Christmas after our daughter Jessica was born, we spent the holiday with my parents. After dinner, Mom and Dad sat next to each other on the sofa, taking turns cuddling their first grandchild. Jessica began to whimper softly, and Susan took her from Dad's arms. "She probably needs to be changed," she said, carrying the baby into my parents' bedroom to diaper her.

When Susan came back into the living room, there was a strange mist in her eyes. She handed Jessica back to Dad before taking my hand and quietly leading me into the room. "Look," she said softly, her eyes directing me to a spot on the floor beside the dresser. To my amazement, there, as if it had never been removed, stood the old pickle jar, the bottom already covered with coins.

I walked over to the pickle jar, dug down into my pocket, and pulled out a fistful of coins. With a gamut of emotions choking me, I dropped the coins into the jar. I looked up and saw that Dad, carrying Jessica, had slipped quietly into the room. Our eyes locked, and I knew he was feeling the same emotions I felt. Neither of us could speak.

A. W. Cobb

"No, enhancing family values does not
mean raising your allowance."

Reprinted by permission of Dave Carpenter.

Geraniums of Love

*Thou are thy mother's glass, and she in thee
calls back the lovely April of her prime.*

William Shakespeare

As the fifth of seven children, I went to the same public
school as my three older sisters and brother. Every year,
my mother went to the same pageant and had parent/
child interviews with the same teachers. The only thing
different was the child. And every child participated in an
old school tradition—the annual plant sale held in early
May, just in time for Mother's Day.

Third grade was the first time that I was allowed to take
part in the plant sale. I wanted to surprise my mother, but
I didn't have any money. I went to my oldest sister and
shared the secret, and she gave me some money. When I
arrived at the plant sale, I carefully made my selection. I
agonized over that decision, inspecting each plant to
ensure that I had indeed found the best geranium. Once I
had smuggled it home, with the help of my sister, I hid it
on the upstairs neighbor's porch. I was very afraid my
mother would find it before Mother's Day, but my sister

assured me that she wouldn't, and indeed she did not.

When Mother's Day arrived, I was bursting with pride when I gave her that geranium. I remember how bright her eyes were, and how delighted she was with my gift.

The year I was fifteen, my younger sister reached third grade. In early May she came to me full of wonder and secrecy and told me that there was going to be a plant sale at school, and she wanted to surprise our mother. Like my older sister did for me, I gave her some money and off she went. She arrived home full of nervous excitement, the geranium hidden in a paper bag under her sweater. "I looked at every plant," she explained, "and I know I got the best one!"

With a sweet sense of déjà vu, I helped my little sister hide that geranium on the upstairs neighbor's porch, assuring her that our mother would not find it before Mother's Day. I was there when she gave my mother the geranium, and I watched them both bursting with pride and delight. It was like being in a dream I had already dreamed. My mother noticed me watching, and she gave me a soft, secret smile. With a tug at my heart, I smiled back. I had been wondering how my mother could pretend to be surprised at this gift from her sixth child, but as I watched her eyes light up with delight as she was presented with that most precious gift, I knew she was not pretending.

Harriet Xanthakos

The Tooth Fairy

*Children are God's apostles, sent forth, day by
day, to preach of love and hope and peace.*

Jane Russell Lowell

He held out the little red felt pillow and pointed to its
tiny pocket, which held a quarter, instead of a tooth.
"Look, Mom! Look what the tooth fairy left me. Twenty-
five cents!"

I shared his excitement, and we chatted for a few minutes about the purposes to which he would put his new
wealth. I returned to my kitchen activities, but he lingered, silent, a thoughtful look on his face. "Mom," he
hesitated, "is there really a tooth fairy, or do you put this
money in my tooth pillow and take away my tooth?"

Of course I knew I would have to answer such questions, but in spite of seven years of preparation, I hadn't
really thought through a suitable reply. I stalled for time
by asking, "What do you think, Simon?"

"Could be either," he reasoned. "It seems like something
you would do, but I know some things are magic, too."

"What would you like to think?" I continued, still

uncertain about whether or not I was about to break his heart.

"It doesn't really matter," he said with confidence. "I like it either way. If there is a tooth fairy, that's pretty exciting, and if it's you, that's pretty nice, too."

I concluded that no disappointment would result from my answer, so I confessed to being his benefactor, and he smiled contentedly. I then cautioned him not to say anything to his younger brother, explaining, "Each child is entitled to the magic until he or she is ready to ask the question that you did today. Do you understand that?"

"Yes," he said, nodding. He took great pride in his older brother role, and I knew he would never spoil anything intentionally. I considered the matter closed, but still he lingered in the kitchen.

"Is there something else, Simon?" I asked.

"Just one more question, Mom. Does Dad know?"

Elaine Decker

The Good Stuff

No man can possibly know what life means, what the world means, what anything means, until he has a child and loves it. And then the whole universe changes and nothing will ever again seem exactly as it seemed before.

Lafcadio Hearn

The cardboard box is marked "The Good Stuff." As I write, I can see the box where it is stored on a high shelf in my studio. I like being able to see it when I look up. The box contains those odds and ends of personal treasures that have survived many bouts of clean-it-out-and-throw-it-away that seize me from time to time. The box has passed through the screening zone as I've moved from house to house and hauled stuff from attic to attic. A thief looking into the box would not take anything—he couldn't get a dime for any of it. But if the house ever catches on fire, the box goes with me when I run.

One of the keepsakes in the box is a small paper bag. Lunch size. Though the top is sealed with duct tape, staples and several paper clips, there is a ragged rip in one side through which the contents may be seen.

This particular lunch sack has been in my care for maybe fourteen years. But it really belongs to my daughter, Molly. Soon after she came of school age, she became an enthusiastic participant in packing the morning lunches for herself, her brothers and me. Each bag got a share of sandwiches, apples, milk money, and sometimes a note or a treat. One morning Molly handed me two bags as I was about to leave. One regular lunch sack, and the one with duct tape and staples and paper clips. "Why two bags?"

"The other one is something else."

"What's in it?"

"Just some stuff—take it with you."

Not wanting to hold court over the matter, I stuffed both sacks into my briefcase, kissed the child and rushed off.

At midday, while hurriedly scarfing down my real lunch, I tore open Molly's bag and shook out the contents. Two hair ribbons, three small stones, a plastic dinosaur, a pencil stub, a tiny seashell, two animal crackers, a marble, a used lipstick, a small doll, two chocolate kisses and thirteen pennies.

I smiled. How charming. Rising to hustle off to all the important business of the afternoon, I swept the desk clean—into the wastebasket—my leftover lunch, Molly's junk and all. There wasn't anything in there I needed.

That evening Molly came to stand beside me while I was reading the paper. "Where's my bag?"

"What bag?"

"You know, the one I gave you this morning."

"I left it at the office, why?"

"I forgot to put this note in it." She hands over the note. "Besides, I want it back."

"Why?"

"Those are my things in the sack, Daddy, the ones I really like—I thought you might like to play with them, but now I want them back. You didn't lose the bag, did you, Daddy?" Tears puddled in her eyes.

"Oh no, I just forgot to bring it home," I lied.

"Bring it tomorrow, okay?"

"Sure thing—don't worry." As she hugged my neck with relief, I unfolded the note that had not got into the sack: "I love you Daddy."

Oh.

And also—uh-oh.

I looked long at the face of my child.

She was right—what was in that sack was "something else."

Molly had given me her treasures. All that a seven-year-old held dear. Love in a paper sack. And I had missed it. Not only missed it, but had thrown it in the wastebasket because "there wasn't anything in there I needed." Dear God.

It wasn't the first or last time I felt my Daddy Permit was about to run out.

It was a long trip back to the office. But there was nothing else to be done. So I went. The pilgrimage of the penitent. Just ahead of the janitor, I picked up the wastebasket and poured the contents on my desk. I was sorting it all out when the janitor came in to do his chores. "Lose something?"

"Yeah, my mind."

"It's probably in there, all right. What's it look like and I'll help you find it?" I started not to tell him. But I couldn't feel any more of a fool than I was already, so I told him. He didn't laugh. He smiled. "I got kids, too." So the brotherhood of fools searched the trash and found the jewels and he smiled at me and I smiled at him. You are never alone in these things. Never.

After washing the mustard off the dinosaurs and spraying the whole thing with breath freshener to kill the smell of onions, I carefully smoothed out the wadded ball of brown paper into a semifunctional bag and put the treasures inside and carried the whole thing home gingerly, like an injured kitten. The next evening I returned it to Molly, no questions asked, no explanations offered. The bag didn't look so good, but the stuff was all there and that's what counted. After dinner I asked her to tell me about the stuff in the sack, and so she took it all out a piece at a time and placed the objects in a row on the dining room table.

It took a long time to tell. Everything had a story, a memory, or was attached to dreams and imaginary friends. Fairies had brought some of the things. And I had given her the chocolate kisses, and she had kept them for when she needed them. I managed to say "I see" very wisely several times in the telling. And as a matter of fact, I did see.

To my surprise, Molly gave the bag to me once again several days later. Same ratty bag. Same stuff inside. I felt forgiven. And trusted. And loved. And a little more comfortable wearing the title of Father. Over several months the bag went with me from time to time. It was never clear to me why I did or did not get it on a given day. I began to think of it as the Daddy Prize and tried to be good the night before so I might be given it the next morning.

Sometimes I think of all the times in this sweet life when I must have missed the affection I was being given. A friend calls this "standing knee-deep in the river and dying of thirst."

So the worn paper sack is there in the box, left over from a time when a child said, "Here, this is the best I've got. Take it, it's yours. Such as I have, I give to thee."

I missed it the first time. But it's my bag now.

Robert Fulghum

Let's Go Fly a Kite

Dads are stone skimmers, mud wallowers, water wallopers, ceiling swoopers, shoulder gallopers, upsy-downsy, over-and-through, round-and-about whooshers. Dads are smugglers and secret sharers.

Helen Thomson

When my son was very small, about five or six, I traveled a lot. I worried all the time about what that absence might mean to him later in his life, not to mention how hard it was for me to be away and miss all his milestones. But I knew how important it was for a boy to have his father near. My own father, although very present in my life, was quiet and mostly kept to himself, and the times I loved the most were the special moments we had together, occasions when we would connect apart from the rigors of everyday life that put such a heavy demand on his time. I cherished those special moments and still, to this day, hold those memories dear. I decided that if I couldn't be with my son as often as I wanted to, I would make a concerted effort to create those kinds of special times for us.

One year I had to be in Europe for most of the summer—one of the hardest times for me to be away. My son was out of school, and it was vacation time for families. My wife eased the separation by sending me little care packages from home. They contained pictures and cute little notes and drawings from my son. He once sent me a candy bar with a bite taken out of it, with a little note saying, "I'm sharing my treat with you."

In one of my letters home I promised my son that I would teach him how to fly a kite. We could go to a nearby beach and fly it as high as it would go. Through my travels I would pick up things for our kite adventure and send it to him. I bought a couple of blueprints on how to make your own kite, and I sent those on. I found special balsa wood for the frame that I sent him one piece at a time, carefully packed. Bit by bit, in each letter or package home, I sent something for our kite. Toward the end of my trip, I had to go to Japan. There I found the most beautiful blue silk with gold threads woven through it. Perfect kite material. I sent it home. I found some multicolored, heavily braided material that would be perfect for the tail. I sent that home, along with a small Buddha figurine that would serve as a weight. I told him it wouldn't be long; I was on my way home.

I arrived home very late one night. I crept into my son's room to find him sleeping soundly, completely sur-rounded by all the items I had sent him for our kite.

For the next week we worked on creating our master-piece. I loved every second of it. We had our exclusive time together, in the garage, after dinner.

Finally, it was finished. It was beautiful. The blue silk made it so elegant, more like a showpiece than a toy. It was all I could do to keep my son from sleeping with it that night. "You don't want to roll over on it and break it, do you?" He tried patiently to explain that he couldn't pos-sibly do that because deep in his mind, even though he was asleep, he would know it was there and he would sleep carefully. Finally we agreed to keep it on a chair next to his bed. "We'll fly it tomorrow, right, Dad?"

"If the weather's right." I explained to him that you need wind to help lift the kite off the ground. Quite frankly, I was afraid we had passed our window for good weather. It even looked like it might rain.

"We'll fly it tomorrow 'cause I'm going to pray with all my heart for the best kite weather." When I checked on him later that night, he had pushed the chair with the kite on it up against his bed. He was sound asleep, with his hand resting on his kite.

The next day, the weather was iffy. There wasn't even a breeze. My son came into the living room with kite in hand, "Let's go, Dad!" We walked outside. I was doubtful, but he was ready. As we walked down to the beach, it was still as calm as it could be. By the time we got on the sand, a robust wind kicked up, and we were able to launch it without a bit of difficulty. The wind held, the day was beautiful, sunny and clear and we flew that kite all day long. "I told you, Dad." He was right. I will never underestimate the power of a child's prayer again.

My son is grown now, with children of his own. The other day we met for coffee. Even though the world spins quickly around us, we still try to make time for each other. While having our coffee he mentioned that he had some new pictures of his daughter that he wanted to give me. When he reached into his wallet to retrieve the photo, something fell out. I reached over to pick it up and hand it back to him. Suddenly, it dawned on me what it was that my son was keeping in his wallet, and I began to well up. He smiled as I handed it back to him. A flood of memories washed over us as he tucked his treasure back into his wallet . . . a small remnant of blue silk with gold threads woven through it.

Robert Dixon
As told to Zan Gaudioso

My Second Birth

We are all born for love. It is the principle of existence, and its only end.

Benjamin Disraeli

My second pregnancy was unexpected in any number of ways. For starters, the whole thing was unplanned. My husband John and I *did* want another baby—someday. At the moment, we were more than busy raising our fifteen-month-old daughter, Katie, and finishing high-pressure Ph.D. programs at Harvard. Then there was the fact that I had an undiagnosed autoimmune disease, which made the pregnancy very difficult. But the strangest things that happened while I was expecting Adam weren't logistical or medical. In fact, they were so difficult to explain that, for months, I didn't even know how to talk about them.

From the moment Adam was conceived, I felt a subtle but powerful sea change occurring in my life. It was like the experience of being in a pitch-dark room by yourself, and then suddenly sensing that the room is full of people; though everything looked the same to my physical senses, I had the feeling I was . . . accompanied. Something within me seemed to have linked up with something around me, making me the center of a strange, warm, benevolent energy. When my pregnancy test came back positive, it resonated in my subconscious mind—*Aha! That's why!*—even as I told myself I was having hormone-induced delusions.

Fate seemed to pile an awful lot of bad luck into the nine months Adam spent getting ready for his birth. Our little family endured a near-fatal traffic accident, almost constant illness, and long, forced separations due to John's work. One day, Katie and I were caught in a high-rise fire that made our apartment building unlivable and sent us to the hospital with smoke inhalation. Even though I was resolutely unsuperstitious, part of me was starting to wonder whether the baby I was carrying might be some kind of bad-luck charm.

It was after the fire, as I lay in a hospital bed with oxygen tubes in my nose, an IV in my arm and deep doubts in my mind, that I dreamt one of the most powerful dreams of my life. I was sitting at a wooden table, in a room filled with slanted light from half-closed shutters. Strewn across the table were hundreds of ancient, yellowed documents. I knew for some reason that I was supposed to find something of great significance in the pages, but I had no idea where to look. I searched desperately through the clutter, knowing I could never find the right page on my own. As soon as this thought crossed my mind, I realized I wasn't alone. I looked up and saw a young man sitting across the table from me. At least, he looked young. I had the sense that he was somehow age-less, but from his appearance I would have taken him to be in his mid-twenties. I remember this even though I have no memory of what he actually looked like.

"Here," said the man. He reached across the table to hand me a piece of paper. His voice was so incredibly resonant and gentle that it brought tears to my eyes. I knew immediately that the page he had given me was the one I'd been looking for. It would teach me what I had to learn. A deep comfort began trickling into my heart, the way the glucose solution was trickling into my arm.

I woke up with this comfort still suffusing me, but it faded very fast. I had no idea what the dream meant, but for some reason I was absolutely, irrationally convinced of three things: the young man in the dream was the fetus I carried in my womb; this being loved and respected me as his equal; and there was "something wrong" with the baby.

Immediately, I began scheduling every prenatal test available, trying to banish my unwelcome suspicions. Doctors assured me the odds of a problem were very slight: John and I were both in our mid-twenties, there was no history of birth defects in either family and I'd had good prenatal care. Nevertheless, they agreed to perform an amniocentesis "to put my mind at rest."

I have never been so unhappy about being proved right. When the results came back, they showed that I was carrying a little boy with Down syndrome. My doctors recommended an immediate therapeutic abortion, but by that time, I was twenty-two weeks pregnant. I'd seen my baby stretch, yawn and suck his finger on an ultrasound screen. Though I would never condemn a parent who did choose therapeutic abortion, I simply couldn't.

Adam was born with Down syndrome, just as the doctors predicted. He was exactly what I'd expected—and nothing like I'd expected. The warm, unearthly energy I had felt throughout my pregnancy continues to hover around Adam, as much a part of him as his corn-silk blond hair and merry, irrepressible grin. One of my friends put it this way: "Adam has angels like a dog has fleas; he brings them in with him, and if you're around him long, you end up getting them, too."

Here is one example, an incident typical of Adam's strange, subtle magic. One symptom of his Down syndrome is seriously delayed speech. Adam has been in speech therapy since he was two weeks old, but the low tone of the muscles in his mouth still makes articulation very difficult. When he was three years old, I began to lose hope that he would ever communicate verbally. This was terribly frustrating for him, and it just plain broke my heart. I worked with him for hours, doing the exercises the speech therapists had taught me but having no success whatsoever. I had to face it: The kid couldn't talk. Not at all.

One day, after hours of unsuccessful therapy, I hit a low point. I took Adam, Katie and one-year-old Lizzie to the grocery store and offered them all bribes to keep quiet—I was too tired and discouraged to enforce discipline any other way. I told the children they could pick out a treat from the candy stand next to the checkout counter. When we got there, Katie chose a roll of Lifesavers and Lizzie selected a chocolate bar. Adam, who seemed to understand everything I had said even though he couldn't speak in return, went over to a bucket of red rosebuds and pulled one out.

"This is what you want?" I asked incredulously.

He nodded.

"No, honey, this isn't candy," I said, putting it back. "Don't you want candy?"

Adam shook his small head, walked back to the bucket, picked out the rose and put it on the counter. I was baffled, but I paid for it. Adam took it gravely as the girls unwrapped their candy. He held the flower with both hands all the way home. When we got there, I was immediately engrossed in putting away the groceries and forgot all about his strange request.

The next morning, just as I was waking up, I heard Adam's small feet padding down the hallway toward my bedroom. He appeared at the door with the rose, which he had put into a small crystal bud vase. I was startled; I didn't realize that he even knew what vases were for, let alone how to get one down from the cupboard, fill it with water and put a flower in it.

Adam walked over to the bed and held out the rose. In a soft, calm, perfectly clear voice, he said, "Here."

It had been years since I thought about my dream at the hospital, years since I had heard the incredible gentleness in the voice of the young man who had sat across the table from me—the same voice I had just heard coming from my mute son's mouth. I stared at Adam, almost frightened, the dream replaying in my mind. He looked back at me with steady eyes, and I knew what I should have remembered all along: that this flesh of my flesh had a soul I could barely comprehend, that he was sorry for the pain I experienced as I tried to turn him into a "normal" child, and that he loved me despite my disabilities. Then he turned around, his little blue pajama feet dragging a bit on the floor, and padded out of the room.

The day I had Adam was *my* second birth—the second time I'd had a baby and the second time *I* was born. Until then, I lived in an ivory-tower universe dominated by competition, harsh criticism and worship of The Mind. My son graciously ushered me into a world where love and joy, not achievement, are the measures of success; where Harvard professors are the slow learners and retarded babies the master teachers; where every child, every one of us, is fully and unequivocally lovable. This world is new and strange to me, but I'm not too worried about being left behind as I learn to live in it. Slow learner though I am, I can always trust Adam to help me understand.

Martha Beck

The Photograph Album

A dad is man haunted by death, fears and anxieties. But who seems to his children the haven from all harm. And who makes them certain that whatever happens—will all come right.

Clara Ortega

It was a lazy Sunday morning, the type of day that getting out of bed requires an effort and when you finally put your feet onto the floor, your impulse is to slip them back under the covers and bury yourself under the blanket. Reluctantly, Marilyn and I left the warmth of our bed and made our way downstairs for a late breakfast. When we entered the kitchen, Lori was already at the table doing her homework.

The conversation between us was sporadic and general. Marilyn and I finished our breakfast and with the three of us engrossed in our own preoccupation, the room was relatively quiet. Marilyn was drinking coffee, I was reading the newspaper and Lori was busily scribbling in her book.

From behind my newspaper, I heard Lori close her

textbooks. Glancing up, I watched her stand and start to walk out of the kitchen. Suddenly, she turned and faced me. "Why are there more pictures of Lisa than there are of me?" she asked. Lisa is our older daughter.

I stared back, not understanding the question. Lori turned and left the room. Caught off-guard by the question, I looked at Marilyn. "Are there more pictures of Lisa than of Lori?" Marilyn shrugged and raised her eyebrows in a motion of puzzlement. "Are you aware that there are more pictures of Lisa than Lori?" I added.

Marilyn said, "I've never counted them. I don't know."

"Kids!" was my immediate response. "They drive you nuts with dumb questions," and I proceeded to raise the newspaper and continue my reading. "There can't be that many more pictures of Lisa than of Lori," I mumbled behind the newspaper, but I was having difficulty focusing on the words.

Marilyn's answer was the same as my thoughts, "I hadn't realized that there was any significant difference." I lowered the newspaper again and continued, "Now why would Lori ask such a question?" I asked.

Marilyn just shook her head and stared back at me. After a few minutes of thought she said, "When Lisa was born, you were taking photographs. You hardly went anywhere without a camera. When Lori was born, you were involved in colored slides. There must be hundreds of slides of Lori somewhere in the house that Lori has never seen or doesn't remember."

After digesting Marilyn's remarks, I agreed. "After Lori leaves, we'll look for those slides. Who knows, we might find more slides of Lori than pictures of Lisa," I joked.

Later that afternoon, when we were alone, we went into the basement where we had stored the boxes that we had brought from our previous home. It wasn't long before we discovered the trays of slides, and for the rest of the afternoon we looked at each tray, pointing out those slides that highlighted Lori.

"What are you going to do?" Marilyn asked.

"It's her birthday in a few weeks," I said. "We'll select about one hundred slides with Lori and convert them into pictures, put them into an album and give them to her as a gift. I don't know if the album will answer her question, but at least she'll know that we cared enough to find her an answer."

Over the next few days, we secretly went through all of our slides, selecting and rejecting pictures until we were satisfied. Marilyn took the slides and had them converted into photographs. When the photographs were returned, we placed them into an album. When the album was finished, we hid the book until her birthday.

The album brought back memories of the early years of our marriage and we hoped it showed how we felt about our daughter. What began as a puzzling question had developed into a need to convey to her how much we loved her and somehow had not made her aware of our feelings.

On November 24, when passing Lori's room to leave for work, I opened her door and slipped the album inside, letting it rest on the carpet. Attached to the album was a birthday card with a note explaining why her mother and I had put the album together. I left the house and drove to work.

It was about eight o'clock when my office telephone rang. I picked up the receiver and identified my company name asking, "Can I help you?"

On the other end of the receiver, a tiny voice spoke with obvious difficulty. "I love you, Daddy," she said and disconnected. The receiver remained against my ear for a few more minutes before I placed it on the telephone. Our message had been delivered and acknowledged.

Alvin Abram

"It's no wonder I have a complex. You have *five photo albums* of Billy and *only one single picture* of me. And it's a picture of me saying my first word, which was 'Billy.'"

The Spinner Plate

*When you look at your life, the greatest happi-
nesses are family happinesses.*

Dr. Joyce Brothers

It was defective and should have been replaced when we
first bought the dishes, but by the time we discovered the
dinner plate's flaw, the packaging and receipt had long
been discarded. Whenever anyone applied the touch of an
eating utensil to the plate, a small bulge on the bottom
caused it to spin freely. This required the unfortunate diner
to hold the plate in place whenever he or she tried to
manipulate fork and knife in unison. Even though it was
one of eight, and there were only four of us, the plate turned
up on the table with annoying regularity. We began to
devise sneaky ways of avoiding ending up with the
dreaded Spinner Plate at our place at the table. The children
began to "offer" to set the table as a ruse for appointing both
the plate's place and theirs at the table. The last one seated
would automatically test the stability of his or her plate,
which often set off a series of cries: "Aaaww! I had it last
night. Aren't there any other clean plates? I didn't want to

sit here anyway!" I can even admit to a few lapses into self-pity myself when landed with the wretched thing.

Having heard the whines and complaints one too many times, my husband decided one evening to try to put an end to the sniveling, or at least compensate the plate's unlucky recipient each time it came into use. "From now on," he announced, "anyone caught with the Spinner Plate will receive extra kisses." He then turned to that evening's recipient, our daughter, and kissed her heartily all over both cheeks. He invited our son and I to do the same. No longer feeling like the helpless victim of defective dinnerware, our daughter felt special and it was the beginning of a complete about-face in our attitudes toward the Spinner Plate.

The children still tried to manipulate the plate's positioning, but now for a different reason. After everyone was seated, one of them would smile smugly and proclaim, "I've got the Spinner Plate" and give the plate a whirl, as if someone might dispute it. If one of the family was known to have had a particularly trying day, the Spinner Plate was purposely set at his or her place. After a round of kisses, dinner would begin with troubles eased, perhaps even forgotten.

The Spinner Plate eventually met an early demise, perhaps from its more frequent use, and so ended the ritual of extra kisses at the dinner table. I hadn't realized the significance of the plate's loss until recently. We were dining out with our children and as the waiter placed my husband's plate in front of him, it gave a familiar spin. The children's faces lit up as I bestowed "extra" kisses to their father, and I resolved to find a replacement for our Spinner Plate as soon as I could. An everyday "something" that would serve as a reminder to express the affection we feel for one another. We all need extra kisses from time to time.

Lori Broadfoot

Coffee Milk and Oreos

The words that a father speaks to his children in the privacy of home are not heard by the world, but, as in whispering-galleries, they are clearly heard at the end and by posterity.

Jean Paul Richter

I like evenings, as the house quiets down and the children are mellowing out after the screaming-giggling-singing-jumping-up-and-down of the day's journey they have taken through school, learning and playing. The evening may end with watching television or playing hide-and-seek—which is to say the children hide in the same places, and I pretend that I cannot find them. Some nights we play *Sorry!*, other nights we read books. Lately, as Sarah has begun to get comfortable with her reading skills, she likes me to listen to her read *Green Eggs and Ham* or *The Tale of Peter Rabbit.* It is nice to find a moment to just sit together after the rush of the day and the animated hullabaloo of dinner when everyone tries to tell everyone else what they did, all at the same time.

And some nights, we just sit and hang out together.

Sarah, Max and I were sitting at the kitchen table one evening, getting ready to call it a night. We were eating Oreos, twisting them open, licking and chewing the filling out, and then eating around the edge of each half in concentric circles until we had tiny bits of cookie left.

To wash down the chocolate and frosting, Sarah had a big glass of milk, and the menfolk each had a cup of coffee milk—for Max, half milk, half decaffeinated coffee, a bit of sugar, and for me, a dollop of milk, some artificial sweetener (to help compensate for the Oreos), and a lot of decaf in a mug the size of a small cat.

There was something wonderfully calming about sitting there with my children at the end of this day. Dinner was done, the dishes dumped into our electric scullery maid (the dishwasher), Sarah had finished a shower and was bundled up in her nightie (the Little Mermaid one), and Max was fresh from the bath, pink-cheeked and pretty cozy in his footie jammies. Every once in a while, they looked up from dissecting the cookies and caught me studying them. And they gave me the most amazing smiles, somewhere around completely cute with just a hint of impishness thrown in, just so I knew that they aren't complete angels. I live for moments such as these.

The kids and I talk about all sorts of things at this time of night. What we did today, what they learned in school, what Max wants for his birthday (which is usually at least six months off when he mentions it), which kids Sarah is currently best friends with at school, and sometimes we even talk about what I did all day. They don't quite understand the tasks that an engineer has, but they at least pretend to be interested. Sometimes, though, the conversations get heavily involved in serious stuff.

My children have inquisitive minds that delve into a diverse group of subjects. They want to know all about science and electricity. They have a particular interest in what makes the world go. Sometimes we get into a very complex discussion about how something works or happened or what have you, and we have to go dig out the dictionary or a science book and see if we can uncover the truth of the matter.

Other times, though, Max and Sarah would prefer to wrestle with the deeper issues of life, the philosophical truths. "Daddy," Max asked this particular evening, "are you getting old?" Out of the blue, no warning.

I allowed as how I was always getting older. Some days my back hurts more than others, now and then the knees crackle and pop ominously, and I notice that a few of the lines that appear on my face when I smile stay when I stop. I guess I am getting older. I asked what he meant by old.

"Your hands are old," he said, changing gears slightly as he grabbed my left thumb and lifted my hand up for me to examine closely. "See, Daddy, your hands are getting wrinkly and you are getting older. Are you going to die soon?" Delivered in utter innocence, wide-eyed, a serious question.

Well, my hands aren't that wrinkled, hardly at all in fact, but I said that I hoped that my end wasn't too near at hand. But it might happen, I told them. There could be an accident, or I could get very sick from a bad disease. Sometimes people just die, I explained, but chances were I'd live a good bit longer. And why did he want to know?

"I was just asking. You are getting old like Grandma and Grandpa, and someday you'll die, but first can you wait 'til I have little children so you can be their gran'pa, and we can all eat cookies and drink coffee milk together?"

How could I refuse a request like that?

I put them to bed in our evening ritual, which included dropping each of them onto their beds so they bounce a little, pulling the covers up to their necks, and being called back at least twice—for a fresh glass of water, for an extra hug or kiss, or maybe just to tease me and giggle. It is a fine way for them to go to sleep. Then I retired to my office in the basement to ponder the evening's subject.

Am I old? Am I going to die soon? Am I going to die someday? The latter question has a resounding yes, I will die someday, and that is probably the ultimate disappointment, that I cannot go on learning and experiencing forever. But if I can last long enough to sit at my kitchen table, drinking coffee milk and eating Oreo cookies with my grandchildren, that'd be fine by me.

Hunter S. Fulghum

THE FAMILY CIRCUS.

PARENTS CAN GIVE CHILDREN THINGS... ...OR TIME.

TIME IS BETTER!

Bil Keane

Reprinted by permission of Bil Keane.

Daddy

I had heard many stories of men who experienced sympathy pains or put on weight as their partners entered their last stages of pregnancy. I really did not believe it until this happened in our home.

When I was pregnant with our second child and nearing the end of my term, it became quite obvious that my husband's waistline had begun to rival mine.

One morning while standing in the kitchen with our then three-year-old daughter, Courtney, we noticed that she had begun to eye us curiously. Though she had been frequently schooled about the arrival of her new baby sister, something seemed to confuse her. Courtney looked at her father, then looked at me. Again she returned her gaze to her father. Thoughtfully, and with all the seriousness a three-year-old could muster, she asked, "Daddy, when are you going to have YOUR baby?"

Laurin Broadbent

Comic-Book Solomon

Children are little hoarders at heart and seldom interested in sharing. They see. They want. They keep.

My five-year-old daughter was listing off her possessions the other day when she brought out her supply of comic books.

"This is mine and this is mine and this is mine and . . . ," she droned on, picking up each comic book separately.

"Wait a minute," my wife said. "That one isn't yours. That's Richard's."

"No, it's mine. It's mine," Jane insisted.

"It's Richard's. It's got his name written on the top."

"It's mine."

"It isn't yours. Look. It has *R-I-C-H-A-R-D* written right there."

The evidence wasn't accepted.

"I don't care. It's my pile of comic books, and it's mine," Jane persisted.

"You have to give it back to Richard," my wife countered.

"No."

"Wouldn't you be mad if Richard had something of yours and wouldn't give it to you?"

Jane then burst into tears, her answer for practically every argument.

"But it's mine!" she blubbered. "Grandma gave it to me."

"Grandma didn't give it to you. Richard got it at Christmas. I can remember. . . . Well, I can recognize Santa Claus's printing. He printed each of your names on a comic book for your stocking."

More tears. More yowls. More Bette Davis. And a tighter grasp on Exhibit A.

The prosecution proceeded to clinch its case by calling upon an independent witness (Jane's older brother, Stephen) and asking him to verify the name on the comic book.

"Richard," he swore.

Even Perry Mason couldn't have helped Jane after that damaging testimony.

The verdict.

"You've got to give the comic book back to Richard," my dishpan Hammurabi decreed.

Then followed a long discourse on the rights of others, the many advantages of being honest (especially in the afterlife) and, finally, the promise of dire consequences if Jane didn't cough up the comic book.

"Now, for the last time, whose book is that?" my wife asked.

"Richard's," Jane admitted sullenly.

Richard was then summoned from the back yard.

"Go on," my wife encouraged Jane. "You know what you have to do."

"Here's your comic book, Richard," Jane said.

"I don't want it," Richard replied, running off to rejoin his pals.

Next case.

Gary Lautens

Driving Me Crazy

You can learn many things from children. How much patience you have, for instance.

Franklin P. Jones

One of the high-water marks in any parent's life is teaching their children how to drive.

I'm hitting this high-water mark in my own life just now, and it's pretty much right up there with labor pains and parent-teacher conferences.

In the week since my boy received his learner's permit, life has changed for me.

I don't "drive" anywhere now. I "lurch." My boy and I have been lurching all over town together now for a week because, he says, there's something wrong with the car.

"Something's wrong with this clutch," he tells me whenever we lurch to a stall, which is pretty much every time he tries to get the thing going.

On those occasions when he does get it going, he generally gets it as far as second gear and then quits bothering with the gearshift.

"We're picking up some speed," I tell him. "It's time to shift to third."

But he doesn't want to do that because it just means he'll eventually have to face the prospect of shifting back into second.

"Something's wrong with third gear," he says. "I'm sticking with second."

And so, when we've finally got the car lurched into motion, we maintain a steady pace by zooming around town in second gear.

Teaching my boy to drive has made us much closer. There was a time before he got his learner's permit that he wasn't that keen on doing some types of things with me, such as going downtown together to buy a carton of milk.

"Would you like to go downtown to buy a carton of milk with me?" I'd say, and he'd say, "Well, no. Actually I don't think that idea appeals to me at all." Getting a carton of milk with me just wasn't his cup of tea back then.

But now, when I try to sneak out of the house with my car keys, he can hear them jingle as well as the dogs can. And suddenly he's standing there in the driveway, anxious to spend some quality time with me going downtown to buy a carton of milk. And this means that we're going to be out in the car together for quite some time.

That's because, not only do we have to go everywhere in second gear, we can't even get out of the driveway until he makes a number of time-consuming "adjustments." All student drivers need to make "adjustments" before they can "go."

They make elaborate adjustments to the seat, for example. Up. "Too close." Back. "Too far." Up. "Too close." Back. "Too far." They can spend a good two, three minutes going up and back, and it never does "feel right."

"Something's wrong with this seat," my boy tells me.

And he spends an inordinate amount of time adjusting

the rearview mirror. My boy's rearview mirror is adjusted to just exactly the precise specifications they should have been using when they adjusted the Hubble telescope for space launch. His rearview mirror is totally, totally adjusted.

Which is somewhat ironic because he *never* uses it.

I've also been spending a lot of time riding around in reverse, which is in no way related to using the rearview mirror. Reverse is different than forward for my boy because, instead of lurching along, he launches away.

The first time he tried leaving our driveway in reverse, he went from zero to sixty in 2.5 seconds and never did stop until he ran into the basketball hoop.

"Something's wrong with reverse," he told me.

And I've learned to look at the roads around town with a new eye. I used to just take it for granted that all the roads were pretty much wide enough for two cars, coming and going. But, by watching my boy swerve onto the shoulder every time a car comes, I realize I've had a limited view of things.

"Why did you drive off the road?" I asked him the first time I noted this habit.

"Something's wrong with that driver," he told me.

Last night my boy said he thinks he's ready for the highway.

I told him I didn't think so, at least not until he was willing to use third and fourth gear. I just can't see how any good could come of zooming down the highway in second gear.

He was disgusted with my fastidious concern about staying alive.

"Something's wrong with you," he told me.

He's certainly got that right.

Beth Mullally

"We aren't waiting up for you.
Your father's waiting up for the car."

Reprinted by permission of Dave Carpenter.

I'm Okay

Motherhood is the most emotional experience of one's life. One joins a kind of woman's mafia.

Janet Suzman

The house is a mess, the dishes are dirty.
I'm too old for this stuff, I'm well over thirty!
The car is not clean, my hair is a wreck,
And I've already spent next Friday's paycheck.

The laundry needs washing, the kids are too rowdy,
And I never have time for a leisurely "Howdy."
With all that I do, it's never enough,
It's never quite finished, it always looks rough.

I looked in my mirror and what did I see?
A harried old stranger, where I used to be.
The hurrier I go, the behinder I get.
Today is tomorrow, and I'm not caught up yet.

My kids are growing at such a fast pace,
That I'm missing their childhood for the sake of this race.

I work and I clean and I cook, and I say
"Hit the books, clean your room!" there's no time for play.

Well, the Lord, for some reason, chose ME with the care
Of three of His children, but I'm rarely there!
I've GOT to slow down lest there's nothing to show
For my role as their mom when they pack up and go!

I'm only one person, but look through my door,
What appears to be one, divides into more!
I'm a chauffeur, a cook, a planter of trees,
A teacher, an umpire, a mender of knees.

Sometimes, I forget that deep down inside,
There's a lady with feelings, and last night, she cried.
She gets tired and lonely, feels taken for granted
She wants to see blooms from the seeds that she's planted.

Then, amidst all the turmoil in this mind-bending pace,
My little ones look at me—square in the face . . .
And just when I need it, they all in one day
Say, "Momma, I love you" and then . . . I'm OKAY!

Rabona Gordon

$\overline{2}$

A MOTHER'S LOVE

Suddenly she was here. And I was no longer pregnant; I was a mother. I never believed in miracles before.

Ellen Green

On Becoming a Stepmother

Children thrive in a variety of family forms;
they develop normally with single parents, with
unmarried parents, with multiple caretakers
and with traditional two-parent families. What
children require is loving and attentive adults,
not a particular family type.

Sandra Scarr

When my stepchildren arrived at the door with a suitcase of dirty clothes, their medical records and confused
expressions on their young faces, it was obvious they
weren't just coming for dinner. In the long—very long—
seconds that followed, I had to make one of several
choices. I could lock myself in my room with every book I
had ever wanted to read but for which I could never find
the time. I could leave the husband I had married for better or worse. Or I could put on a smile, assume the responsibilities that loomed before me and start their laundry.

Needless to say, I chose option number three. I went
out and bought the economy-size box of detergent, three
loaves of bread, a ton of lunch meat, a bushel of fruit and

several extra-large bags of chips, and I plunged headfirst into being a stepmother.

Unfortunately, the only models I had for stepmothering came from fairy tales. And those stepmothers were not what I wanted to be.

In fact, I wasn't yet that good at being a "real" mom. My daughter was only two and a half, and I was still learning how demanding a child could be.

What made it even more difficult was that, although I had accepted responsibility for these children, they had not yet accepted me. There they were, a six-year-old boy and an eight-year-old girl, watching me, studying me, waiting for me to do all the things their "real" mother had done and wondering why she had sent them to us in the first place.

They hadn't asked to come live with their father and me. As day followed day, I could feel how much they missed their "other mother," feelings they were too young to deal with. Some days, I didn't want them around, feelings I was too ashamed to admit having.

At first, they were as nervous around me as I was around them. Sure, we knew each other. We had spent many a visitation weekend at the zoo or the beach. We had gone on picnics and out to dinner. We had played hide-and-seek. I had read them bedtime stories and tucked them in. But during all those hours, they had been my guests, and I had been their father's special friend. What we needed now was to become special friends ourselves, and to find the boundaries of our new relationship.

Then, of course, there was my own daughter to consider. And it was through her that I finally learned to be a stepmom.

Suddenly, she had a brother and a sister. Not a stepbrother or half-sister. Simply a brother and a sister. I had been her mother, and now I was their mother. When people asked her if she had any brothers or sisters, she would answer yes, without any qualifying explanations, without any hesitation at all.

She was too young to comprehend the situation in any other way. And was there really any other way to see it?

At first, yes. Because no matter how hard I tried, I kept running into a version of myself created by my stepchildren. Even though I did all the "mom" things—made lunches, did laundry, corrected homework—it was never enough.

I would hear them playing "orphanage" or "foster home." I heard my stepdaughter whispering about me in the night. She told the other children how mean I was. How I didn't have straight hair like mothers were supposed to and how I put too much mustard on her sandwiches. I was too thin and too loud. In other words, I was the opposite of her natural mother. I suppose that's the closest I ever came to fitting the evil stepmother description.

I would walk away from their room, a heavy pressure against my heart. And while they played "moving" and "let's live somewhere else" games, I would cry myself to sleep.

And then something happened. The everyday motions of life took over.

We began to fill the photo albums and create memories. The days stacked one on top of the other, like well-worn measuring cups. We began not only to look like a family but to feel like one.

And we definitely did look like a family. The dentist certainly didn't know any different, not when he was filling a cavity and the child was holding my hand. The checker in the market only saw three rambunctious children fighting over a package of cookies, yelling for Mom to intervene.

Sometimes I wanted to yell out, "They're not really mine." But what mother doesn't?

What mother doesn't have days when her children are driving her crazy?

When the school nurse called to tell "Mom" that her child had a fever, I showed up at the office. I sat on one hard bench after another watching my son sit on one hard bench after another at football games.

I took my daughters door to door selling Girl Scout cookies. I walked the windy streets on Halloween.

"So how many children do you have?" someone will ask. "Three," I say, "a boy and two girls." I give their names. And I leave it at that.

Of course, there is one complication that other families don't have. Some day, they might just pick up and leave us. But all children leave home eventually.

Now that I'm a pro, a new stepmom friend of mine asked me the other day: "How will I ever get them to like me?"

"First, you have to like them," I said. "And don't think of a stepmother as someone removed, as being a step lower than the mother who gave birth."

Because when you get right down to the nitty-gritty, to the dirty laundry and the scabbed knees, there really isn't any difference between a stepmom and a natural mom. What's important is that there is a mom who loves and cares.

Janie Emaus

The Other Mother

Loving a child is a circular business. The more you give, the more you get, the more you want to give.

Penelope Leach

Born in 1931, the youngest of six children, I learned to share my parents' love. Raising six children during the Depression took its toll on my parents' relationship though, and when I was eighteen years old, they divorced. Daddy never had very close relationships with his children and drifted even farther away from us after the divorce.

Several years later a wonderful woman came into his life, and they were married. She had two sons—one of them still at home. Under her influence, we became a "blended family" and a good relationship developed between the two families. She always treated us as if we were her own children.

It was because of our *other mother*—Daddy's second wife—that he became closer to his own children. They shared over twenty-five years together before our father passed away. At the time of his death, the question came up of my mother (Daddy's first wife) attending his funeral.

I will never forget the unconditional love shown by my stepmother when I asked her if she would object to Mother attending Daddy's funeral. Without giving it a second thought, she immediately replied, "Of course not, Honey—she's the mother of my children."

Jewel Sanders

Daddy's Hair Is Red

A young woman named Mary gave birth to her first child and because her husband was on military duty, she spent a couple of weeks after the birth at the home of her parents.

One day Mary mentioned to her mother that she was surprised the baby's hair was reddish when both she and her husband were blonde.

"Well, Mary," said the grandmother, "you must remember, your daddy's hair is red."

"But Mamma," said Mary, "that doesn't make any difference, because I'm adopted."

With a little smile, Mamma said the loveliest words that her daughter had ever heard: "I always forget."

The Best of Bits & Pieces

I Live with an Alien

Parents are the bones on which children sharpen their teeth.

Peter Ustinov

There's an alien living in my house. He doesn't have three eyes or six legs. He doesn't peel off his skin at night to expose a hairy, scaly body. And he doesn't feed himself through a hole in his nose.

But he does change moods quite frequently. In fact, from one second to the next he has been known to go from laughing uncontrollably to shouting at the top of his lungs and slamming doors. He communicates in a non-verbal language that consists of rolling eyes, shoulder shrugs and an occasional grunt seasoned with words like "dude" and "pal." And he inhales food as if it were going to evaporate before it reached his mouth.

By now, anyone with one of these creatures living in their home knows that I am referring to the teenage boy. More specifically, the teenage boy not old enough to drive but too old to be seen with Mom in the car while being chauffeured around the Valley.

"Drop me off here, Mom. Stop. That's close enough." God forbid he should be seen in the car with a real live mother.

His hormones are raging through his body (like the Viper roller coaster at Magic Mountain), turning him into a virtual alien unable to relate to the rest of his perfectly normal family.

He can eat a package of cookies, two pot pies and a burrito, and drink a quart of milk before dinner and then complain there's nothing left to eat in the house.

He leaves bowls of Jell-O under his bed to develop into fungal specimens that no living creature should be forced to breathe.

He is the center of his foreign world and completely misunderstood by everyone else in it. Over the past few years, I have come to accept his membership in this alien existence. I have watched as he grew to my height and beyond, as he grew out of his sleepers and into jeans. I have listened as he went from the Muppets singing "Sesame Street" to rappers dancing in the street.

I have gone from bathing his imaginary friends to reminding him to shower before going to school.

And things would be okay if I could live with him. IF. That's a very big word in the English language.

If I, his mother, could remain myself as he goes through his transformations into manhood. But that seems to be impossible.

I find that, as hard as I may try to remain calm at the sight of his strewn-about clothes, at an empty package of my favorite crackers, at one of his innocent shrugs and that roll of the eyes, I simply cannot.

Even though I know there's an end to this, somewhere, I go berserk. I look at myself in the mirror and see an alien face. *What is happening to me?* I scream uncontrollably. I rant, making no sense at all.

Logically, I can understand it.

He has reached that point in his life where my memories begin. I can remember those heartaches. The sight of that pimple the day of a big date. The phone calls into the night. The rapid heartbeat as the boy I had a crush on walked by without giving me a glance. The indecision, insecurity and that ever-present sexual drive. I was once there myself. But that alone is not enough to help.

A "Thank you, Mom," a kiss on the cheek and an "I love you" would be nice.

And you know what? It does happen. When I least expect it, he comes up and plants a soft kiss on my cheek. Then the next minute he is once again communicating with that spaceship.

Sometimes I pray for them to come and take him away. Let him grow up, I plead, and then bring him back. Taller, wiser, with a beard and kids of his own.

Then I walk into his empty room and listen to the sounds he would have left behind. That beep, beep of the Nintendo game. The whisperings late at night into the phone. The heavy bass pulsating against the doorway. Standing there, in the center of his world, his mess, I realize that he is going to leave someday.

He is going to pass these memories of mine and move on to a new set. Some that I will have lived through, others that I will have not.

Then one day he'll get what he deserves. One day an alien will move into his house, eat all his food and slump around as if nobody understands him.

And he'll love that child as much as I love him.

Janie Emaus

A Time for Love

The way to love anything is to realize that it may be lost.

G. K. Chesterton

The time that your child deserves your love the least is the time that your child needs it the most.

Over and over in my mind, I heard my own mother's wisdom. Her words echoed in my head, driving me forward, giving me determination and courage.

As I backed the rented truck up to the dilapidated steps of the shoddy, yellow crackhouse, I fought back the tears. My body trembled in terror. My mind raced with the fierceness of two wild tigers darting at each other. Two young men, old friends of my daughter and well-muscled, jumped out of the back of the truck. Armed with baseball bats, they stormed the door and disappeared into the house, searching for my daughter or her body. Full of fear, I prayed for everyone's safe return.

How had we ever come to this? As a single mother, I had tried hard to instill in my two daughters the values that I had been brought up with, as I did the children in the school where I taught. One of my delights as a teacher was having my two young daughters often there helping me out in the classroom. We had been a team.

But when the teenage years hit, things started to go downhill. When she was seventeen, my youngest daughter Rebecca rebelled and hit the streets after we fought about the rules that I deemed so important to living under my roof. She had stormed out of the house. With no energy left for any more agony and turmoil, I willingly let her go. The rage and frustration on both sides had become unbearable. The abuse she had dished out over the past few years had made me feel like I was living in the twilight zone. I had given up all hope, so I set her free. I suppose I thought I was setting myself free, too.

Then one afternoon, that dreaded but expected phone call came from an unnamed friend. "Your daughter has walking pneumonia. She is wavering in and out of consciousness. She hasn't eaten for days. You are her mother, her only hope for life over death. Please come and get her out of here."

The feelings of anger and hatred that I harbored deep down inside me swelled up again. But then I heard the whisper of my own mother's voice as she proclaimed once again, "The time that your child deserves your love the least is the time that your child needs your love the most."

I thought about all the times my mother had come to me when I so desperately needed her love. She had never abandoned me and now it was my turn. My child needed me, and I could not abandon her.

I quickly took action. A phone call to one of her old friends, a rented truck and here we were.

Now, full of anxiety, eyes glued to the door, prayers screamed out in my head. *Please let them find her alive. Please let my child come home. Please, please, give me another chance to love her, nurture her and guide her back to health and life.*

In that moment, the two young men reappeared, supporting a third figure between them. My heart began to race. I choked back my tears as I cautiously unlocked the door of the truck. Carefully, they eased her up onto the seat beside me. As she slumped against my shoulder, I whispered my silent prayer of gratitude to God for this second chance.

Through my tears I spoke my first words to Rebecca in many months. "Oh, I'm so glad. Oh, I love you so much." She tilted her weary face upward and whispered faintly, "Thanks, Mom . . . I love you, too."

Several years later, I was sitting quietly one night when a friend called and said, "There's an e-mail here for you from Rebecca."

Having regained her health, she went back to night school and was now a young woman. She traveled abroad to finish her healing and discover herself. Now she was in Korea teaching English as a second language.

As I read her message, tears once again came to my eyes.

Dear Mom:

I love you more than anything in the world, and I thank you for all you have done. If it hadn't been for you, I wouldn't even be alive today. I can never repay you, but I can let you know every day. I have grown up a lot, and I can never go back to being the person I was, or knowing the people I did. I am so much more, and so much better. I am very smart, beautiful and full of life. I am back, and I am ready to start over. I'm coming home.

And then, in that moment of tearful gratitude, I remembered my own mother again, her own love and her timeless words of wisdom.

Noreen Wyper

When He Sleeps

He acts his age,
which at sixteen,
Is twelve.
He hides his insecurities behind a boisterous
And cocky facade.
Like others of his age and gender,
He lives for weekends and strives for mediocrity,
Giving his parents grief and grey hair.

But if you could see him when he sleeps,
You would see the truth,
A perfect freckled face, framed by
An irreparable cowlick.
You would see the little boy who once stopped
His dad's busy lawn mower to rescue a flower.

Now, you will hear him shout macho threats at his
    opponents,
While playing basketball.
He spews forth statistics of teams and players
With a know-it-all glint in his eye.

The biceps he sees in the mirror are twice as large
As those the rest of the world sees.

But if you could see him when he sleeps,
You would see the scrawny boy
Who was always the last pick for childhood games.
You would see eyes that idolized
Sports heroes, like his dad.
You would see big aspirations inside
A little body.

These days, you may know him as a confident and fickle
"Ladies' Man,"
A teenage Casanova, whose greatest talent is dating.
Indeed, on any given day he can be heard saying,
"What a babe!"

But if you could see him when he sleeps,
You would see the neighborhood weakling
Who would defend his sisters to the death.
You would see the soiled little hands
That were always happiest inside his mother's.

Today, he excuses his behavior as that of the
"Normal guy."
He claims to be average,
But I know better.
I've seen him, as he truly is,
When he sleeps.

Josie Lauritsen

"But Mom, Webmasters set their *own* hours."

Defining Love

About five years ago, "spring fever" was officially in the air, and love and romance were exploding all over the place. I knew that because my then nine-year-old son saw his babysitter kissing her boyfriend good-bye when he dropped her off. My son immediately wanted to know, "What's so great about all this kissing and love stuff, anyway?" I knew that this wasn't the "birds and bees talk" because we'd been having those since he could understand the difference between blue and pink. This was the *LOVE* talk.

Defining what "love" is and why it always seems to happen in the spring was quite a challenge. I thought that love would be a concept best understood by sharing my personal experiences with him. I realized that the more ridiculous you appear to your children, the more fully they will believe you. So, for ease of explanation (and minimum embarrassment), my romantic explanations were broken down into two areas: the first kiss and first love.

For the first kiss I told him that every woman (and most men) on this planet can tell you exactly where they were, how old they were and who the co-kisser was. I was at summer camp (truly a hotbed of romance for a twelve-year-old), and I was so excited about it that I wrote a postcard to my mother and asked her if she minded that I was a woman now (you can imagine the phone calls and letters that followed that little bit of correspondence). I said that a first kiss is exciting and scary and a lot of weirdness all rolled into one big, clumsy (possibly wet) smack somewhere in the vicinity of your lips. His response: a "yeech" followed by a very rude noise.

First love explanations were a little trickier. Trying to rationalize that the side effects—sweaty palms, total acne attack over your appearance and the roller-coaster feeling in the pit of your stomach—accompany a good thing just didn't quite make it. Saying it feels like you're coming down with the flu impressed him more.

I told him my first love was a high school classic. He was the sophisticated older man; I was the younger woman. To this day I've convinced myself that he's never gotten over me. It's been over twenty years and I still smile when I think of us plastered to each other's side, holding hands and being a nervous wreck waiting for him to call. I told my son that I didn't remember why we broke up but I do remember it broke my heart. When I got to this point in the explanation I could see that my son's eyes were glazing over. My son was old enough to ask the questions but too young to understand the answers.

I realized that trying to explain "spring fever" and falling in love to a child who still "loves" his comic books, "loves" the Indiana University basketball team and really, really, really "loves" his Rollerblades is sort of like asking a fifteen-year-old with a learner's permit to parallel park a semi truck on Mt. Everest. Technically, they know how to park (no pun intended), but they have absolutely no real frame of reference.

I decided to tell my son that first kisses and first loves have to be experienced to be understood. Spring is when love seems to happen because that's when all new things start to grow. He seemed satisfied with that answer but I felt sure that about thirty seconds after this conversation he'd have filed it away, never to be seen again. I'd forgotten about our heart-to-heart until yesterday, when my now fourteen-year-old came home with a slightly glazed look in his eye, a sappy grin on his face and a yearbook signed by the girl of his dreams. I asked him if he was feeling okay. As he breezed past me on his way to "graze" in the fridge, he stopped, got that grin on his face that reminds me why I fell so hard for his dad, and said, "I hate to admit it, Mom, but you were right. It does feel like the flu." I started smiling and that's when he said, "Don't worry, it's probably only a twenty-four-hour bug and I'll be fine by tomorrow." Thinking he was just being a smarty-pants I asked him how he could be so sure. "Oh, that's easy," he said. "She's not enough like you to make me really sick."

Eileen Goltz

Housewife's Prayer

Cleaning your house while your kids are still growing is like shoveling the walk before it stops snowing.

Phyllis Diller

Thank you dear Lord,
For things to do;
Tasks to complete,
That are never quite through.
Thank you for the laundry,
That piles up so fast;
For the tub I just cleaned,
Though I know it won't last.
Thanks for the toys,
That litter my floor;
For the mud-caked shoes,
That sit by the door.
Thank you for the fingerprints,
On once-clean glass;
Thanks for my carpet,
Now covered with grass.

Thanks for the kitchen,
That never stays clean;
For the skillets to scrub,
That lay in my sink.
These things in my life,
Just prove that I'm blessed;
God gave me a family,
I can live with the mess.

Sheila Hammock Gosney

"Say something! I want to make sure you're my child
before I give you a bath."

My Wife Doesn't "Work"

Any mother could perform the jobs of several air-traffic controllers with ease.

Lisa Alther

Is there anything more embarrassing today than being married to a woman who doesn't "work"?

Take Jackie.

She weaves, spins wool, attends classes twice a week at art college and is currently putting together a seven-foot tapestry she designed for the living room. She also whips up a hundred meals a week, irons a dozen shirts, waxes and washes the floors, walks the dog and throws a dinner party once a week.

But she doesn't "work."

She feels a minimum of two foreheads a week (to see if they're warm), listens to enough homework to get a degree from Oxford, runs the family budget, finds things in the basement no other living human being can find, reminds Richard to comb his hair every morning, cheers up Jane when she gets a zit on her face and refinishes furniture.

She does the shopping, locates the bargains, washes gym stuff, keeps track of everybody's underwear, answers family mail, makes certain nobody leaves a ring around the bathtub and takes care of minor medical problems.

But she doesn't "work."

She cuts hair, cleans the filter on the furnace, clips the dog's nails, provides waltz lessons for male members of the family, vacuums, puts treats in school lunchbags for a noon-day surprise, hangs up coats, rubs feet when they get cold, provides laughs whether needed or not, removes splinters, gives instruction on the application of eyeshadow, announces if it's a boot day, smiles through the recounting of old Monty Python skits and files class photographs.

She doesn't let anyone out of the house without a hug; she tucks Jane into bed every night (even though Jane is fourteen and almost as big as her mother); she knows the postal rates, moves sofas, listens solemnly when someone in the house says he or she is going to be Prime Minister, a famous athlete or just an astonishing detective (Richard's current ambition); she hangs pictures (eighty on our one wall), sews on buttons, visits art galleries.

But "work"? I'm afraid not.

Jackie lengthens jeans, unplugs plumbing, remembers to serve spaghetti once a week (the kids' favorite), picks out newspaper items that might make columns, does thirty sit-ups every morning to stay trim, explains patiently to Richard why he can't wear the same shirt eighteen days in a row and makes the Christmas cards.

Mind you, she doesn't jog three times a week now, act as a lifeguard at the Y, or take German at night school, and her university class on great books is over.

But she did broadloom Jane's bedroom, make our front-room coffee table (from an old dining-room suite), and (just last week) figured out how to replace the bulb in our slide projector when Daddy had failed.

That is, unfortunately, besides the point.

Jackie does not go to an office, perform brain surgery, drive a truck, belong to a union, type up letters, sell real estate, host a TV show or even wrestle.

In short, she doesn't "work."

Mind you, she did "work" the first three years we were married and trying to get a start, but she quit a month or two before she had Stephen.

So she's just a homemaker, wife and mother now.

Perhaps one day when the kids are a little more grown up, Jackie will "work" again, but in the meantime, I'm afraid she's too busy.

Gary Lautens

The Gift of Life

I was born in England, just prior to the Second World War. My family was poor, and by the time I was twenty, I was the main breadwinner in the family.

Then I met Tim. He was eleven years my senior, and we soon became a serious item. Then, in March 1957, the sky fell! I discovered I was pregnant.

Tim offered to marry me, but I wasn't sure I really loved him. I considered abortion, but couldn't go through with that either. I decided to have the baby and place it for adoption. I had made the mistake, I accepted the consequences.

The following months were a nightmare. I was sick the entire time, I hated the way I looked, I hated Tim, I hated everything and everybody.

When I went into labor, a neighbor took me to the maternity hospital. I felt terribly alone and very frightened. No one came, not even my mother. It was a disgrace in those days to conceive a child out of wedlock.

With every contraction, I kept telling myself everything would be okay, I wouldn't have to look at the baby, it would be adopted right away and my life would go back to normal. Finally, after some frightening complications, the baby arrived.

A few moments later, all my plans were blown away. A small bundle was placed in my arms as I heard the nurse say, "Here Beryl, say hello to your son." I looked down at this tiny, crumpled little being—he was so beautiful. The pain of a love so intense I could hardly breathe shot through me. I started to sob, quietly at first, then uncontrollably.

The next few hours were spent in a hazy, fitful round of sleeping and crying. When I finally awoke, I couldn't wait to hold him again. The nurse brought him to me, all pink and smelling of baby powder. As I looked down at him I thought, *There is no way I will ever part with him, this is part of me, this is my baby.* I named him Steven.

My sudden change of heart caused a lot of problems. I had already signed the adoption forms, and the adoptive parents had been selected. But I was adamant. I was keeping my baby.

When I arrived home, my mother was distraught. She couldn't bring herself to even look at Steven. She said she couldn't bear to hold him and then say good-bye to him. When I told her I was going to keep him, she started to cry, begging me to reconsider. I felt torn in two directions, but I stood firm. I was keeping my baby.

I was totally unprepared for the emotional roller coaster that followed. One day I would be resolute I was keeping him, the next day I would look around me and see the futility of my dreams. I kept asking the same questions. *How could I raise this child and still support the household? Who would look after him while I went to work?* My mother couldn't, and there was no way I could trust my father. There was no subsidized day care in those days, and I didn't even have a pram. I had to borrow one from the neighbor. Even the baby's clothes were given to me. Thank goodness I was breast-feeding; at least I could provide him with regular food.

Finally, I forced myself to face reality. The only thing of importance was the welfare of my baby. I came to realize that his needs were greater than mine. As I looked around our dingy house at my poor, defenseless mother and my father, who had so many problems, I made the hardest decision of my life. I would give up my baby. Tearfully, I told the social worker my decision. The prospective adoptive parents were still eager to take Steven.

On January 24, 1958, I wrapped my son in a beautiful white shawl, put the silver bracelet that I had bought him on his arm, and held him tightly to my body. I felt as if every fiber of my being was flowing from me into him. I had never before felt such intense love.

The social worker arrived with a sympathetic smile on her face. "Poor Beryl," she said, as she gently took Steven from my arms. I watched her walk to the top of the street, turn the corner and disappear from sight. It was all over—my son was gone.

No words can describe my feelings during the next few weeks. It was a continuous round of tears, anger and even thoughts of suicide. I phoned the social worker's office every week for three months and then periodically over the next two years. I just could not let go. I received letters from her, telling me how well Steven was doing. His new parents were thrilled with him, so thrilled they had adopted a little girl a year later. I was grateful to know he was healthy and well-loved, but it did not heal my broken heart and my deep remorse.

I buried myself in my work. I became a perfectionist, constantly having to prove how good I was at everything I did. My entire personality changed.

My relationship with Tim resumed, and over the next few years we kept setting dates to get married. Finally we drifted apart. I was now thirty-four years old.

Then in January 1972, I met Matt. We had such a connection.

He eventually asked me to marry him, and without hesitation I said, "Yes." Two months later we were married.

Matt and I seemed made for each other. The only thing that marred our relationship was that Matt loved children and he wanted to be a dad. I had been told that because of the complications during Steven's birth, my chances of conceiving again were one million to one. This now caused me enormous distress and was constantly at the back of my mind.

Then, while on vacation, I became terribly ill. I thought it was food poisoning. When we got home, I saw my doctor and later that day he phoned me. Sounding very serious, he told me to sit down; he had something very important to tell me. I feared the worst. There was a long pause, then he said, "Beryl, you're pregnant!" I couldn't believe my ears. I thought there had to be some mistake. But there was no mistake, I was pregnant! Matt and I were ecstatic at the news, as was my now-widowed mother.

Nine months later our son was born, and it felt to me like a miracle. I felt redeemed. I felt I had been given a second chance; I had been blessed with another son.

When all the excitement quieted down, I found myself reflecting on that cold day in January 1958, when I was forced into the depths of despair at the loss of my firstborn. For the very first time since that day, I allowed myself to imagine the joy the receivers must have felt when they first saw that tiny, crumpled little being, the thrill of holding him and calling him "Son." It was only then that I realized there is a definite purpose to all things, for being here, for things that happen.

I have tried, unsuccessfully, for forty years to find Steven, and will continue to do so for as long as I live. I just want to tell him I love him, and that his purpose in life has already been fulfilled—twofold.

Beryl Paintin

A Mother's Love Revealed

Some things . . . arrive in their own mysterious hour, on their own terms and not yours, to be seized or relinquished forever.

Gail Goodwin

As tears streamed down my face, I handed my five-day-old son to the nurse for the last time. *Be strong my precious little one. I know your new mommy and daddy will love you as much as I do. You will never be forgotten.*

Several years after the birth and relinquishment of my only child, my Aunt Amanda was visiting the family farm, collaborating with my grandmother on a family genealogy project. Grandma opened her "treasure box" to retrieve some of the priceless genealogy papers and came across the letter I had written fourteen years earlier, pleading with my grandparents to help me so I could keep my child. "Have I ever shown you this letter?" she asked Amanda. As she had not, she and Grandma read it together. Their eyes filled with tears as they reflected back on the difficult decision I had made.

Grandma then said, "By the time Grandpa and I

responded to Nicole's letter, she had changed her decision from what she so badly wanted to what would be best for the baby. I've kept this letter all these years. I know in my heart that Nicole will be reunited with her son again some-day. When that happens, this letter will be very important for her to share with him." Amanda agreed and the letter was carefully tucked back into the treasure box.

A year later, my grandma died of a sudden heart attack. It was difficult for all of us to deal with the loss of such a won-derful person. My grandpa, however, struggled the most. He was so lost without his companion of fifty-three years.

Over the next several months, my Aunt Amanda returned to the farm several times to try and help Grandpa. During one of her visits, she noticed that several personal items of Grandma's were missing. As she gently broached the subject with Grandpa, he confessed that it was too difficult to have Grandma's personal items around. Fear arose in Amanda. She quickly, yet discreetly, made her way to the treasure box. The box was still there, but when she opened it, her worst fears were confirmed—the treasure box was empty. Indeed, while trying to cope with his anger and grief, he had thrown away all the genealogy papers, the letters and the pictures received from their children and grandchildren over the years, including the precious letter I had written all those years before. Amanda raced to the paper bin on the back porch that stored the paper items waiting to be burned in the incinerator. Empty. All the treasures lost—burned by a grieving man in an attempt to ease his pain.

Another year passed and Amanda was again spending a few days on the farm with Grandpa. As was her practice, she helped him clean the house. As she was mopping the porch that morning, she pulled the paper bin out from the wall to mop under it. She immediately noticed what ap-peared to be a small white triangle beside the baseboard.

Leaning closer, she realized the "triangle" was actually the corner of several folded pieces of paper. She gave it a tug, and out from under the baseboard came a letter. When she examined it, she realized in amazement it was the letter I had written seventeen years before—the letter Grandma knew she would need someday. Amanda stared in disbelief at the letter. How could this be? She had mopped this area several times during the past year. The paper triangle had never been there before! She quickly tucked the letter in her pocket, making a vow to fulfill the dream of my grandma. She would keep the letter for the day I would be reunited with my son.

The years passed. The curiosity regarding his birth mother continued to increase in the young man, and he began to entertain thoughts of a reunion. His curiosity became surrounded by fear when his adoptive sister tried to contact her own birth mother. The message she received was one of abandonment—her birth mother wanted nothing to do with her relinquished daughter. *What if my birth mother feels the same about me?* he thought. He also had a fear that his adoptive parents might see themselves as failures because he chose to seek his birth mother. *I have to know,* he thought. *I have to know if she cared for me, or was just kicking me out.*

"Nicole," the voice on the telephone said. "There's someone who would like to meet you for his twenty-first birthday." The call was from the adoption agency I had worked with nearly twenty-one years before. "Your son is curious, excited, but also nervous. His adoptive parents are very supportive. What do you think?" I slid to the floor. I could hardly breathe. Fear ran through my body. I had always dreamed of this moment. Now that it was happening, how would I ever find the words to tell my son of the struggle I had in making such a difficult decision? How would he really know that I loved him so much that I gave him a life with parents who could offer him everything? But how could I say no? Through the tears, I managed to say, "Of course. Of course, I want to meet him."

Later that evening, after hearing the reunion would be a reality, my son listened as the caseworker shared details about me. "She's my birth mother! She's real! She's scared to death, and I'm going to meet her!" he said, grinning from ear to ear. In his soul, however, he still struggled with the question about why I gave him up for adoption and whether or not I really cared about him.

Two weeks later, as my son handed me a bouquet of flowers, I put my arms around this precious child for the second time in his life. We spent the next ten hours talking about our lives, our feelings and the future. Although our reunion was wonderful, I still sensed a lingering doubt in my son. Had I really tried everything in my power to keep him twenty-one years earlier? Had I really cared about him?

When I returned home from the reunion, I called my Aunt Amanda to share the incredible news. Amanda started crying as I shared the experience. "He knows everything there is to know," I said. "I only hope I was able to convey how much I loved him to be able to relinquish him."

When I finished talking, Amanda said quietly, "I have something for you." She then shared the story of how Grandma had decided to save the priceless letter. A few weeks later, I handed my son the now-yellowed pages that contained these special words:

Dear Grandma and Grandpa,

　　I've been trying to get up the courage for the past two weeks to ask you this but couldn't seem to think of the right words to say. I hope you don't get mad because I asked.

As you probably know, I can't go home unless I give this baby up for adoption. And that's just the problem—I don't want to. I want this baby more than anything in the world. I have thought very seriously about the pros and cons of both keeping and not. I've discussed it many times with the people at the adoption agency. There are many reasons behind each way to go, but I have decided that I want to keep this baby. This is what I'm asking. Would you help support the baby and me long enough for me to get back on my feet and get a job? I know it's asking an awful lot, but after I start working I could pay you back. It would probably be a few months that I'd need help. I've thought of every other way to go about this without involving you with money, but nothing is working out. I hope you can understand why I am asking you. I want this baby so much. You are the only hope I have left. If you don't think you should, I'll understand. I've tried to explain this to Mom, about how badly I want to keep him, but she doesn't seem to understand. I always get the same reply, "I know exactly how you feel." But she doesn't know how I feel! She kept me and had both of you on her side to help her out all the way. I've fought this thing out almost totally on my own. Grandma and Grandpa, you're all I have left. You couldn't let me go after Mom had me. What about your first great-grandchild? What more can I say? Please. Please. I need you. I've never begged for anything before, but I'm begging—please.

Love,

Nicole

P.S. Throughout this letter I have referred to the baby as "he." The doctors have said it's a boy.

As I sat next to my son, I watched the look on his face as he read the letter. I hoped the power of the words would show him the depth of my love. He placed the letter in his lap and looked into my eyes. "Whatever doubt might have lingered deep down inside of me is now gone," he said. "We will be a family from this day forward."

Indeed, six years later, we continue to be a family. I was able to attend my son's wedding last year and just found out I am going to be a grandma. I am truly blessed.

We will never know how the letter mysteriously found its way under the baseboard and how it seemed to reveal itself when it was ready to be found. I will always believe my grandma had her hand in this, somehow, and for that, I am eternally grateful.

Nicole Smith

Cyberstepmother

Only a mother knows a mother's fondness.

Lady Mary Wortley Montagu

I've often felt that "stepparent," a label we attach to men and women who marry into families where children already exist, was coined merely for the simple reason that we need to call them something. It is most certainly an enormous "step," but one doesn't often feel as if the term "parent" truly applies. At least that's how I used to feel about being a stepmother to my husband's four children.

My husband and I had been together for six years, and with him I had watched as his young children became young teenagers. Although they lived primarily with their mother, they spent a lot of time with us. Over the years, we all learned to adjust, to become more comfortable with each other, and to adapt to our new family arrangement. We enjoyed vacations together, ate family meals, worked on homework, played baseball and rented videos. However, I continued to feel somewhat like an outsider, infringing upon foreign territory. There was a definite boundary line that could not be crossed, an inner family circle that excluded me. Since I had no children of my own, my experience of parenting was limited to my husband's four, and often I lamented that I would never know the special bond that exists between a parent and a child.

When the children moved to a town five hours away, my husband was understandably devastated. In order to maintain regular communication with the kids, we promptly set up an e-mail and chat-line service. This technology, combined with the telephone, would enable us to reach them on a daily basis by sending frequent notes and messages, and even chatting together when we were all on-line.

Ironically, these modern tools of communication can also be tools of alienation, making us feel out of touch and more in need of real human contact. If a computer message came addressed to "Dad," I'd feel forgotten and neglected. If my name appeared along with his, it would brighten my day and make me feel like I was part of their family unit. Yet always there was some distance to be crossed, not just over the telephone wires.

Late one evening, as my husband snoozed in front of the television and I was catching up on my e-mail, an "instant message" appeared on the screen. It was Margo, my oldest stepdaughter, also up late and sitting in front of her computer five hours away. As we had done in the past, we sent several messages back and forth, exchanging the latest news. When we would "chat" like that, she wouldn't necessarily know if it was me or her dad on the other end of the keyboard unless she asked. That night she didn't ask and I didn't identify myself either. After hearing the latest volleyball scores, the details about an upcoming dance at her school and a history project that was in the works, I commented that it was late and I should get to sleep. Her return message read, "Okay, talk to you later! Love you!"

As I read this message, a wave of sadness ran through me and I realized that she must have thought she was writing to her father the whole time. She and I would never have openly exchanged such words of affection. Feeling guilty for not clarifying, yet not wanting to embarrass her, I simply responded, "Love you, too! Have a good sleep!"

I thought again of their family circle, that self-contained, private space where I was an intruder. I felt again the sharp ache of emptiness and "otherness." Then, just as my fingers reached for the keys to return the screen to black, Margo's final message appeared. It read, "Tell Dad good night for me, too." With tear-filled, blurry eyes, I turned the machine off.

Judy E. Carter

3

A FATHER'S LOVE

But after you've raised them, and educated and gowned them, they just take their little fingers and wrap you around them.

Ogden Nash

My Ray of Hope

Safe, for a child, is his father's hand, holding him tight.

Marion C. Garretty

When I was five years old, I became gravely ill. My parents were terrified and the doctors were stymied. Finally, a diagnosis was made. I had spinal meningitis. At that time, there was not that much known about the disease, and the only hospital that would take me was County General in downtown Los Angeles. Because the disease was thought to be highly contagious and always fatal, the only place for me in the hospital was in the men's contagious disease ward.

They put me in a crib amongst terminally ill men. Invariably, someone died on a daily basis and their bodies would lie there until the night shift attendants could take them away. When the attendant would come in to retrieve the body, I peered out through the bars of my crib and watched them being wheeled away. I can still remember the eerie sound of the iron lungs whirring through the night and then the even odder sound of the silence, when the man inside would die.

My parents drove out every single night to visit me. From Santa Monica to downtown Los Angeles the trip would take an hour or more, depending on the traffic. To make matters worse, my parents couldn't even touch me. The warmth of their arms wrapping around my little body was something I missed more than anything. Their arms would be down at their sides and inside a sterile gown. Masks would cover most of their faces. All I could see were their eyes, and more often than not, they were tearful. Shortly after I was admitted, I fell into a coma. My spine was a veritable pin cushion, being subjected to daily spinal taps. Even though I was in a coma, I can remember hearing the doctors talk about how I was going to die.

My mother started a prayer vigil at church, and around the clock someone would be praying for me. My father felt helpless and so alienated from his baby boy, his only child. I know he spent hours trying to figure out how he could break through this strange world I was living in. He desperately wanted to let me know that he was there . . . that I wasn't alone. Soon he devised a simple plan, and he prayed earnestly, perhaps for the first time in his life, for me to live.

The day I came out of the coma, the words of the doctors came flooding back to me. I thought I was going to die. I was scared, and I was confused. Suddenly, I felt something in the bed next to me. I soon learned that my father had left me a present. A small flashlight that had been run through the autoclave—the hospital's sterilizer— so that I could use it. There was a note on it that said, "I love you, Pop."

Better than any toy that I had been given, that flashlight became my world. Careful not to shine it anyplace that would have been considered intrusive, for fear that it would be taken away, I played with that little beam of light all day long. I would shine it at my toes and under my blankets.

That night something so exciting happened. When it came time for my parents to visit, I noticed a ray of light coming in through the window at the head of my bed from the parking lot far below. I shined my light back at it. It shined back at me with two blinks, then I blinked back twice, then three times. I felt joy for the first time in months. It was my dad! He had found a way to reach into my world and pull me away from my terror.

My father and I played the flashlight game every night from that day on, and I stopped thinking about dying. He had found a way for me to participate in my own life— even if it had to be in a hospital bed. At Christmas time, my parents put up a fully decorated Christmas tree in my room at home. Under the tree were some beautifully wrapped presents and a brand-new, shiny, red two-wheeler bicycle. They took pictures of that tree, with all those presents, and my Dad taped them to the foot of my crib. This happy collage embodied all the joy of the holiday. I would shine my flashlight on the pictures, spending hours trying to guess what goody each package held. It became my determination to get better so that I could open my presents and ride my new bike. At night I would wait for my dad to shine his flashlight in my window, announcing his arrival. We would flash back to each other in different sorts of code that we had concocted, and our game always made me laugh. The nightmare was ending; I was getting better. Five months later, I was released from the hospital.

My parents went on to have another baby. I was healthy again, and life seemed back to normal. But throughout my life, my father and I would share the secret world that lived tucked into a ray of light, emanating from a flashlight.

Many years later after my sister and I had turned our parents into proud grandparents, my father suffered a stroke. He was unable to communicate, and I saw so much fear in his eyes. That night I went back to the hospital, found his window and shone through it the brightest flashlight I could find. There would be no response.

Shortly after that, my father passed away. At that moment it dawned on me that my father, whose name was Ray, became the only ray of hope that kept me alive by devising a simple plan of a flashlight and a ray of light.

At the funeral, one particular story recounted to me cut through my grief better than any words of consolation could have. A nurse, who was with my father the night he died, said that he had been agitated and uncomfortable that entire day. "But at one point he looked up, towards the heavens, I thought, and he grinned a smile as wide as a river, and his whole body seemed to relax. *Strange,* I thought. I looked up to see what he was looking at, and there was this light coming in through the window. Kind of like someone was shining a flashlight from the parking lot into his window." She laughed and said, "Maybe it was just the angels trying to light his way up to heaven . . . guess we'll never know."

Robert Dixon
As told to Zan Gaudioso

Hidden Green Words

My youngest daughter and I have not always seen eye to eye. As with many parents, different opinions and different generations don't always add up to a smooth relationship. In an attempt to communicate with this small person who was this female version of myself, I found that I was too corporate for my own good. Thirty-one years with the same company gave me the skills to conduct one hell of a business meeting, yet I couldn't even talk to my own daughter.

"I love you" or "good job" could have been wiped clean from our spoken language with very little consequence—they were rarely used between us. Dinners were spent in front of the television, weekends taught us avoidance and special events were rehearsed. This was neither the way I imagined fatherhood to be, nor was it what I wanted.

However, in my sincere desire to change the situation, I stumbled upon a "common interest" that was able to communicate for us the love we so deeply shared. I thankfully unearthed an alternate method of communicating, more emotionally effective than I could have ever hoped, and after ten years it's still going strong.

One year, while working at the Indianapolis 500, I came across a liquor salesman with a briefcase full of what we now affectionately call "Greenie Men." A green, fuzzy pompom formed the body. Two white antennas protruded from the top, and two large white plastic bubble eyes with black pupils floated aimlessly from side to side when shaken. Ten little toes that shared the same self-adhesive foot were glued to the bottom of these amusing little creatures. I decided to take about ten of the funny little guys home, not realizing how significantly they were about to change my life. I was about to embark on a journey that my family now refers to as "The Greenie Man Wars."

My youngest daughter, who was away at college in Florida, would be coming home to Indiana for the Christmas holiday. I knew she'd be arriving in the midnight hours, and I was on heart medication that didn't always allow for a clear mind late at night. I decided if I couldn't be awake to kiss her tired head, I would deploy my green troops to warmly welcome her home. I stationed two of the fuzzy green men on her desk in her bedroom. I balanced a small yellow sign, comprised of two Post-it Notes stuck together like a tent, between the tiny twins. Using my best handwriting, I carefully wrote the note, "Welcome Home—Luv, Pop" onto the miniature billboard. The arrangement decorated the well-preserved room nicely. My hopes were that she would giggle a tiny laugh to herself before crawling into bed.

Looking down at the lonely bed, I remembered the tiny body that barely used to stretch halfway down the endless mattress. It had not been slept in for months. I sat on the bed, looked up at the ceiling and wondered where all the time had gone. Just then, for no other reason than to try to get one more laugh, I peeled off the adhesive layer from the bottom of a third "Greenie man's" large foot, jumped up on the bed and stuck it to the ceiling directly above her awaiting pillow. Disappearing into my room for the night, I was pleased with the risk I was taking. I had convinced myself that it didn't even matter if the only reaction I garnered was the rolling of a teenager's eyes over the silliness of her father.

The following morning, I got up, went to the restroom and proceeded to lift the toilet seat . . . only to find two cockeyed plastic eyes staring back at me from underneath the lid.

The wars had begun. . . .

"Greenie men" would be cleverly placed in the most unexpected places: medicine bottles, gift boxes, sock drawers, cassette recorders, shoes, coffee beans and glove boxes. Any place they would fit, no matter if it was Indiana or Florida. These were the most well-traveled toys on the East Coast.

Some of them were hidden so well, we'd all forget where they were, only to have them pop up unexpectedly in the oddest of places. The numerous "ambushes" made new and creative places difficult to discover. A new approach needed to be taken . . . a challenge originated by my daughter, a response I could have only dreamt of receiving from that "childish" act from many months before.

I was taking a business trip to Florida where my daughter would meet me for a visit between seminars. As I was checking into my hotel, I noticed the desk clerk staring quizzically at something over my shoulder. I turned to see six enormous green balloons with gigantic staring eyes, large rigid antennas and mammoth feet emerging from the escalator, followed by my daughter. The balloons were so immense, I was sure that at any moment she would float away.

The smile on her face was as tremendous as the balloons

she carried. I realized a bond was maturing where there was once a void. These whimsical, funny-looking creatures were bridging a gap between my daughter and me. There were still times we weren't always able to talk about the day's problems, whether it was school, boys or life; however, we did have another form of trust slowly developing that many parents only wish for.

From then on the "greenies" grew in size and splendor. To cheer me up after the death of my mother, a homemade "greenie" the size of a large head of lettuce, sporting a red Santa hat, appeared under the Christmas tree. When my daughter had foot surgery, I had a cane handcrafted for her with a "greenie" at the top. After I underwent a heart procedure, my family showed up at my bedside in green baseball caps with large eyes and bobbing antennas. They came to deliver a "greenie man" sweatshirt to keep me warm in a cold hospital. There was not a more welcome sight in the world. And when my daughter graduated from college, custom-designed "greenie" stationery said, "I'm proud you graduated from college."

And the wars continued . . . greenie men lurking around each twist and turn of life. Little soldiers communicating love, compassion, kindness and understanding.

I would have never thought these little green toys could have made such an enormous impact on my life. Communication between a parent and a child can, in fact, be a fun thing. Just when I thought there was none . . . there they were—two plastic eyes staring back at me. Teaching, giving, sharing, loving . . . risking. All shouting a hidden message with each "gotcha . . ."

Sarah J. Vogt with Ron Vogt

Hey Son, I Love You, Too

Your children will become what you are; so be what you want them to be.

David Bly

If I wanted to, I could come up with a dozen excuses. I was tired after a long day. Caught off-guard. Or maybe I was hungry. The simple truth is, when I walked into the living room and my twelve-year-old son looked up and said, "I love you," I didn't know what to say.

For several long seconds all I could do was stand and stare down at him, waiting for the other shoe to drop. *He must need help with his homework.* That was my first thought. Or he's going to hit me up for an advance on his allowance. Or he's assassinated his brother—I knew it would happen someday—and he's preparing me gently for the news.

Finally I said, "What do you want?"

He laughed and started to run from the room. But I called him back. "Hey, what was that all about?" I demanded.

"Nothing," he said, grinning. "My health teacher said

we should tell our parents that we loved them and see what they said. It's sort of an experiment."

The next day I called his teacher to find out more about this experiment. And, to be truthful, to find out how other parents had reacted.

"Basically, most of the fathers had the same reaction you did," my son's teacher said. "When I first suggested we try this, I asked the kids what they thought their parents would say. They all laughed. A couple of them figured their folks would have heart attacks."

Some parents, I suspect, resented what the teacher had done. After all, a health teacher's job is to teach children how to eat balanced diets and brush their teeth properly. What does saying "I love you" have to do with that? It is, after all, a personal thing between parents and their children. Nobody else's business.

"The point is," the teacher explained, "feeling loved is an important part of health. It's something all human beings require. What I'm trying to tell the kids is that it's too bad we don't all express those feelings. Not just parents to children and not just boys to girls. A boy should be able to tell his buddy that he loves him."

The teacher, a middle-aged man, understands how difficult it is for some of us to say the things it would be good for us to say. His father never said those things to him, he admits. And he never said them to his father—not even when his father was dying.

There are a lot of us like that. Men and women who were raised by parents who loved us but never said so. It is a common reason for the way many of us behave.

But as an excuse it is starting to wear thin. Our generation has devoted a great deal of attention to getting in touch with our feelings, to verbalizing our emotions. We know, or should know, that our children—sons as well as daughters—need more from us than food on the table and clothes in the closet. We know, or should know, that a father's kiss will fit as comfortably on the cheek of a son as on that of a daughter.

It's no longer enough for us to say that our fathers were Archie Bunkers who raised us to be "that way." We have done too many other things that our fathers never did. Our fathers didn't stand in the delivery room, vacuum floors or cook desserts.

If we can adapt to all of these changes, surely we should know what to do when a twelve-year-old son looks up and says, "I love you." I didn't . . . not at first. It's not always easy to make the leap from John Wayne to Alan Alda. But when my son came to me that evening for his bedtime kiss—a kiss that seemed to be getting briefer every night—I held on to him for an extra second. And just before he pulled away, I said in my deepest, most manly voice, "Hey, I love you, too."

I don't know if saying that made either of us healthier, but it did feel pretty good. Maybe next time one of my kids says, "I love you," it won't take me a whole day to think of the right answer.

D. L. Stewart

My Dad Henry

A son can be guaranteed to astound you all through his life—astound, bewilder, unnerve, flabbergast. . . . You name it. He'll do it.

Charlotte Gray

In the summer of 1980, my dad Henry was seventy-five. He had been getting weaker, and so I went down to Los Angeles often to see him. He was as crabby as ever, and not easy to be around when he felt weak. It wasn't a feeling he could deal with easily. But I was more stubborn, and I wouldn't let him take me down to his level. Sometimes, I took on the part of the father, remembering the times in Connecticut when I was so ill. I worried for him. I knew he could not stand to be around weakness. There hadn't been any work, so far, in '80, so I decided to write and direct a little home movie, as it were.

Dad and I had been on the phone one autumn afternoon, and the spirit was in me. "Dad, if I have enough ego to call myself an actor, writer, producer and director, there is this little scene I am going to write and direct. And you're going to star in it."

"What are you talking about, son?"

"I'm really saying, 'Your clock is running, and there are no time-outs.'"

"Sometimes I can't follow what the hell you're saying, Peter."

"Well, you watch a lot of sports, so you're familiar with the phrase 'the clock is running and there are no time-outs.'"

"Jesus, Peter, I can't keep up with your thought pattern. I don't understand what you're getting at."

"What I'm getting at is, your heart is not going to get better, and there is nothing you can do about it. Your clock is running, and there are no time-outs." I wasn't going to let him get away. "So I'm writing this scene and I'm going to direct this great actor in it—that's you, Dad—and the name of the scene is 'I Love You Very Much, Son.'" He sputtered for a moment then hung up the phone. A few days later, I called him and told him about the news at the ranch, how the apples were doing, how the boys were doing. Things one says to someone who doesn't do much talking during a phone conversation. "Conversation" is giving Dad too much of an active role, given the way that he normally played on the phone, in the kitchen, in his garden, or even as a captive in a car. Anyway, at the end of our "conversation" I said, "I love you very much, Dad." No preamble. Right to the quick. He sputtered again and hung up.

After five or six of these exchanges on the phone, and after I had said I loved him very much, he spat the words "loveyoutooson," into the phone. "No, no, no, Dad, you don't say the line as a response to something I've said, it has to come from the heart. It has to be an original idea that is not a repeated phrase. You have to fill its moment with your own reality. Now, we won't do the scene again today, but think about what I've just said, okay? And I'll

call you again in a few days. I love you very much, Dad."
He said yes, and hung up.

Soon, he was beating me to the end of the telephone
"conversation" with his very own, "I love you very much,
Son." With the distance and the plastic between us, I had
given him a chance to ease into the scene. But I knew it
would only count if we could do it looking down the bar-
rels, person to person, live. I told him that there were
some things I had to do in "Smell A," and I would drop by
for a visit, the next week. I had nothing really important
to do in my business, but I had this very important thing
to do with my dad.

A week later, having called first, I drove over to his
house in the early afternoon. He was out of bed and walking around the lower floor with the aid of a walker. "I
really hate this thing, Son, but my cane doesn't work well
on the tiles." He was embarrassed about his weakness,
although he needn't have been in front of me. We went
into the library-bar and he poured himself a shot of
tequila with a beer back. I was astounded. I passed on the
tequila but shared a beer with him.

He was more animated than usual, and spoke about the
neighbors' complaints over his chickens. But there was no
stalling about the reason I was there.

I could see that he was tiring, so I made the noise of
having to go to some meeting. That relieved him a bit. I
had taken the initiative to get to the end of the scene. We
both walked slowly to the front door. Once outside, he
took me by the shoulders. It was as if he were pushing me
away, and at the same time drawing me close. Tears were
streaming down his cheeks. Ever so slowly, and choking
on the high-powered emotion, he said, "I love you very
much, Son. I want you to know that."

I hugged him so hard I could feel the pacemaker in his
chest. Tears streaming down my own cheeks, I told him I

loved him very much and kissed him on his lips. Something we had never done before. I quickly drove off, stopping at a nearby park to have the good hard cry I needed. It had been done, and done with real emotions and originating feelings. Years of frustration fell off my heart like melting snow sliding off a roof.

On August 11, 1982, Dad lay in his bed in the ICU at Cedars, very weak. We were all there around him, we knew the Big Bell was tolling. At about ten o'clock, he opened his eyes and looked around the room. After looking in turn at each of us, he looked at me, pinning me with both of his beautiful blue eyes. "I love you so very much, Son. I want you to know that." And he closed his eyes and lay his head back on the pillow. These were the last words he spoke before he died. There are not many sons who get to have that moment with their fathers. Everything that had gone so wrong for so long was wiped from the slate. He died early the next morning.

There are times when I still get angry with him for some omission or other meaningless thing, but those times are immediately pushed away as I hear my dad's last words ringing like the Chimes of Freedom in my heart.

Peter Fonda

It Takes a Special Man to Fill a Stepfather's Shoes

With Father's Day coming up, it's occurred to me that this country is missing a holiday, Stepfather's Day.

If anyone deserves a special day, it's these brave souls who've had to carve out a place for themselves in ready-made families with the care and caution of a neurosurgeon.

That's why we have a Bobber's Day in our family. It's our own version of Stepfather's Day, named after Bob the stepfather. Here's why we celebrate it.

The Bobber has just moved in.

"If you do anything to hurt my mother, I could put you in the hospital, you know," says the college boy, who is far bigger than the stepfather.

"I'll keep that in mind," says the Bobber.

"You're not going to start telling me what to do," says the junior-high schoolboy. "You aren't my father."

"I'll keep that in mind," says the Bobber.

The college boy is on the phone. His car has broken down forty-five miles from home.

"I'll be right there," says the Bobber.

The vice-principal is on the phone. The junior schoolboy has been in a fight.

"I'll be right there," says the Bobber.

"I need a tie to go with this shirt," says the college boy.

"Pick one out of my closet," says the Bobber.

"You need to get your ear pierced," says the junior schoolboy.

"You need to stop burping at the table," says the Bobber.

"I'll try," says the boy.

"I'll think about it," says the Bobber.

"What did you think of my date last night?" asks the college boy.

"Does it make a difference?" asks the Bobber.

"Yes," says the boy.

"I need to talk to you," says the junior schoolboy.

"I need to talk to you," says the Bobber.

"We should have a stepfather-stepson bonding experience," says the college boy.

"Doing what?" asks the Bobber.

"Changing the oil in my car," says the boy.

"I knew it," says the Bobber.

"We should have a stepfather-stepson bonding experience," says the junior schoolboy.

"Doing what?" asks the Bobber.

"Driving me to the movies," says the boy.

"I knew it," says the Bobber.

"If you drink, don't get in the car. Call me," says the Bobber.

"Thanks," says the college boy.

"If you drink, don't get in the car. Call me," says the college boy.

"Thanks," says the Bobber.

"What time do I have to be home?" asks the junior schoolboy.

"11:30," says the Bobber.

"Okay," says the boy.

"Don't ever do anything to hurt him," the college boy says to me. "We need him."

"I'll keep that in mind," I say.

And so we have Bobber's Day. The boys buy their step-father a new toy they can all play with. The Bobber grills steaks. And I am awed by our great fortune that the Bobber earned his way into this family with such grace that it now seems he was always there.

Beth Mullally

The Toaster

*Dads don't need to be tall and broad-shouldered
and handsome and clever. Love makes them so.*

Pam Brown

When selecting gifts for others, a toaster probably tops
the list of risky items. It's fine for a shower of a cousin you
barely remember or an inept bachelor who can't master
much more than bread and peanut butter; it's definitely
taboo for your wife on her birthday or your wedding
anniversary. But the toaster my father bought for me was
one of the most touching and memorable gifts I had ever
received.

During my third year of university, I had gone home for
the weekend to my parents' farm where I had grown up.
Most of the weekend had been spent catching up with my
sisters, chatting with my mom and recounting stories
about my classes, my roommates, my boyfriend of the
moment. I had even brought home some photos of the
cheap town house I had rented with two other students.
My mom and sisters roared with laughter as they came
upon a picture of me desperately fanning a smoke alarm

with one hand and grasping a piece of black toast with the other (a temperamental secondhand toaster was an ongoing joke at our student house). My father, as usual, was on the fringe of this noisy female world.

On the last day of my weekend at home, I stood over the kitchen sink, my hands immersed in steaming, soapy water, and gazed out the window towards the shed where my father was working. He and his hired man were leaning over a manure spreader, examining axles and chains, tapping here and there with wrenches. As I watched the two of them, intent and purposeful, I recalled the times that I had joined my father in that shed, handing him tools, holding rusty fragments of farm equipment as requested, but mostly watching, as I was now, not really part of the picture. I was an outsider, a foreigner in this world of grease and dirt and steel. I wondered then what they talked about while they worked. The weather? The hockey game? Nothing at all? That secret male world of barnyard conversation seemed beyond my grasp. In truth, I imagined nothing more than essential grunts, orders, requests, curses, sighs of success. It would be nothing like the endless chat sessions that my mother, my sisters and I enjoyed, sprawled across one of the farmhouse's large beds.

On this particular day, during the last couple of hours before I would return to the city for school, I felt an overwhelming sense of loss as I watched my father in that world of his, which seemed so remote to me. I wondered if he preferred this seemingly voluntary isolation, or if he too longed to be part of a world that seemed equally remote and impossible for him to reach.

Having finished the lunch dishes, I went upstairs to do some final reading, pack my things and get ready for the hour-long drive back to university. I was to pick up my mother from work at two o'clock so that she could

drive me back. I had heard my dad come in from the barn;
I heard the shower and the electric razor and the noisy
drawers of his dresser opening and closing. When he
emerged from his room, I noticed his clean shirt and pants
and wondered where he was heading for the afternoon.
Thirty minutes later I descended the stairs, bags and
books weighing me down as I headed for the car. Dad
stood in the doorway to say good-bye as I hurriedly
crammed my baggage into the back and got into the driver's seat.

When I arrived at my mother's workplace, she was surprised to see me alone in the car and asked where Dad was.
She told me that he had been planning to come for the
drive and finally see the house and the university where I
had spent the past two and a half years. Immediately I realized why he had shaved and abandoned his usual pair of
green coveralls. He had intended to come, but I had made
no signs of inviting him. I had no idea that he would have
wanted to go with us. Shocked and ashamed, I hurried to a
telephone booth to call home and tell Dad that we would
be back in ten minutes to pick him up.

This time, Dad slid into the driver's seat and I crawled
into the back beside my pile of books and my suitcase. I
couldn't think of a word to say. The only thing on my
mind was what I hadn't said before. On our way back
through my hometown, Dad pulled over on the main
street and disappeared into the local hardware store. A
few moments later, he got back into the car and handed
me a small box containing a brand-new toaster.

"Sounds like you girls can use one of these," was all he
said.

I thanked him, though the words, I'm sure, were barely
audible. With the toaster on my lap, clutched between my
trembling hands, I stared at the back of my father's head
and his strong, straight shoulders. I thought of hugging

him, even touching his arm and saying thanks again, but we had never been accustomed to physical gestures of that sort. So instead, I sat and stared at the shiny picture on the box. At the time, that toaster seemed to say enough for both of us.

Even now, on a calm quiet morning as I stare out of my own kitchen window and wait for the breakfast toast to pop out of my new silver toaster, I can still vividly recall that day, fifteen years ago. That day, when I had sat in the back seat of my parents' car with another toaster on my lap, staring at my father's head, tears running down my cheeks. Sometimes as parents and as children, we can't always find a way to reach each other or find the right words to say. Sometimes there are no words to say, but a toaster still can warm my heart.

Judy E. Carter

A Letter to the IRS

Fatherhood, for me, has been less a job than an unstable and surprising combination of adventure, blindman's bluff, guerrilla warfare and a crossword puzzle.

Frederic F. Van De Water

Dear Sirs:

I am responding to your letter denying the deduction for two of the three dependents I claimed on my 1994 federal tax return. Thank you. I have questioned for years whether these are my children or not. They are evil and expensive.

It's only fair that since they are minors and not my responsibility that the government (who evidently is now taxing me more to care for these waifs) knows something about them and what to expect over the next year. You may apply next year to reassign them to me and reinstate the deduction. This year, they are yours!

The oldest, Kristen, is now seventeen. She is brilliant. Ask her! I suggest you put her to work in your office where she can answer people's questions about their returns. While she has no formal training, it has not seemed to hamper her knowledge of any other subject you can name. Taxes should be a breeze. Next year she is going to college. I think it's wonderful that you will now be responsible for that little expense. While you mull that over, keep in mind she has a truck. It doesn't run at the moment so you have the immediate decision of appropriating some Department of Defense funds to fix the vehicle or getting up early to drive her to school.

Kristen also has a boyfriend. Oh joy. While she possesses all of the wisdom of the universe, her alleged mother and I have felt it best to occasionally remind her of the virtues of abstinence, and in the face of overwhelming passion, safe sex. This is always uncomfortable and I am quite relieved you will be handling this in the future.

Patrick is fourteen. I've had my suspicions about this one. His eyes are a little close together for normal people. He may be a tax examiner himself one day if you do not incarcerate him first. In February, I was rudely awakened at three in the morning by a police officer who was bringing Pat home. He and his friends were toilet-papering houses. In the future, would you like him delivered to the local IRS office or sent directly to Ogden, Utah? Kids at fourteen will do almost anything on a dare. His hair is purple. Permanent dye, temporary dye, what's the big deal? Learn to deal with it.

You'll have plenty of time as he is sitting out a few days of school after instigating a food fight. I'll take care of filing your phone number with the vice principal. Oh yes, he and all of his friends have raging hormones. This is the house of testosterone, and it will be much more peaceful when he lives in your home. DO NOT leave any of them unsupervised with girls, explosives, inflammables, inflatables, vehicles or telephones. (I'm sure that you will find the telephones a source of unimaginable amusement, and be sure to lock out the 900 and 976 numbers!)

Heather is an alien. She slid through a time warp and appeared quite by magic one year. I'm sure this one is yours. She is ten going on twenty-one. She came from a bad trip in the sixties. She wears tie-dyed clothes, beads, sandals and has hair that looks like Tiny Tim's. Fortunately you will be raising my taxes to help offset the pinch of her remedial reading courses. *Hooked on Phonics* is expensive so the schools dropped it. Good news! You can buy it yourself for half the amount of the deduction that you are denying! It's quite obvious that we were terrible parents (ask the other two) so they have helped raise this one to a new level of terror. She cannot speak English. Most people under twenty understand the curious patois she fashioned out of valley girl/boys-in-the-hood/reggae/yuppie/political doublespeak. I don't. The school sends her to a speech pathologist who has her roll her *R*s. It added a refreshing Mexican-Irish touch to her voice. She wears hats backwards, baggy pants and wants one of her ears pierced four more times. There is a fascination with tattoos that worries me, but I am sure that you can handle it. Bring a truck when you come to get her as she sort of "nests" in her room, and I think that it would be easier to move the entire thing than find out what it is really made of.

You denied two of the three exemptions, so it is only fair you get to pick which two you will take. I prefer that you take the youngest. I'll still go bankrupt with Kristen's college, but then I am free! If you take the two oldest, then I still have time for counseling before Heather becomes a teenager. If you take the two girls, then I won't feel so bad about putting Patrick in a military academy. Please let me know of your decision as soon as possible as I have already increased the withholding on my W-4 to cover the

$395 in additional tax and made a down payment on an airplane.

Yours truly,
Bob Mullen

Note: The taxpayer in question added this caveat at a later date: "Rats, they sent me the refund and allowed the deductions."
Our response: "Gee Bob, sometimes you just can't get a break."

Bob Mullen

"Hey, Dad, can I set up a Web site
to trash my science teacher?"

Advice from the Groom's Dad

Words have an awesome impact. The impressions made by a father's voice can set in motion an entire trend of life.

Gordon MacDonald

I have the most useless job in the world.

Father of the groom.

Our Stephen is getting married this weekend and, as father of the groom, I'm expected to do absolutely nothing.

Okay, I have to show up.

But that's all. I have no duties. Don't have to hire a string quartet, arrange for flowers, select a modest but saucy little wine or walk down any aisle.

I could nod off and no one would care. Or notice.

Well, the role of nonparticipant is not for me; I want to get in my two cents' worth.

So, as my contribution to the wedding, I offer Stephen and his bride, Rhea, this advice on marriage.

Always eat a good breakfast. A good marriage requires lots of energy, and you shouldn't start the day on an empty stomach.

Always put the other person first.

Never leave home without a kiss. It's nice. If you can work in a little pat, I'm all for that, too.

Have fun. If you don't make each other laugh, there is something wrong.

Accept early in marriage that there are some things you'll never agree on—the proper room temperature, station wagons, pedal pushers, the *Three Stooges*. This is normal. Don't panic.

Don't try to win every argument. Compromise with dignity. And no gloating.

Live within your means. Money management is a lot more important than you may think in marital bliss. Don't be afraid to do without things. Things won't keep you together. When you look back, it isn't things you remember.

Surprises. You need lots of them. Just the other morning, I found a little poem left at my place at the table. Now you know why I think I have the finest life partner in the galaxy.

Don't sulk, whine or leave things in your pockets on washday.

Don't save your best smiles for strangers, people at the office or clients. Get your priorities straight.

Talk to each other. I'm a big believer in this.

Have a nice, big, cozy bed where you can start and end each day with a cuddle. If you're too busy to cuddle, you are probably suffering from a bad case of self-importance— fatal in a marriage.

Don't take each other for granted even if you're celebrating your golden anniversary.

Be faithful.

Don't figure romance is over once you're married. It's just started, if you play it right.

Have dinners at night with everyone around the table

discussing the day's events. Don't have the television on. Don't read the newspaper. Don't just complain. It's time to lighten up and relax.

Serve whipped cream now and then. Whipped cream puts everybody in a good mood.

A little lace never hurt a marriage.

Have children. And when you have them, take care of them, love them, enjoy them, spend time with them, say no to them, play with them, hug them. Children are probably the most important contribution you'll make to the world, so don't treat them like a hobby or leave them to strangers to raise.

Have a porch as soon as you can. And a couple of nice chairs. Sit out on summer evenings and watch sunsets. You don't always have to be on the go.

Be around when things go right, but also when they go wrong.

Listen, listen, listen. You'll be surprised what you learn.

No double standards.

Early in the morning, when you're still just half-awake, reach over and touch your partner to reassure yourself that he or she is there, and that things are all right. Tenderness is still legal.

And finally:

Invite the father of the groom over for dinner when you have meat loaf or Swiss steak. He promises not to give any more advice.

Gary Lautens

4

SPECIAL CONNECTIONS

If we have not peace, it is because we have forgotten that we belong to each other.

Mother Teresa

Against All Odds

Martin Wall was a prisoner in Siberia during the war. He had left behind in the Ukraine his wife Anna and his son Jacob. Unbeknownst to him, Anna had given birth to a daughter after his departure and named the little girl Sonya.

When Martin was released from prison he was a frail, old-looking man, bearing the evidence of torture on his hands and feet, and knowing he would never father another child. Yet he was free. He immediately began an intensive search for Anna and Jacob. Finally he received word through the Red Cross that his family had died en route to Siberia, and he was heartbroken. He still did not learn that he had a little daughter.

Anna was fortunate in the early stages of the war, having fled to Germany. She worked for a caring farm couple and was treated kindly. It was there her little Sonya was born. It seemed like many ages since she and Martin had been children in a peaceful home in a village in the Ukraine. *Could life ever again be free from pain, suffering and separation?* she wondered. She believed it could, if only Martin, too, could come to Germany and they could start anew.

It was not to be. The war ended with Germany's defeat, and Anna and her children were rounded up by Stalin's forces and told they were going home. Crammed into cold cattle cars, often without food and water, Anna knew in her heart she was headed for the terror-filled death camps of Siberia. Her hope was dead, and she was ill. "Oh God, protect these innocent little ones," she pleaded over and over again. Her labored breathing and her continuous chest pains were getting worse.

"Jacob," she breathed to her son, "I am so sick. Maybe I will die. I will go to heaven, and I will ask God to protect you. Don't ever leave little Sonya. God will take care of you both."

In the morning Anna was dead, and her body was carried away on a wagon to be buried in one of the many mass graves. Her children were removed from the train and sent to a communist orphanage. They were truly alone in the world.

When Martin received the news that his family was dead, he stopped praying. God had let him down at every turn, he felt. He was assigned to a job on a commune. There, as he worked mechanically, he slowly began to regain his health and strength. But his feelings and his heart felt dead. Nothing mattered to him anymore.

Then, one morning he met Greta, who was also working on the same commune. If she had not smiled at him, he would never have recognized the girl he had once known back home as a happy, intelligent schoolmate. What good fortune that they should have found each other here, of all places, after all this time and all that had happened.

Soon they were married. Life became worth living again. But there are some women whose arms ache until they are filled with a little child to love. Greta was such a woman. She knew Martin could never father a child and still she longed for children.

"Martin, the orphanages are full of Mennonite children. Why don't we adopt one as our own?" she begged.

"Greta," Martin replied, "how can you want to bring a child into our home to love? Don't you know what happens to them?" His heart could not bear to be broken again, and he had closed it.

Yet Greta's longing continued and love won out. Finally one morning Martin said, "Greta, you can go and bring one home."

When her day off came, Greta, having already chosen an orphanage, boarded the train and headed out to find a child. When she entered the long, dark hall of the orphanage, and saw the silent, pleading faces lining it, she wished she could scoop them all into her arms and carry them away.

Just then, a little girl came along and smiled shyly. *This is God's way of helping me choose,* Greta felt. She knelt beside the little girl and asked, "Would you like to come home with me to a real home with a father and a mother?"

"Oh yes, so much," the child replied, "but wait until I call my brother. We go together, and I could never leave him."

Sadly Greta shook her head. "I can only bring one child. I wish you would come with me." The girl again shook her head vigorously. "I have to stay with my brother. We had a mother once. She told him to care for me. She said God would take care of us both."

Greta found herself unable to look for another child. This one had stolen her heart. "Martin," she pleaded when she came home, "please, please, I need to bring two. The one I chose has a brother, and she will not come without him."

"Really, Greta," Martin answered, "of the thousands of children to choose from, you can only bring this one or none at all? I do not understand you."

Martin saw that Greta was sad and did not go back to the orphanage. Again, love won out. He suggested they both return and look at her little girl. Maybe he could persuade her to come alone, leave her brother behind. Then he thought of his little Jacob. What if he had ended up in an orphanage? Would he not want him adopted by a kind person like Greta?

"You came back for us," whispered the wide-eyed little girl as she greeted them in the hall. This time she held the hand of a frail, thin boy with gentle eyes. "I promised not ever to leave her," he said. "When my mother died, she said I must promise. And I promised. I am very sorry she cannot come to you."

Martin regarded the two small children in silence, and after a moment announced in a very decided voice, "We will take them both." He had been instantly drawn to this frail boy.

While Greta went to collect their clothes, Martin went on to make arrangements with the desk and to sign them out. When Greta arrived at the desk with a child on each hand, she found Martin standing in a daze. He was pale as a sheet, and his hands were shaking so badly he was unable to sign the papers.

She immediately rushed to him crying, "Martin! What is it?" Surely he was not taking sick here.

"Greta, read the names!" He thrust a paper in her face. Taking the paper she read the names of the two children: "Jacob and Sonya Wall, mother Anna (Bartel) Wall. Father, Martin Wall." All the birthdays matched.

"Oh Greta, these are *my own children!* This is my beloved son Jacob that I believed to be dead, and a daughter I never knew I had! If it had not been for your pleading for a child, and your heart full of love, I would have missed this miracle!" He wrapped his arms around his son, and cried, "Oh, Greta, there is a God."

Elizabeth Enns

A Hundred and One Atlantic Nights

A proud parent boasts little of a son's abilities and his achievements. But glories in his kindness, his gentleness, his quiet courage.

Pam Brown

I arrived home to a message light flashing on the answering machine. Nothing really out of the ordinary, and yet I had an uneasy sense about it. I pushed the button and listened to the devastated voice of my twenty-one-year-old son, Daniel:

"I'm guttered, Mum, Jaish can't do it!"

I gasped, feeling his disappointment and my own as well. Three months before, in the fall of 1995, Daniel's old school chum Jaishan had asked Danny to team up with him and enter the Great Atlantic Rowing Race and row from Tenerife, Canary Islands, to Port St. Charles, Barbados. He had accepted with great excitement. They paid the entrance fee, and planning began immediately.

I was excited to be able to use my background in public relations to help promote them, get the specially designed rowing boat custom built and help raise the needed funds. We had two years.

Both boys were British army cadets and needed permission for the time off. Danny's request had been accepted. Now we knew Jaish's request had been turned down. I reassured Daniel that he would easily find another partner.

"It's not that easy, Mum. I need someone who can commit the next two years to promotion, fund raising, training and skills acquisition. But mostly it has to be someone I can spend three months alone with on a twenty-three-foot boat!"

I'm not really sure what happened next. I don't know whether he asked or I offered. All I know is that at the end of the conversation I had agreed to become his new partner and row across the Atlantic with him—we were a team!

My beloved second husband Keith had died of cancer a few years before, and my old life was gone. I was fifty years old and a widow. My life felt empty and had no direction. The prospect of spending the next two years preparing for an adventure was very exciting, and the opportunity to share this unique experience with my son was irresistible. Once I had decided, there was no going back. He was offering me a once-in-a-lifetime opportunity, and I was going to seize it.

The commitment to row the Atlantic had been made. Now came the logistics. Money was a major issue. I had a marketing job, but there was no way it would begin to finance this project. So off I went to the bank.

As the former mayor of my hometown of Chipping Norton I was fairly well known, so I did have some hopes. But when all was said and done, my presentation still sounded like a fifty-year-old widowed woman asking for a loan so she could row the Atlantic with her son. Right!

So I mortgaged my home, my two-hundred-year-old little stone cottage.

We were officially a team.

When our custom-built ocean-going rowing boat was completed, we ceremoniously named it *Carpe Diem*—Seize the Day! We began training sessions together, mostly on the Thames. Daniel began to feel quite guilty because of the financial burden he felt he had placed on me. At one point I realized, *My God, if this doesn't work, I could lose my house!* But we didn't have time for thoughts like those. We each brought our own unique skills to the venture. I knew it was my job to get us to the starting line in the Canary Islands, and Captain Daniel would get us to the finish line in Barbados.

When I finally got up the courage to tell my own mum of our plans, to my delight she offered no guilt, fear or negativity. Instead her response was: "The years between fifty and sixty go like that!" and she snapped her fingers. "DO IT! And I'm utterly behind you."

October 12, 1997, finally arrived. After two years of hard work, we departed Los Gigantes Tenerife along with twenty-nine other teams. At fifty-three, I was the oldest participant, and we were the only mother-and-son team. Our boat was designed with two rowing seats, one behind the other. For the first six hours we rowed together. After that, we began the routine we would maintain for the next one hundred days. Two hours of solo rowing, and then two hours of sleep in the tiny cabin in the bow. For the first week out, Danny was sick with food poisoning, and I had to be captain and in charge. It proved to us both that I could in fact pull my own weight on the water.

Once Daniel was better, we fell into a comfortable routine that bonded us together into a wonderful new partnership. Sometimes he would be sleeping so soundly that I would row for another hour or so. Often Dan would do the same—row for another hour or so and let his mum sleep. Our obvious kindness toward each other was awesome, and I found my son's kindness toward me to be overwhelming. We were a rowing team, yes, but in the larger picture we were still mother and son, loving and caring for each other unconditionally. If either of us could have given the other a full eight hours' sleep, we would have done so in a flash.

The constant rolling and heaving of the boat, the constant dampness and humidity, the lack of sleep and comfort and, of course, the heavy rowing all began to take a toll on my body that deeply worried us both. My hands were red and raw and stiff like claws. I had boils on my bottom and I began to suffer from sciatica. There was swelling in my hip from a muscle I had torn prior to departure, and my shoulder was injured from being thrown across the boat in high seas. Danny was worried that his drive to achieve his goal was going to permanently damage his mum, and I was worried that the frailty of my fifty-three-year-old body was going to destroy my son's dream. I suddenly felt old and a burden on the venture. But then Daniel began to experience many of the same pains, and I knew it wasn't just me, but the extraordinary conditions we were living under.

Throughout the trip, there were many things that made us think about giving up. There were the hard days when we blamed each other. "How could you do this to your poor mum?" I would shout. "This is all YOUR fault!" And Daniel would yell back, "I didn't expect you to say 'Yes!'" But in truth, we decided that the only thing that would have *really* made us give up was if a whale had smashed our boat. Daniel laughs now and says, "And oh my God, how many times we prayed for that!"

We were astonished as to how something as small as a rainbow, or a fish leaping out of the water could instantly cheer us up when we were low. In addition, before we left, we had all our friends and relatives write poems and letters to us, and seal and date them. That way, we had mail to open on each day of our journey. The humor and love in these letters picked us up and carried us when times got really rough.

We also had on board a radar beacon that allowed us to be tracked exactly. Each night the positions of all the boats were posted on the Internet, and our friends and family were able to track us. My own sweet mum rowed the Atlantic with me every night in her dreams. My stepfather drew a map to scale on the wall, and each night friends would call and report our position to my mum. They would then plot our course on that map. In a way, it was three generations rowing the Atlantic.

Both Daniel and I took a careful selection of books and taped music along. If you think rowing the Atlantic is boring, you should try *not* rowing! After a while, for variety, we began to trade books and listen to each other's music. Daniel began to appreciate my classical choices, and I began to enjoy listening to his reggae and UB40!

Every team in this race had its own reasons for participating. Some were committed to winning. We, however, were doing it for the challenge and the opportunity to spend this unique time together. Knowing we would not win, we took two hours off each night, and sat and enjoyed dinner, and talked. We told each other the stories and anecdotes of our lives, things that might not otherwise have been shared over a lifetime. One night over dinner I said, "This is a little bit like Scheherazade, you know, the story of *A Thousand and One Arabian Nights!*" Daniel replied, "Yes, Mum! Perhaps we should call our book *A Hundred and One Atlantic Nights!*" By complete coincidence (or was it?), that's exactly how many nights it took to cross—101!

On the night of January 22, 1998, we were approaching

Barbados, thinking we still had twenty miles to go. We were loafing, savoring the last night of our long adventure together. One last time, my son began to make me a cup of hot chocolate and turned on his headlamp for a few moments. Suddenly the radio began to squawk. It was an escort boat, and they were looking for us. When we identified ourselves as *Carpe Diem*, we heard a lot of screaming and shouting on board: "It's them, it's them, they're safe!" They had seen Daniel's light for those few moments and were hoping it might be us. Then they told us to our shock and delight that we actually had only six miles left to go! Daniel rowed the first four, and allowed me, his aching but ecstatic mum, to row the last two. I would be the one to take us across the line of longitude that was the official finish line.

To our amazement, an entire flotilla of waiting boats carrying family and friends began to cheer. They then set off fireworks, lighting up the night sky, accompanied by the triumphant cannons of the 1812 Overture to welcome us and celebrate our safe arrival. The thrill of our accomplishment filled me in that moment, and I burst into tears and cried out "We've done it!! Oh Daniel, we've done it!"

Because of the heavy headwind, and our great fatigue, we chose to board the waiting escort boat, while our own weary little *Carpe Diem*, half filled with water and listing to one side, was towed in behind us. We were almost two months behind the winning KIWI team and thought that everyone would have forgotten about us—after all, we were the last boat in. But we were surprised and truly overwhelmed at the enormous welcome we received upon our arrival! Everyone wanted to meet and congratulate "Jan and Dan," the British mother-and-son team who had successfully rowed across the Atlantic and completed the race.

Aboard the escort boat we had an emotional reunion

with my daughter, Daniel's sister Becky. And there was one more lovely surprise! Waiting for us on shore with tears and hugs was my own sweet mum, come all the way from her home in France, to welcome her jubilant daughter and grandson.

When I try and put into words what we will remember most, my journal entry from day sixty-nine speaks most poignantly of the things only my heart would know. I wrote:

> *I don't believe it is the beauty, the dolphins, whales, dawns and sunsets, although they will be with me forever. The brilliant night sky, stars, delicate new moons, brilliant full 'bright as day' moons. The power and the glory of the ocean.*
>
> *No. It is finding out how one's body and mind learn to cope. Seeing how Daniel bears up. I have found such pride in his unfailing good temper and optimism—his intrinsic kindness and thoughtfulness. I have loved the baby, the child, the boy, I have been proud of them, but now I love and admire the man, Daniel, with all my heart.*

For the rest of our lives, no matter where they may take us, we will always have the memory of this special time together, and the pride in the spectacular accomplishment that was ours, and only ours.

We did it. Together.

Jan Meek with Daniel Byles
As told to Janet Matthews

From the Heart

The older I become, the more I think about my mother.

Ingmar Bergman

When I was fourteen years old (same age as my daughter is today), my mom and I didn't have money for a Christmas dinner, much less gifts. I knew she was sad about it, and I was determined we wouldn't let it get us down. Homemade gifts are nice, but I wasn't very imaginative and too broke for supplies. I decided to give my mom something I treasured myself—the one nice piece of jewelry I owned, a gold cross necklace.

I cleaned it, made sure there were no knots in the chain and wrapped it in the prettiest paper I could find. I was so excited, I couldn't wait for her to open it.

Single moms have it hard (as I know firsthand now), and I really wanted to see her smile. We always opened our gifts on Christmas Eve night, and that afternoon, I could wait no longer.

I asked if we could "have Christmas" early. I anticipated that Christmas more than when I knew I was getting a lot of nice gifts. I didn't expect to get anything that year. It was about giving.

I handed her the little box, hugged and kissed her and wished her a Merry Christmas. I waited anxiously for her to open it but she just sat there with the box in her hands and looked at it.

I remember the look on Mom's face was a mixture of sadness and serenity. She knew her greatest gift to me was her love. After what seemed a long time, she looked at me and said, "I have something for you, too."

She reached into her pocket, pulled out another small box, placed it in my hands and told me although it was not much, it was filled with love.

I was quite curious and a little scared. I knew money was tight and hoped Mom hadn't spent money on something we couldn't afford.

There was a little velvet box inside and when I lifted the lid, there was a tiny ring with a diamond chip in the center. In a note, she told me the ring was twenty-three years old, she hoped it brought me good luck . . . and "I love you."

I got a huge lump in my throat and looked at her. She smiled and told me it had been her wedding band from my dad. It was now mine. I slipped it on my finger and hugged my mom.

She opened my gift and when she saw the necklace, big tears filled her eyes. She asked me to put it on her. She held the necklace and told me she thought it was our best Christmas ever. I could only nod my head in agreement.

This Christmas, I give thanks for Mom and treasure every memory we shared. You see, my mom has advanced Alzheimer's disease and no longer knows me. But I look at "our" ring and remember her gentle, wise spirit and give thanks God blessed me with her.

But that's not the end of the story.

Our home was burglarized four years ago. One of the

items stolen was that little ring. I had left all my jewelry at home for safekeeping, because it was Memorial Day weekend and I was going to the lake. I was totally heartbroken when I found out the ring was gone. Of course, so were her diamond rings, my wedding band, engagement ring, etc., but it was *that* ring I grieved for the most.

I wrote a letter to our local paper and begged whoever stole it to "PLEASE return it by mail anonymously."

A few weeks went by with no response and then one day a police detective showed up at my door. He held out a tissue and asked me to identify the item inside.

It was my ring! I have never found out where or how he got it, but it remains on my finger to this day.

Nancy McBee

The Navy's Baby

It is a peg big enough on which to hang a hope,
for every child born into the world is . . . an ever
fresh and radiant possibility.

Kate Douglas Wiggin

In the summer of 1953, the Navy escort carrier the USS
Point Cruz arrived in Inchon, Korea, fresh from combat.
The city had been devastated by three years of war. Food
was scarce, and the orphanages were full of leftover children. The ship's chaplain, Lt. Edward O. Riley, received an
urgent message from his old friend Sister Philomena, a
remarkable Irish nurse who ran the Star of the Sea
Children's Home. Like all the orphanages, it was over-
crowded, and short of food and medicine. When he
arrived, Father Riley was startled to find a sick, starving
infant with blue eyes staring up at him.

"Where did he come from?" he asked. Sister Philomena
told him. The baby had been left outside the corpsman's
building in ASCOM (Army Service Command Post) City.
Marine Corpsman Lyle Van Meter had gone out at midnight on a hot night in July, and discovered the sick,

emaciated one-month-old child wrapped in some filthy rags. After a short investigation, Lyle and his buddies realized the best place for this white baby in Korea was with Sister Philomena.

Sister received him with open arms, but when she saw the blue eyes, she was dismayed. She knew that as a half-Caucasian baby, he had no future in Korea. If he lived, he would be despised in this culture, an object of ridicule and scorn. But her first concern was his desperate need for medical attention. The Marines who found him called him George ASCOM, she told Father Riley. "He's an American, Father, and he's very sick. I have no food for him, no medicine. Can you not help?"

A man of action, by sunset he was back on board the *Point Cruz* and in conference with his skipper.

Now Captain John T. "Chick" Hayward and Father Riley were of the same rugged school. As soon as he understood the situation, the captain ordered Father Riley to bring the baby aboard the *Point Cruz,* and "keep him here until he's healthy." He said: "Go ashore and get a visa for him to enter the States, and don't come back to this ship without it." The *Point Cruz* then put to sea, leaving Father Riley behind on shore to face the red tape on his mission of mercy.

A short time later, the hospital ship the USS *Consolation* arrived in Inchon Harbor. On this steaming hot morning, Navy surgeon Lieutenant Hugh Keenan finally had shore leave, and he and several companions talked of going to a beach that day for some badly needed R&R. They decided instead to head for the Star of the Sea Children's Home. They also knew Sister Philomena and thought she might appreciate a visit. Perhaps there was some way they could help.

Sister welcomed them in out of the heat and quickly ascertained that the young doctor was married and a father. She led him to the nursery, and there amongst the dozens of Korean babies, he noticed the tiny white baby with blue eyes. No more than three months old, he was scrawny and listless, and covered with a rash. He clearly had an American father—totally unacceptable in Korea.

Picking up the child, he cuddled him close. He and his wife Genevieve had lost four babies over the last few years. Something about this baby reminded him of the boy they had lost most recently. He was so taken with the child he decided on the spot he wanted to adopt him.

The next day, he returned with some ointment for the rash. Then he took little George in his arms and began to feed him. With a smile, he told Sister his plan. He would take him home to Genevieve, and they would raise him as their own—as an American. She smiled with satisfaction and told him that their mutual friend Father Riley was already working on a visa to get George out of Korea.

That evening he sought out his own captain, who proved unmoved by the situation. Disappointed, Dr. Keenan realized he would have to rely on Father Riley for the paperwork and find another way to get George to the States.

Meanwhile, Father Riley had finally managed to procure a Korean passport for George. But the U.S. Consul flatly refused to issue a visa. The *Point Cruz* had returned to Inchon, and the captain ordered, "Bring that baby aboard!" Father Riley was a bit worried about how the Navy would feel about a baby on board. The captain was more concerned about the reaction of the crew. He needn't have been.

By now the entire crew knew about George and was preparing for his arrival! The armistice had been signed in July, Christmas was coming and the men just wanted to go home. Morale was low, as low as it ever gets on board ship, so the men turned their attention to the baby. A nursery was prepared, and a crib and playpen were built. Homemade toys and rattles were lovingly crafted for the baby, who represented to all of them family they missed. Sheets were cut into diapers, and a bomb cart was converted into a baby carriage so they could wheel him around the ship. Anticipation built as they waited for the baby to arrive.

When Father Riley finally brought George up the gangway, the entire crew of the *Point Cruz* lined the rail cheering and waving. *Their baby was finally on board!* He was named "George Ascom Cruz," but mostly the crew called him "Baby-san." And they volunteered in droves to tend to him. Six men were chosen to be his caregivers: The qualification was they had to know how to fold a three-cornered diaper!

Little George quickly responded to all the love and care. He put on weight, the rash disappeared and, to everyone's delight, he was soon gurgling and smiling. The men soon discovered that when George gazed up at them with his blue eyes, their hearts totally melted! So many of them wanted to visit the nursery that Captain Hayward began posting bulletins to apprise them of his improving condition. Each day, George was wheeled up on deck in his bomb-cart carriage, and the ship's PA system would announce: "Attention all hands! Baby-san on the hangar deck from 1400 to 1430." The men would then line up to visit *their* baby, fuss and cluck, and take his picture. They treated him with as much love and pride as if he were their own. Surrounded by a sea of fatherly love, it was as if he had eight hundred fathers! Sometimes Captain Hayward would even order George onto the bridge to enjoy some private time with him.

On laundry day, the men replaced the Admiral's flag and hung a half-dozen or so diapers on the yardarm to dry. When a passing ship radioed that it didn't understand the signal, *Point Cruz*'s response was always just "Baby-san on board!"

Dr. Keenan finally had shore leave, and met with Father Riley. Captain Hayward had agreed that because Keenan still had a year to serve, George should remain on the *Point Cruz*, while the captain arranged passage for him to the States.

When Hugh Keenan wrote to his wife and told her he was making arrangements to have a baby in her arms by Christmas, he held his breath waiting for her reply. When it arrived, it was an emphatic YES!

A cheer broke out that night at dinner on the Point Cruz when it was announced over the PA that their baby was going to the States to have a real family, a real home.

Meanwhile, Father Riley still had no luck with the visa. Then, in mid-November, Vice President Richard Nixon arrived and dropped a word in the right ear. A few days later, the visa arrived! Captain Hayward then completed arrangements to fly George to Japan to meet the transport ship *General Gaffey* which would carry him home to Seattle.

In late November as the *Point Cruz* prepared to sail, Hugh Keenan kissed his new baby son good-bye and handed him to Father Riley, who would escort him all the way home to the U.S. Ten days later, eight hundred men lined the rail and cheered as George Ascom Cruz Ibfc. (Infant Boy first class) was piped over the side to begin his journey home to America.

On a cold day in Seattle, a few days before Christmas, Genevieve Keenan stood anxiously waiting dockside to meet her new son. All eyes were on the now eight-month-old baby coming down the gangplank in the arms of a Navy nurse, with Father Riley close behind. As the crowd watched, Mrs. Keenan scooped up her new baby, a special

Christmas present from her husband, and exclaimed, "Oh, Father, what a beautiful child!"

George was renamed Daniel Edward Keenan. Daniel for Hugh's father, and Edward for Father Riley. A year later, Hugh Keenan finished his naval tour, came home to his wife and two children, and returned to his residency at the Mayo Clinic. Later he moved to Spokane where he set up his own surgical practice. Danny grew up in Washington state, graduated from university, married and had his own family.

As the years passed, the men from the *Point Cruz* never stopped wondering about their baby. In 1993, Bill Powers, the former hangar deck chief, organized a reunion and was determined that Dan should be there. When word got out that "George" had accepted, the veterans began to buzz with excitement! *Their baby was coming!*

When Bill Powers stood up to formally introduce Dan to the seventy men in attendance, he concluded by saying, "And now gentlemen, after forty years, here is our baby," and then just stood there and cried. There wasn't a dry eye in the house. The former crew members crowded around him just as they had done all those years ago in his bomb-cart carriage. They were excited to see him and shake his hand, and they regaled him with tales and anecdotes from the early months of his life on board the *Point Cruz*. Some shared the one special time they got to hold him, another would declare that he'd had the privilege of changing his diapers. One gentleman came up to him with tears in his eyes, and simply said: "You just don't know how much this means to me to have this opportunity to finally meet you." And then he planted a big kiss on his cheek.

Dan Keenan struggled with his words as he rose to bid them farewell. He wondered what he could say to these men to express his gratitude for saving his life. He looked out at the aging faces—all strangers to him. But they had all loved him; to them he was like a son. He meant so much to them, and he was deeply moved. As he stood on the podium, the words began to flow.

"How do I thank you for my life? Without you men and your good captain, I wouldn't be here. Not in this hotel, not in this country. And maybe not even on this earth."

There was a long silence that followed as the men of the *Point Cruz* looked at the man who had grown from the baby they had loved. He had lifted their spirits and given them hope for life and peace, and the end of the war. And they in turn, led by their captain, had given him his life and his future.

Janet Matthews with Dan Keenan

Embassy of Hope

Luck is a matter of preparation meeting opportunity.

Oprah Winfrey

When Mark was five years old his parents divorced. He stayed with his mother, while his father enlisted in the armed forces.

As Mark grew up he occasionally had recollections of the brief time he shared with his father and longed to see him again one day. However, as he grew into his late teens, thoughts of his father began to subside. Mark was now more into girls, motorcycles and partying.

After he graduated from college, Mark married his high school sweetheart. A year later, she gave birth to a healthy bouncing baby boy. The years passed.

One day when Mark's son was five years old and as Mark was preparing to shave his face, his son looked up at him and laughed, "Daddy, you look like a clown with that whipped cream on your face."

Mark laughed, looked into the mirror and realized how much his son looked like him at that age. Later, he remembered a story his mother had once told him of him telling his own father the same thing.

This event started him thinking about his own father a lot and he began quizzing his mother. It had been a long time since Mark had spoken of his father, and his mother told him that it was now over twenty years since she had spoken to him. In addition, all her knowledge of his whereabouts ceased when Mark became eighteen.

Mark looked deep into his mother's eyes and said, "I need to find my father." His mother then told him that his dad's relatives had all passed away, and she had no idea where to begin searching for him but added, "Maybe, just maybe, if you contact the United States Embassy in England, they might be able to help you."

Even though the chances seemed slim, Mark was determined. The very next day, he made an overseas call to the American Embassy and the conversation went something like this.

"U.S. Embassy, how may we help you?"

"Ahh . . . hi, my name is Mark Sullivan and I am hoping to find my father."

There was a long pause and the ruffling of some papers, and then the man said:

"Is this Mr. Mark Joseph Sullivan?"

"Yes," Mark answered anxiously.

"And were you born in Vincennes, Indiana, at the Good Samaritan Hospital on October 19, 1970?"

"Yes . . . yes," he answered again.

"Mark, please don't hang up!"

Mark then overheard the man as he made an excited announcement to his co-workers: "Everyone listen . . . I have terrific news . . . Lieutenant Ronald L. Sullivan's son is on the phone . . . he found us!"

Without a pause Mark heard in the background the roar of a crowd—obviously the entire staff of the embassy, clapping, cheering, laughing, crying and praising God.

When the man returned to the phone he said: "Mark, we are so glad you have called. Your father has been coming here in person or calling almost every single day *for the past nine years,* checking to see if we had located you."

The following day, Mark received a phone call from his overjoyed father. His father explained to him that he had been traveling to the United States every six months trying to find him. Once he was even given an address, but when he got there the landlord told him that Mark and his mother had moved out just two weeks prior, leaving no forwarding address.

Having found each other, Mark and his dad enjoyed an emotional reunion. They are now part of each other's lives, and see each other as often as possible.

David Like

What Odds?

*The happiest moments of my life have been the
few which I have passed at home in the bosom
of my family.*

Thomas Jefferson

On the first day of school, as I introduced myself to my
new class, one little girl named Patricia caught my attention. She looked so much like my own daughter, Darcie, I
had to give my head a shake. As the months went by I
noticed how her mannerisms and even certain behaviors
were similar to Darcie's, even though she was only eight
and Darcie was now nineteen. She even wore her hair the
same way Darcie had in grade school.

At the parent-teacher meetings in November, I enjoyed
meeting Patricia's mom, Jenny. I shared with her how
much her daughter resembled mine, and wished I had
brought a picture along to show her the similarity. I then
mentioned that Darcie was adopted, even wondering
about the possibility of the two girls being related somehow—the resemblance was so uncanny. As Jenny was
leaving, I said, "Yes, Darcie was born on July 19, 1975, so if

you had a relative who gave up a baby for adoption, maybe it was Darcie." Being a fairly private person, I was startled at myself at this sudden confidence. I attributed it to my nervousness about the interviews and put it out of my mind.

I forgot about this episode until the March interviews rolled around. This time Patricia's father, Garth, was also present. Again, I had forgotten to bring a picture of Darcie to show Jenny. *Oh well, I will one of these days,* I thought.

Then, at the end of June, on the last day of school, my phone rang. To my surprise, it was Jenny. In a strange voice, she said, "I've been struggling with whether or not to make this call all year. But today, it was now or never." And then, out of the blue, she said: "I think I'm your daughter's natural mother."

I was stunned. This possibility had honestly never entered my head. It's a good thing there was a chair by the phone because my legs felt like rubber. I thought back to our first interview last November. Poor Jenny—what a shock she must have had that night!

Over the phone, Jenny and I exchanged the information we had both been given at the time of the adoption. It was emotionally draining, and we were both choking back tears as we spoke. I learned that day that Jenny's husband, Garth, was Darcie's natural father as well. Patricia and Darcie were truly full genetic sisters. No wonder they looked and behaved so much alike.

Afterwards, I sat down and had a good cry. I wasn't feeling insecure or threatened, but rather totally drained and somewhat relieved. As an adoptive mom, I always knew that someday my children might want to find their natural parents. I had just hoped that they wouldn't find out that their mother had died of an overdose, or that their dad was in jail. Jenny and Garth seemed to be fine people, and I was as pleased as could be. Patricia had been in my class for a whole year, and I knew a fair bit about her life. Had Darcie been raised in their family, her life might have been quite similar to the life she had in ours. All in all, I thought, Darcie could feel very proud.

Jenny had asked me to tell Darcie if I wanted to. She and Garth would put no pressure on her. If she wanted to contact them—great! If not, they would respect that.

On a Tuesday when Darcie got home from work, I called her upstairs to talk. After reassuring her that nothing was wrong, I put my arm around her and said, "Darcie, I spoke to your birth mother on Friday." She was shocked and totally speechless. When I asked her if she thought she might like to meet her, she replied, "I don't know, this feels weird." When I explained that I'd actually met Jenny on several occasions, she wondered if she looked like her.

As the week passed, she asked for more information as she was ready. She found it easier to absorb small pieces of information, and she couldn't decide whether or not she wanted to meet Jenny and Garth. I said: "Look Darcie, it took Jenny almost a whole year to decide to call me. Please take all the time you want. There is no pressure to make a decision."

A few months later, she felt ready, but definitely wanted me with her. I was glad about this—adoption doesn't just happen to the baby, it happens to the parents, too. I needed to be a part of this.

Darcie was feeling a bit insecure. With us she knew unconditional love, but with Jenny and Garth she felt she'd have to gain acceptance by some accomplishment or look or both. Over the next few months, she lost some weight, found a new job, dyed her hair three times, and had it permed, straightened and cut.

My adopted son, Dale, wondered why she was in such a flap. "These people are just strangers," he said, "why does she even want to meet them?" I replied, "It must be meant to be, Dale. Look at the odds here. This city has a population of over 600,000! We adopted Darcie when we lived in the west end, Jenny and Garth lived centrally, and now we all live in the east end!" I was truly in awe of the strange trail of unlikely coincidences that all these years later had brought us to the same neighborhood, and placed Patricia in my classroom.

By June 1997, Darcie asked me to arrange a meeting with her birth family. Jenny was pleased but cautious, wanting to be sure that Darcie was ready. She also wasn't sure she was prepared for Patricia and her son, Jordan, to know about Darcie.

When the day finally arrived, Darcie was so nervous that I had to greet Jenny and Garth, and bring them into the kitchen. After my introduction, Jenny walked towards Darcie and wrapped her arms around her. They both began to cry as Jenny held the daughter she had given up so many years ago.

When we had all calmed down, we settled in the family room and the conversation flowed easily. Darcie showed them her baby album and school pictures, and asked lots of questions. She learned that Garth had been sixteen, and Jenny only fourteen, when she was born. They had given her up out of love, knowing they were not ready to be parents. Six years later they were married and had always longed to know her. When they learned from me she had grown up close by in a good family, it seemed like a miracle, and they were overjoyed. When Jenny and Garth finally left late that night, there were lots of hugs all around.

Jenny and Garth had told their children they had given up a child for adoption, but they hadn't shared the recent contact or my involvement. A week later, they did, and Jenny asked Darcie if she would like to meet Jordan and Patricia, who were her full brother and sister.

Darcie excitedly agreed, and this time, I was excited, too! Everyone had lots to say, and it felt a lot like a family party! When Patricia entered our home and saw Darcie for the first time, she was over the moon with excitement and exclaimed: "Oh Mom, she looks like you!" She was so excited to have an older sister, she was like a kid in a candy store. She wanted to see Darcie's room, her shoes, the rest of the house, our back yard. She couldn't sit still!

Darcie and Jenny keep in touch by phone from time to time and exchange birthday cards.

Darcie is married now, with a baby of her own. Patricia loves to baby-sit for Darcie and her husband, and Jenny and Garth are thrilled to know their first grandchild. The sad loss of their youth has been replaced with joy and healing, and I can honestly say it is a feeling of contentment and peace that we all share.

Lou Ogston

The Bungee That Binds

A mother is not a person to lean on but a person to make leaning unnecessary.

Dorothy Canfield Fisher

I'm standing in the middle of High Street in downtown Columbus, Ohio. There are hundreds of women all around me waiting to Race for the Cure, an annual fundraiser for breast cancer. The most important of these, to me, is standing at my left side, a bungee cord dangling from her right hand. She is my daughter, Kara, and it's her twenty-sixth birthday today, May 16, 1998.

Kara has found a spot for us to stand somewhere in the middle of three thousand women. We are far from six-minute milers, but we do want to run, not walk, so slipping into a spot about halfway between the beginning and the end of the mob seemed like a good idea. This would be our first race together, and Kara's first ever.

"Did you ever think, twenty-six years ago today, that we'd be doing something like this together?" she asks.

"Not in my wildest dreams," I say, but I am so proud of what she is about to do that I find it hard to speak.

I'm a little nervous, and I know she is, too. With my left hand, I fiddle with the other end of the bungee cord, the tether that would keep me on course. As a blind runner, I had learned that holding onto a short tether, the other end of which is held by the sighted companion runner, is the most effective way of guiding me through the course. I had left my Seeing Eye dog, Sherry, at home. Crowds frighten her, and it might be dangerous for her, so Kara would be my guide.

When I first mentioned this race to Kara and showed her the brochure, she read it thoroughly and thoughtfully. "This would be a nice thing to do on my birthday," she said. I didn't know if she was being sarcastic or not. After all, she had never run for three miles straight, and it would mean getting up before noon on a Saturday. Nonetheless, without further mention of it, I sent our registrations in, hopeful that she would really do this with me. I had run in two other races with a friend, but the thought of running with my daughter to help fight breast cancer was more exciting than running one hundred races with anybody else.

We did several training runs together at a nearby track and practiced staying together with the bungee cord. "I'm going to like this," she said as she playfully jerked me from side to side and forward and backward. I was laughing so hard I couldn't run, and Sherry, who was along for the exercise, looked at us like we didn't have any sense.

"Don't make me laugh. I can't run and laugh at the same time," I said. It was then that I knew for sure that I was going to like this, too.

"On your mark! Get set! Go!" yells the starter. I expect to be pushed forward with the rushing crowd, but instead we find ourselves standing still, not able to take even one step. Minutes pass, while we wait for the hundreds of people ahead of us to get started. Finally, slowly, we

arn more about Minnesota Relay services
- **Schedule a free presentation**
  - **Request brochures**

innesota Relay Consumer Relations Office

1-800-657-3775 (voice/TTY)

Email: tam.commerce@state.mn.us

U V W

Y Z Z

To call a person
who is deaf,
hard of hearing or
speech disabled,
just dial

7 1 1

MINNESOTA
RELAY

began to move. Our impatience mounts as we discover we are trapped in the middle of the walkers, who apparently comprise most of the participants.

"Okay," we say to each other. "We'll walk for the cure." But we're both disappointed. We want to run. That's what we have trained for. Walking three miles for us is nothing; it's the running that's the challenge.

Suddenly, Kara starts finding ways to pass people. Soon we are darting first to the right and then the left, weaving our way through and around the walkers. "I have to think of myself as two people wide, and find gaps in the crowd wide enough for us both," Kara says. I clutch her arm as we run a few steps in one direction and then suddenly the other. At last there is a little space for running, so Kara says, "tether," signalling me that the coast is clear and "let's go for it." I drop my death grip on her arm and hold the hook of the bungee cord as we had practiced. We realize we've gone a mile when Kara spots the first water stop just ahead.

"Do you want to stop for water?" she asks me.

"No," I reply. "I'm afraid we'll lose our position and be overtaken by the walkers."

Our first left turn takes us over cobblestone streets. "Pick up your toes," I warn her. "You don't want to trip and lose our place." The crowd is thinning now, and we pick up our pace. People are standing on the sides of the street, cheering us on.

Now we're having fun. We turn left onto Third Street, and I notice for the first time in my life that it goes uphill. We're proud of ourselves, not only because we have passed all the walkers, but we're now up with the runners, and even pass a few of them. We grin with each little victory. "We're up with the big kids now," I say.

Kara begins to read aloud to me the signs on the backs of some of the runners and we choke back our tears. "In memory of my mother who died May 16, 1997." That's one year ago today. Others are running in celebration of friends and family who are breast cancer survivors.

We're on the last mile, and the bungee cord technique is working well. We're hot and thirsty, but we don't dare stop. "Look!" somebody calls out toward us. "They're hooked together so they won't get separated."

"There's our first idiot," says Kara. She has a tendency to be a bit intolerant of those who aren't as observant about people with disabilities as she is. It happens again about two blocks later, but we just laugh and keep running.

Then I hear a familiar voice shouting our names. It's my friend Eve, standing on the sidelines. She is here to cheer us on. "Looking good! You're doing great, Mary!" The sound of Eve's encouragement is better than a drink of water.

We turn left onto Broad, and I know we're nearing the end. In a matter of minutes, we'll be heading toward the finish line. My mouth is full of cotton, and my legs feel like lead.

Kara counts down as we head for the finish line. "Fifty yards! Twenty yards! Ten feet!" The finish line! We've done it!

We slow to a walk. Someone hands us a ribbon, and someone else hands us bottles of water. We toast each other with our water bottles and begin to make our way to the lawn where the award ceremonies will be held.

We settle on the grass for one of the most moving and touching experiences we will ever share, not just as mother and daughter, but as two women.

A breast cancer survivor speaks to the crowd about her struggle out of the "valley of darkness and fear." As the mother of twin six-year-old boys, she tells us her goal was to be strong enough to walk them to their first day of school. She feels triumphant, having met that goal. She also won the race in her division today. We all applaud, and many of us cry. What a great day this is for her, for us all.

Other survivors are recognized and applauded. We observe a moment of silence for those who are not with us today. Every one of us in this crowd today has been touched by cancer in some way. We each have our private sorrows and fears, but united in hope and prayer, maybe, just maybe we've taken a step toward conquering this dreaded disease.

"I'm glad we did this today," Kara tells me. I am, too. I'm grateful that we, as women, could participate together in an event that touches all women. We didn't win any trophies or prizes, but we are winners because we did it, we did it together and we'll do it again.

The bungee cord lies between us in the grass. Its work is done for the day, but its meaning will continue to give me strength and courage. Connection is what it's all about, one child to her mother, one woman with another.

Mary Hiland

Joey Comes Home

Children are the hands by which we take hold of heaven.

Henry Ward Beecher

The phone rang at three thirty that day. It was the Children's Aid Society, and they had a child they wondered if we could take. We weren't given much information, only that his name was Joey, he was five years old, he came from Djibouti, Africa, and he spoke no English. My husband's family had been missionaries in Africa for many years—there was a vague hope that he would be able to communicate with the boy.

Our family became very excited, and we hurriedly got things ready. My daughter Julie and her five-year-old daughter Amanda had been living with us for some time, and my other daughter Tammy and her four-year-old son, Freddy, lived right next door. We were all excited, anticipating Joey's arrival.

When the doorbell rang and I opened the door, I stood there in shock. Standing there was the smallest five-year-old boy I had ever seen. But what made me gasp was seeing how badly he had been abused.

I asked the social worker to come in, and Joey quietly followed him. At his suggestion, we went straight to the kitchen. Freddy and Amanda came running in to meet the newcomer, then stopped short and just looked at me. They got very quiet, turned around and walked away. They sat down on the couch and didn't say a word. They seemed very frightened, but we could say nothing to explain or to calm them.

Joey sat down, and I gave him supper. He ate without speaking, and then walked over and sat silently on the couch. Sadly, he spoke a different language than the one my husband knew. After the worker left, we tried doing our normal routine. I got Amanda ready for bed, and Joey just watched while I got his clothes. When I bent down to change him, he became very upset. When I tried explaining, he just backed away into a corner. I didn't dare touch him then, he was so afraid.

My daughter put Amanda to bed, and then Tammy took Freddy home. Now it was just me and Joey. My heart ached for this little boy. For several hours we sat there, Joey on the loveseat sucking his thumb, and me on the couch. He just sat watching me. I put on a movie, and he stayed in the room with me, but remained wary. If I moved, he'd jump. I got him a drink, which he drank only after I sat down again. I talked to God a lot that night, and asked for help in reaching this child.

About two A.M. he fell asleep on the loveseat. I slept until seven on the couch. When I got breakfast ready, everyone came down, but he just sat in the corner sucking his thumb until Amanda came in. Slowly, Joey sat down beside her. I gave him breakfast, and he ate it all. Then, Joey and Amanda walked into the living room together, and Amanda wanted a movie on. She sat down to watch, and Joey sat with her. And so it began.

Joey let Amanda do things for him, but never anyone else. By the second day we needed to bathe him, and this proved to be quite a challenge! I knew I had to get him into the tub, but didn't know how. Joey came up the stairs that night with Amanda, and he stood watching as we put her into the tub, but he wouldn't come past the doorway. Amanda finished her bath, and I changed the water. He had to have a bath!

My husband picked him up and after a struggle, finally got him in clothes and all! All of a sudden as he went to get up, he fell in! I started to laugh, and then Amanda started laughing, and then everyone was laughing. Joey sat looking at us with his thumb in his mouth, with his soaking wet clothes on. And then Amanda started bringing in toys. Suddenly Joey stood up and took off all his clothes, sat down and started playing. I just sat on the floor and watched. How sad I felt looking at this little boy—he was so hurt all over. Over and over I thought, "Thank God he's with us tonight."

When Joey got out, he let Amanda put cream on his back. I sat still, so amazed at this little girl rubbing cream on him and talking softly to him. Joey didn't understand a word, but he let her do it and he relaxed as long as I stayed back. We went to the bedroom, and Joey followed Amanda, just sucking his thumb and watching. Amanda passed him his pajamas, and he put them on. When Amanda got into her bed, he got into his.

Joey lay so still and quiet, thumb in, eyes closed, I knew he wasn't asleep. When I went to bed, I again asked God for guidance, to help me in reaching this child.

Around 5:30 A.M., I woke suddenly and listened. I could hear Amanda talking quietly. I tiptoed down the hall, and could see the light in their room was on. Peeking in, I was amazed to see Amanda with Joey on her knee, rocking him and rubbing his head saying softly to him, "It's okay

Joey, my nanny won't let anyone hurt you." Joey was crying softly and talking to her in his own language. This little five-year-old girl just kept rubbing his head and repeating, "It's okay Joey, my nanny doesn't let anyone hurt little children."

I felt the hot tears stinging my eyes. I had asked God for help in reaching this little boy, and help had come through Amanda. They spoke different languages, but Amanda and Joey were able to reach each other. He wouldn't let me do much, but he would let Amanda! I could help him a bit if she was there. When Joey started having nightmares and wake up screaming, Amanda would wake up and call me. I wouldn't touch Joey, but I would hold Amanda and rock her, because I knew she was also upset. Joey would sit with his thumb in his mouth and watch.

After a month or so, Joey began to allow my daughter Julie to help, but still not me. He would watch me with the other kids, and say nothing. I just kept doing my work every day, and the other children always came to me for hugs and kisses. The break finally came on Christmas Eve. I had just sat down for a cup of tea, and the children were getting ready for Santa. Joey didn't know what Christmas was, but knew the other children were very excited. I watched as he slowly walked over to where I was sitting. Suddenly, he put his arms around me! I lightly hugged him back. Then he kissed my cheek! I looked into his enormous dark eyes, then bent over and kissed him lightly on his cheek. It felt like a miracle!

From then on, everything was different. I watched Joey turn from a frightened little boy, to a trusting, happy and loving child. I watched in awe as against all odds, this courageous little boy went forward. The friendships he forged with Freddy and Amanda were rich and amazing to watch. We have often heard Joey and Freddie talking away well into the night about all the things that make life work. They became like brothers in every way.

We decided that we wanted to make this family relationship permanent and adopt him as our son. It involved a lot of legal battles, and his future was very uncertain for a long time. But through it all he continued to grow in love and trust and courage. As I watched, I often felt totally humbled by him, and still do.

Finally, in May of 1998, we signed the papers to start the adoption and patiently waited for the court date to make it final.

Joey's eleven now, happy, loving, and we hug all the time. He and Freddy and Amanda have this wonderful relationship, and he is officially and permanently our son. The friendship between the three children goes beyond family, beyond race, beyond what I could have ever dreamed possible. They are true sisters and brothers of the heart. And I know in my heart that when Joey was sent to us, he was not being sent away, but was in fact coming home.

Cheryl Kierstead

5

SPECIAL
MOMENTS

*Love the moment, and the energy of that
moment will spread beyond all boundaries.*

Sister Corita Kent

Something to Make Me Happy

The world is not divided into the strong who care and the weak who are cared for. We must each in turn care and be cared for, not just because it is good for us, but because it is the way things are.

Sheila Cassidy

I was doing some last-minute Christmas shopping in a toy store and decided to look at Barbie dolls for my nieces.

A nicely dressed little girl was excitedly looking through the Barbie dolls as well, with a roll of money clamped tightly in her little hand.

When she came upon a Barbie she liked, she would turn and ask her father if she had enough money to buy it. He usually said "yes," but she would keep looking and keep going through their ritual of "Do I have enough?"

As she was looking, a little boy wandered in across the aisle and started sorting through the Pokémon toys.

He was dressed neatly, but in clothes that were obviously rather worn, and wearing a jacket that was probably a couple of sizes too small. He, too, had money in his hand, but it looked to be no more than five dollars or so, at the most.

He was with his father as well, and kept picking up the Pokémon video games. Each time he picked one up and looked at his father, his father shook his head, "no." The little girl had apparently chosen her Barbie, a beautifully dressed, glamorous doll that would have been the envy of every little girl on the block.

However, she had stopped and was watching the interchange between the little boy and his father. Rather dejectedly, the boy had given up on the video games and had chosen what looked like a book of stickers instead. He and his father then started walking through another aisle of the store.

The little girl put her Barbie back on the shelf, and ran over to the Pokémon games. She excitedly picked up one that was lying on top of the other toys, and raced toward the check-out, after speaking with her father.

I picked up my purchases and got in line behind them.

Then, much to the little girl's obvious delight, the little boy and his father got in line behind me.

After the toy was paid for and bagged, the little girl handed it back to the cashier and whispered something in her ear. The cashier smiled and put the package under the counter.

I paid for my purchases and was rearranging things in my purse when the little boy came up to the cashier. The cashier rang up his purchases and then said, "Congratulations, you are my hundredth customer today, and you win a prize!"

With that, she handed the little boy the Pokémon game, and he could only stare in disbelief.

It was, he said, exactly what he had wanted!

The little girl and her father had been standing at the doorway during all of this, and I saw the biggest, prettiest grin on that little girl that I have ever seen in my life. Then they walked out the door, and I followed, close behind them.

As I walked back to my car, in amazement over what I had just witnessed, I heard the father ask his daughter why she had done that. I'll never forget what she said to him.

"Daddy, didn't Nana and Paw Paw want me to buy something that would make me happy?"

He said, "Of course they did, Honey."

To which the little girl replied, "Well, I just did!"

With that, she giggled and started skipping toward their car. Apparently, she had decided on the answer to her own question of, "Do I have enough?"

Sharon Palmer

A Father's Day Phone Call

It is the nature of grace, always to fill the spaces that have been empty.

Goethe

It was a typical June day in San Francisco, cool and overcast. Reading the newspaper, I noticed the East Coast was suffering a heat wave, and Father's Day was approaching. Father's Day, like Mother's Day, never meant much to me. I've generally regarded those days as good for merchants and convenient for children.

Putting the paper down, I looked at a photograph on my desk. My sister had taken it several summers ago in Biddeford Pool, Maine. Father and I stood together on the porch of a cottage, our arms around each other's shoulders. By the looks of us the apple didn't fall far from the tree. *Father's Day,* I mused, and thought about calling to see how he and Mother were doing.

Picking up the photograph, I examined it closely. With his top teeth out, my old man grinned like a grizzled ex-hockey player. His eyes were set deep in a sun-creased face, with a cocky stance at seventy years old.

It was a younger man who used to chase me along the beach and take me into the water, a stronger man who taught me to row, skate and split firewood. That was before his plastic knee, false teeth and hearing aid. I decided to give the old man a call.

"Good afternoon!" he shouted.

Mother picked up the other phone and told him to put his hearing aid in.

"I've got it here in my pocket," he said, and I heard him fumbling for it.

Mother said the air-conditioning was a godsend, her plastic hip was alright, but the new dog was driving her nuts.

"Actually," she said, "it's not the dog, it's your father."

"What's the matter?" I asked.

"Shep jumps over the fence whenever the mood strikes him, then takes off into God knows where. Your father worries and waits up until he comes back. He's out there at two in the morning, calling the dog and making an awful racket. Then, when Shep comes back, he scolds him 'Malo perro, malo, malo,' as if we were back in Peru and the dog understands Spanish."

"I think he's learning," said Father, back on the line. "Your mother thinks I'm a damn fool, and she's probably right."

"You're still shouting," said Mother.

He ignored her and asked me how I was doing. I told him.

"Freelancing is fine," he said loudly, "but you need security. You're too old to be cooking on yachts, tending bar and working construction. You've got a college education. Why don't you use it? What are you going to do if you get sick? You know how much it costs to stay in a hospital?"

"You know," I told him, "I can't figure you out. You

smoke too much, drink too much, don't exercise, you eat all the wrong foods, and still you're a tough old goat."

"You're right. And I'm outliving all my classmates." He said it without bragging.

There was something I wanted to tell him, and I was having a difficult time getting it out.

"Do you read the newspaper clippings I send you?" he asked.

"Sure I do."

"I don't know whether you do or not, you never write."

I wasn't forgetting that he and I had had our differences over the past forty-four years and that we had angered, disappointed and cursed each other often. But those times seemed long ago and I wanted to tell him I loved him. I wanted to be funny and I wanted the phone call to flow.

"Listen," I told him, "I understand Father's Day is coming up."

"Oh?" he said, uninterested. He never kept track.

"It's the seventeenth," said Mother on the other phone.

"I'm sorry I jumped through the top of your convertible."

"You were six," he said and chuckled. "I couldn't believe it at first."

I wanted to thank him for the hockey games, chess games, books and lobster dinners. I wanted to apologize for punching him in the eye when I was eighteen.

"Thanks for being my father," I said.

He was quiet on his end and mother was too. A long-distance microstatic filled the void.

"I wish I'd been better," he said, his voice subdued for the first time.

"You were just fine," I said. "A guy couldn't have had a better father."

"Good of you to say, old boy, but not true. I wish it were," he said with regret in his voice.

"It is true," I said, and hurried on. "Do you remember when I wanted to feed sugar to the donkey at the Cricket Club and you patted him on the rump and he kicked you?"

"Yes," chuckled Father. "Smashed my knee, damn beast. You always thought that was funny."

"And all those ships you took me aboard," I added.

"There were a few of those," he conceded. "Boy, you're really taking me back."

"I loved the ships," I told him.

"But still I couldn't convince you to go in the Navy."

"I wanted you to go to college after high school," said Mother.

"But you wouldn't listen," said Father. "You had to be a Marine."

I didn't say anything. I heard them remembering.

"And we flew out to California," he went on, "to say good-bye before you left for Vietnam."

"We stayed at The Newporter Inn," said Mother, "and went to Disneyland."

"I remember I had to leave that Sunday night by helicopter to catch a flight out of Los Angeles," he continued. "Your mother and the girls stayed in the motel and you walked me to the helipad. You were in uniform and we shook hands. . . ." His voice trailed off. "It tore me up. I didn't know if I'd ever see you again. I cried on that helicopter. It tore me up, your leaving."

"I know," I said, and felt a lump in my throat.

"We prayed for you," he said, his voice beginning to tremble. "We lived for your letters."

"And I for yours," I told him. This was crazy, I thought. My eyes were damp, and I swallowed to clear the lump.

"I called to wish you a happy Father's Day," I managed.

"That was good of you, old boy. I'll hang up now, don't want to run up your bill." His voice was shaking.

"Don't worry about the bill," I said. "I love you."

"I love you, too. Good-bye and God bless you," he said hurriedly and hung up.

"You know how he gets," said Mother quietly on the other phone.

"I know," I replied, and after another minute we said good-bye and hung up. I looked at the photograph of Father and me on the porch in Maine. *Yes*, I thought, *I know how he gets*. I wiped my eyes, smiled at the picture and blew my nose loudly. The apple didn't fall far from the tree.

George Eyre Masters

Monsters Under the Bed

My husband and I faced each other across the pristine sheets of the hospital bed. Four-year-old Kate was still happily cranking the foot of it up and down. This was an adventure to her, the first of Daddy's overnights in the hospital. "When is Daddy coming home?" she had asked me that morning. "In a week," I told her, though it wasn't the whole truth. Serge would need to be hospitalized for one week in every three for eight months. A lot of overnights. A lot of "When is Daddy coming homes?"

Nervously I smoothed the already smooth pillow. Serge fingered his beard. *How long,* I wondered, *before the chemotherapy stripped it away?* My husband had worn a full beard for more than twenty years; I had never seen him without it. The bogeyman of cancer was literally going to change the face of our lives.

We both studiously avoided looking at the IV drip. The thought of the strong chemicals that would soon flow through Serge's body was as frightening as the lymphoma they would attack. We were setting a monster to catch a monster, and it was a scary prospect.

We faced each other across the bed in silence. All the words had already been said: the complex medical ones, the philosophical supportive ones, the loving, comforting ones. Still, fear persisted.

When I was a child and afraid to go to sleep in the dark, I always trusted my father to chase away the dragons under my bed. I wished life was still that simple. I wished I could slay Serge's dragon.

A nurse popped her head in the door. "Time to go," she said. "Visiting hours are over."

Kate stopped cranking the bed. She took a quick peek under it as though she were checking for something, then picked up her backpack from the chair and carefully unzipped it. She carried that pink and purple backpack with her everywhere. Usually it contained crayons, paper, a couple of picture books, "stuff to do" as Kate called it, for whenever she got bored in the car or in a waiting room. Today she carefully lifted out a stuffed bear named Mishka. Mishka had sat at the foot of Serge's bed while he was growing up and had been spruced up and awarded a new red bow when Kate was born. Kate believed Mishka had special powers. "He's a guard bear," she said, and he always slept at the foot of her bed. Kate whispered something in Mishka's ear, hugged him tightly for a minute and then put him in her father's arms. "He'll protect you in the night, Daddy," she said, "whenever monsters come."

It was impossible not to cry. All the technical jargon I'd been reading about coping with illness, the support groups, the struggle to find the right words to say were swept away in a moment by the innocent compassion of a four-year-old. She believed that Mishka would stand guard for Serge through all the hospital overnights to come. Her belief was magic. My daughter had given her father more than a stuffed bear; she had given him a talisman against fear.

Anne Metikosh

The Special Olympics

At a Special Olympics track meet, a young girl had just won the fifty-yard dash and was jumping up and down all excited.

She yelled out to her parents, "Look, Mom and Dad, I won!"

Her parents instantly burst into tears.

At the awards ceremony, the young girl proudly stood there as a medal was placed around her neck.

Then she ran over to her parents, who were crying now even more than before.

The three of them hugged . . . as the parents kept crying.

A Special Olympics official who had watched this whole scene became concerned and went over to the parents and said, "Excuse me, is there anything wrong?"

Through her tears, the mother said: "No, nothing's wrong. Everything's right. . . . We just heard our daughter speak for the first time!"

Bits & Pieces

Keeping the Magic

Kevin came running from one end of the house to the other screaming with the telephone in hand, "It's Santa, Mom! It's Santa! He's called our house! It's really him!"

I took the phone and tentatively said, "Hello?"

I heard my friend Sandra, laughing, "All I said was, 'Hi, Kevin, it's Sandra!'"

I smiled into the phone. I was about to speak when I caught the sparkle in Kevin's eye. In those beautiful blue eyes the magic of Christmas reflected back, with all the hope and excitement that the season brings. I smiled into the phone and spoke over my friend's laughter: "Yes, Santa, Kevin and Sean have been really good boys. It was so nice of you to phone. Thank you."

I paused a moment as there was a silence on the other end of the line. "And Merry Christmas to you too, Santa," I said, and then I gently hung up the receiver.

Kittie Ellis

Love of a Child

Fifteen years ago, Karen was born with a debilitating condition. At the age of one year, because of surgical complications, she suffered a heart attack and was clinically dead for one hour, resulting in harm to her brain. However, with all of these challenges in her life she has grown to be a very beautiful and inspirational young lady, with a clarity that usually humbles and brings a smile to those around her.

Regardless of her condition, her greatest fear in her life has been Santa Claus, solely because of the lyric in a particular Christmas song that says, "He sees you when you're sleeping. . . ." She has always imagined this big, red-clad, hairy-faced man watching her as she is sleeping, and it has scared her so much throughout her life that in recent years her mother has thought that she should really tell her the truth about Santa Claus, but was concerned about the disappointment that might bring.

Karen recently began having these dreams again in quite a severe manner and became so anxious and irrational about the whole thing that her mother decided, in a panic, to tell her the dreaded news. Holding Karen close and looking straight into her eyes, her mother said,

"Karen, listen to me, calm down and listen to me. . . . THERE IS NO SANTA CLAUS! MOMMY IS SANTA CLAUS, MOMMY HAS ALWAYS BEEN SANTA CLAUS! You don't have to be scared anymore." Karen looked at her mother with a blank expression and went off to sleep.

The next day when Karen went to school she looked disturbed, so much so that her teacher made a point of asking her what the problem was. Karen answered in a very serious and concerned voice, "I am *very* worried about my mom." When the teacher asked her why, she answered in an equally serious voice, "She thinks she's Santa Claus!"

Brian Locke

Self-Esteem at Five

I was blessed with three beautiful, intelligent and terrific children, who are now thirty, twenty-nine and twenty-eight. But at one point in their lives, they were seven, six and five.

My youngest daughter, the five-year-old who was always asking questions, came home from kindergarten one day and asked, "Mommy, how many children did you want?"

Thinking for a minute, I looked at her and said, "Two."

She thought about it for a moment and then asked, "Me, and who else?"

Kathrine A. Barhydt

The Window

Life is a flame that is always burning itself out, but it catches fire again every time a child is born.

George Bernard Shaw

Kathy and I sit in her doctor's office, stunned. Dr. Hurley, ob-gyn, shuffles reports and test results on her desk while we absorb the impact of what she's just told us. Her words hang in the air like a thunderclap.

"Each of you has specific fertility issues. If it was just one we could possibly work around it. But both . . ."

She shrugs, averting her gaze.

"Short of extraordinary measures, there's no way you'll ever be able to conceive."

We look at each other, struggling to process the news. Once again she taps her pen on the papers, pointing to temperature graphs, percentage points, motility factors. We gaze at the figures. I squeeze Kathy's hand as she fights back tears.

We drive home in silence. Each of us wonders how this could be happening. We each feel personally responsible for the failure to have the family we'd always planned for. I remember growing up, throwing the baseball in the backyard with my dad, running across the room, jumping up into his arms after he returned from a business trip, how happy I felt to be his "biddy buddy." All the things I'll never get to share with a son of my own.

In the next few days, Kathy and I decide to get a second opinion. Expensive or not, it will be worth it if somehow, some way the numbers turn out different.

They don't. Short of extremely invasive, extremely expensive procedures, natural conception is still out of the question. Once again we're heartbroken.

We discuss other options. One couple we know had twins by a surrogate mother. Another had five in-vitro fertilizations before the last one finally took. The cost was astronomical, the procedure trying and far from romantic. We talk about the possibility of adoption while struggling with the very real chance we'll never hear the pitter patter of little feet after all.

Six weeks later we arrive at a joint decision. We'll find another doctor, one with a more positive, upbeat attitude. Maybe do some research, investigate alternative remedies if necessary. If it's God's will we shouldn't have children, then we'll both try to find the strength to accept that. If we're meant to have a family then we'll do whatever it takes to heal whatever needs to be healed and give it our best shot, then pray for a miracle.

Dr. Cornelia Daly, fertility specialist, walks around her mahogany desk and offers her hand to Kathy, then myself. It's firm, confident. Her smile is bright. She sits on the edge of the desk and listens to our story. She nods, holds eye contact, seems to really understand. On a shelf behind her desk I notice framed pictures of her own family. She and a happy husband smile in a variety of holiday poses with three adorable daughters.

She dismisses the reports we'd faxed with a wave of her hand and goes on to outline some less radical possibilities we hadn't thought of. She discusses diet, abstinence until ovulation, and the pros and cons of various fertility drugs. Her energy and optimism are catchy. We feel the first glimmer of hope we've had in months.

"My advice to you both is get more exercise, watch those foods that tend to slow you down: caffeine, sugar, alcohol. Look through magazines and cut out pictures of babies: bouncy, happy babies. Tape them on your bathroom mirror and your refrigerator. Go through baby books. Pick out names you'd like for your children, both girl and boy."

I feel my stomach muscles tense, my chest tighten, and I feel Kathy stiffen next to me. Can we really allow ourselves to hope that much? The words from a recent discussion ring in my mind.

"We'll do whatever it takes."

I take a deep breath. *Whatever it takes.* Okay then. I set my resolve and relax, listening.

"Oh, yes, go to the drugstore and ask the pharmacist for a pre-ovulation test. This measures your luteinizing hormonal level. The LH surges twenty-four to forty-eight hours before you're about to ovulate. That's your monthly window of opportunity. Once it opens," she shrugs and smiles, "just have fun."

Two and a half months later, Kathy wakes in the middle of the night with severe cramps. Immediately we think back to the cyst on her ovary that mysteriously appeared, then disappeared half a year earlier. Had it returned? Our minds worry overtime the rest of the night. If it doesn't clear up by next morning we're definitely on the way to the doctor's office if not the emergency room. Again we pray.

Kathy sits on the examination table, pale and drawn, waiting for Dr. Daly to enter the room. I hold her hand, whispering that everything will be fine. I struggle to make myself believe it as well. After all we've been through, she could actually wind up losing her ovary. What would that do to our already slim chances of conceiving? What if it's worse? What if it's cancer? I worry even more. Imagine how empty my life would be without my sweetheart. I fight not to let it show. I reach over and squeeze her hand.

The nurse takes the requisite urine sample. Fortunately there's a lab on the floor below. We can get the results today if we're willing to wait a little longer. We take deep breaths, try to think positive thoughts, put on strong faces for each other. It's hard.

We hear whispers outside the room. The nurse practitioner is briefing Dr. Daly on the lab results. We strain to hear.

She opens the door and steps inside. We search her face. Nothing. She reaches into the pocket of her lab coat and rests her gaze on Kathy. We lean forward to hear what she's about to say, fearing how this new news will change our lives.

"Congratulations. You're going to have a baby."

The doctor's face breaks into a wide grin. We look at her, then at each other. How could this be?

"The first test we ran was to rule out pregnancy and guess what? That's the prognosis. You're going to have a baby."

"But . . . but . . . ," I stammer. "We only made love once during the window, a couple of weeks ago." I'm in shock.

She nods.

"Some women notice or complain of cramps once the zygote or pre-fetus attaches itself to the wall of the uterus. Other women hardly notice at all. Either way it's perfectly normal. The cells are attaching themselves to Kathy's womb."

We look at each other as the wonder of it sinks in. Then

we smile, big beaming smiles. We hug. Finally we cry, big tears running down our cheeks.

Dr. Daly moves Kathy's paper gown aside, squeezes out a glob of colorless gel from a tube, smears it onto her belly and feels around with the ultrasound receiver. There it is on the screen, clear as day. The tiniest ball of cells about the size of a BB. It's nestled against the curve of her uterine wall, our future son or daughter.

Kathy reaches over and touches the black and white image. After all this time, all the worries, doubts and fear, it's true. We're going to have a baby. Miracles really do happen. We're going to be parents after all.

C. J. Herrmann

Reprinted by permission of Steve Nease.

"You're Having a Baby!"

A sweet little someone is coming your way,
Perhaps it will happen even today.
The time has come for getting things ready,
So start buying diapers, a crib and a teddy.

A new little baby will make lots of noise,
You'll miss out on sleep and trip over toys.
Soon old pots and pans will strike up a tune
Banged out by "Maestro" with a wooden spoon.

This child you carry so close to your heart
Will be all you imagined from the start.
Your voice has become so familiar and warm,
Baby knows who you are and it's not even born!

Don't think about hospitals, labor and such,
But dream instead of the gentle touch
Of a tiny hand against your face,
And a heart that beats by God's own grace.

When you stand in the nursery gazing in love
At this marvelous gift sent down from above,
It's then you'll discover deep in your heart
What being a parent is all about.

So whenever it happens, love your child well
And you'll learn much more than tongue can tell,
This precious child will be like none other.
"Dad" will be proud...and so will *you*, "Mother!"

Louisa Godissart McQuillen

Welcome, Levi!

It was midnight on Sunday when I realized our fifth child was getting ready to arrive, and it was time to get moving. My husband Tim woke our four kids, and they grabbed blankets and pillows as they had planned for weeks, and we all headed off together to the hospital!

As we drove to the hospital, I reflected back to the events that had brought us here. After our fourth child, and first boy, Sammy, was born, Tim and I had decided that four kids was enough, and Tim went ahead and had a vasectomy. But as time passed, we decided that maybe we had been a little hasty. We found ourselves longing for another baby.

Changing our minds presented a bit of a challenge, as Tim had to face another surgery to reverse the vasectomy. Reversals are not always successful, but this one was, and shortly afterwards we were jubilant to discover that I was once again pregnant!

Our first three children were girls, and then our son Sammy arrived, and now we were really excited—perhaps we would have another boy. But the most exciting part by far was our decision to have all four of our children present during the birth of this new baby. . . if they wanted to be.

Well, asking our children if they wanted to be present and watch this baby's birth was like asking them if they wanted to go to Disneyland! Having made this major (and, let's face it, somewhat unusual) decision—we next needed to prepare them for this powerful life experience.

We first explained how we might have to wake them in the middle of the night to get up and go to the hospital. They nodded their heads. We told them that if this happened, they would need to get out of bed quickly and be as independent as possible. They nodded again. We explained how they would not be allowed to go to Mom for *anything* as she would be working very hard. We told them that even though Mom might seem uncomfortable, she really was okay, and in good care in the hospital with the doctors and nurses and Dad right there. With wide eyes, they agreed.

We told them that they would have to be very respect-ful of what was going on, and if they were uncomfortable to just leave the room and wait nearby. We explained how the baby might not look like what they would expect at first, and there would be some blood. Having heard all this, they showed that they understood and continued to be keen and very excited about being there.

Next, we faced the very real challenge of finding the right doctor. We were very clear amongst ourselves that we would find and choose a doctor who supported and was in full agreement with our unusual family plan. The clarity of the vision we created together worked so well we were amazed! The very first doctor we went to, Dr. Brian Siray of the Black Diamond Medical Clinic, was intrigued, and quite open to the idea, even though he had never been part of this kind of a delivery before. As the day approached, he also became very excited about the event, making his own plans to ensure the arrival of this new baby was a truly successful family experience!

The big night finally arrived, and after loading our family van with kids and pillows and blankets and packed bags, we were off to the High River Hospital. Once there, Tim and the kids crashed in the lounge area, while Mom went to work. The night passed slowly and quietly, and then at seven in the morning, the baby got serious. It was almost time. Tim woke the kids and had them come and join us in the delivery room—they were fresh and excited having had a good night's sleep. The doctor set them up alongside me, as he coached me as to what was going on with the baby. As the baby's head crowned, the children were anxious to see, so our wonderful doctor moved them alongside him so that they could have a full view of the baby's head emerging.

Our kids gasped in silent awe. Next, of course, the baby's full body appeared, and the ecstatic doctor shouted the traditional "It's a boy!" as our second son emerged to greet not just the world, but his entire family!

The children were awestruck, aglow and totally radiant! They were silent, yet beaming and full of wide-eyed expression. The doctor was so moved he had tears in his eyes—he said he'd never experienced anything quite like it before! This truly was an amazingly miraculous event for us all, and we are so grateful to have shared it together.

The bond between the children and the new baby is phenomenal. Tim and I will never have to answer the age-old question: "Mom, Dad, where do babies come from?" They know where he came from, and how he arrived. There is no rivalry or jealousy, they simply adore him for the special little person he is, and all because we invited them, and shared with them, the very special event of Levi's birth!

Dawn and Tim Johnson

There Is So Much to Learn

My father moved through dooms of love,
through sames of am, through haves of give,
singing each morning out of each night,
my father moved through depths of height.

e.e. cummings

Papa had a natural wisdom. He wasn't educated in the formal sense. When he was growing up at the turn of the century in a very small village in rural northern Italy, education was for the rich. Papa was the son of a dirt-poor farmer. He used to tell us that he never remembered a single day of his life when he wasn't working. The concept of doing nothing was never a part of his life. In fact, he couldn't fathom it. How could one do nothing?

He was taken from school when he was in the fifth grade, over the protestations of his teacher and the village priest, both of whom saw him as a young person with great potential for formal learning. Papa went to work in a factory in a nearby village, the very same village where he later met Mama.

For Papa, the world became his school. He was interested

in everything. He read all the books, magazines and newspapers he could lay his hands on. He loved to gather with people and listen to the town elders and learn about "the world beyond" this tiny insular region that was home to generations of Buscaglias before him. Papa's great respect for learning and his sense of wonder about the outside world were carried across the sea with him and later passed on to his family. He was determined that none of his children would be denied an education if he could help it.

Papa believed that the greatest sin of which we were capable was to go to bed at night as ignorant as we had been when we had awakened that day. This credo was repeated so often that none of us could fail to be affected by it.

"There is so much to learn," he'd remind us. "Though we're born stupid, only the stupid remain that way."

To ensure that none of his children ever fell into the trap of complacency, he insisted that we learn at least one new thing each day. He felt that there could be no fact too insignificant, that each bit of learning made us more of a person and insured us against boredom and stagnation.

So Papa devised a ritual. Since dinnertime was family time and everyone came to dinner unless they were dying of malaria, it seemed the perfect forum for sharing what new things we had learned that day. Of course, as children we thought this was perfectly crazy. There was no doubt, when we compared such paternal concerns with other children's fathers, that Papa was weird.

It would never have occurred to us to deny Papa a request. So when my brother and sisters and I congregated in the bathroom to clean up for dinner, the inevitable question was, "What did you learn today?" If the answer was "Nothing," we didn't dare sit at the table

without first finding a fact in our much-used encyclope-
dia. "The population of Nepal . . ." etc.

Now, thoroughly clean and armed with our fact for the
day, we were ready for dinner. I can still see the table
piled high with mountains of food. So large were the
mounds of pasta that as a boy I was often unable to see
my sister sitting across from me. (The pungent aromas
were such that, over a half-century later, even in memory
they cause me to salivate.)

Dinner was a noisy time of clattering dishes and endless activities. It was also a time to review the activities
of the day. Our animated conversations were always
conducted in Piedmontese dialect since Mama didn't
speak English. The events we recounted, no matter how
insignificant, were never taken lightly. Mama and Papa
always listened carefully and were ready with some
comment, often profound and analytical, always right to
the point.

"That was the smart thing to do."

"*Stupido,* how could you be so dumb?"

"*Cosi sia,* you deserved it."

"*E allora,* no one is perfect."

"*Testa dura,* (Hardhead), you should have known better.
Didn't we teach you anything?"

"Oh, that's nice."

One dialogue ended, and immediately another began.
Silent moments were rare at our table. Then came the
grand finale to every meal, the moment we dreaded
most—the time to share the day's new learning. The
mental imprint of those sessions still runs before me like
a familiar film clip, vital and vivid.

Papa, at the head of the table, would push his chair
back slightly, a gesture that signified the end of the eating
and suggested that there would be a new activity. He
would pour a small glass of red wine, light up a thin,

potent Italian cigar, inhale deeply, exhale, then take stock of his family.

For some reason this always had a slightly unsettling effect on us as we stared back at Papa, waiting for him to say something. Every so often he would explain why he did this. He told us that if he didn't take time to look at us, we would soon be grown and he would have missed us. So he'd stare at us, one after the other.

Finally, his attention would settle upon one of us. "Felice," he would say to me, "tell me what you learned today."

"I learned that the population of Nepal is . . ."

Silence.

It always amazed me, and reinforced my belief that Papa was a little crazy, that nothing I ever said was considered too trivial for him. First, he'd think about what was said as if the salvation of the world depended upon it.

"The population of Nepal. Hmmm. Well."

He would then look down the table at Mama, who would be ritualistically fixing her favorite fruit in a bit of leftover wine.

"Mama, did you know that?"

Mama's responses were always astonishing and seemed to lighten the otherwise reverential atmosphere. "Nepal," she'd say.

"Nepal? Not only don't I know the population of Nepal, I don't know where in God's world it is!" Of course, this was only playing into Papa's hands.

"Felice," he'd say, "get the atlas so we can show Mama where Nepal is." And the search began. The whole family went on a search for Nepal.

This same experience was repeated until each family member had a turn. No dinner at our house ever ended without our having been enlightened by at least a half dozen such facts.

As children, we thought very little about these educational wonders and even less about how we were being enriched. We couldn't have cared less. We were too impatient to have dinner end so we could join our less-educated friends in a rip-roaring game of kick-the-can.

In retrospect, after years of studying how people learn, I realize what a dynamic educational technique Papa was offering us, reinforcing the value of continued learning. Without being aware of it, our family was growing together, sharing experience and participating in one another's education. Papa was, without knowing it, giving us a sense of dignity, listening to us, hearing us, respecting our opinions, affirming our value. He was unquestionably our most influential teacher.

I decided upon a career in teaching fairly early in my college years. During my training, I studied with some of the most renowned educators in the country. When I finally emerged from academia, having been generously endowed with theory and jargon and technique, I discovered to my great amusement that the professional educators were imparting what Papa had known all along. He knew there was no greater wonder than the human capacity to learn, that no particle of knowledge was too insignificant not to have the power to change us for the better.

"How long we live is limited," Papa said, "but how much we learn is not. What we learn is what we are. No one should miss out on an education."

Papa was a successful educator. His technique worked and has served me well all my life. Now, when I get home, often exhausted after a long working day's adventure, before my head hits the pillow I hear Papa's voice resounded clearly in my room. "Felice," he asks, "what did you learn today?"

On some days I can't recall even one new thing I have learned. I'm surprised at how often this is the case (since

most of us move in a world of the familiar and are too pre-
occupied to be bothered or challenged by the unfamiliar).
I get myself out of bed and scan the bookshelves to find
something new. Then with that accomplished, Papa and I
can rest soundly, assured that a day has not been wasted.
After all, one never can tell when knowing the population
of Nepal may prove to be a very useful bit of information.

Leo Buscaglia

6

INSIGHTS AND LESSONS

The parents exist to teach the child, but also they must learn what the child has to teach them; and the child has a very great deal to teach them.

Arnold Bennett

True Generosity

Nothing will ever make you as happy or as sad, as proud or as tired, as motherhood.

Ella Parsons

When a tornado touched down in a small town nearby, many families were left devastated. Afterward, all the local newspapers carried many human interest stories featuring some of the families who suffered the hardest. One Sunday, a particular picture especially touched me. A young woman stood in front of a totally demolished mobile home, an anguished expression twisting her features. A young boy, seven or eight years old, stood at her side, eyes downcast. Clutching at her skirt was a tiny girl who stared into the camera, eyes wide with confusion and fear. The article that accompanied the picture gave the clothing sizes of each family member. With growing interest, I noticed that their sizes closely matched ours. This would be a good opportunity to teach my children to help those less fortunate than themselves.

I taped the picture of the young family to our refrigerator, explaining their plight to my seven-year-old twins,

Brad and Brett, and to three-year-old Meghan. "We have so much, and these poor people now have nothing," I said. "We'll share what we have with them."

I brought three large boxes down from the attic and placed them on the living room floor. Meghan watched solemnly as the boys and I filled one of the boxes with canned goods and other nonperishable foods, soap and other assorted toiletries. While I sorted through our clothes, I encouraged the boys to go through their toys and donate some of their less favorite things. Meghan watched quietly as the boys piled up discarded toys and games. "I'll help you find something for the little girl when I'm done with this," I said.

The boys placed the toys they had chosen to donate into one of the boxes while I filled the third box with clothes. Meghan walked up with Lucy, her worn, faded, frazzled, much-loved rag doll hugged tightly to her chest. She paused in front of the box that held the toys, pressed her round little face into Lucy's flat, painted-on face, gave her a final kiss, then laid her gently on top of the other toys. "Oh, Honey," I said. "You don't have to give Lucy. You love her so much."

Meghan nodded solemnly, eyes glistening with held-back tears. "Lucy makes me happy, Mommy. Maybe she'll make that other little girl happy, too."

Swallowing hard, I stared at Meghan for a long moment, wondering how I could teach the boys the lesson she had just taught me. For I suddenly realized that anyone can give their cast-offs away. True generosity is giving that which you cherish most. Honest benevolence is a three-year-old offering a treasured, albeit shabby doll to a little girl she doesn't know with the hope that it will bring this child as much pleasure as it brought her.

I, who had wanted to teach, had been taught.

The boys had watched, open-mouthed, as their baby

sister placed her favorite doll in the box. Without a word, Brad rose and went to his room. He came back carrying one of his favorite action figures. He hesitated briefly, clutching the toy, then looked over at Meghan and placed it in the box next to Lucy. A slow smile spread across Brett's face, then he jumped up, eyes twinkling as he ran to retrieve some of his prized Matchbox cars. Amazed, I realized that the boys had also recognized what little Meghan's gesture meant. Swallowing back tears, I pulled all three of them into my arms.

Taking the cue from my little one, I removed my old tan jacket with the frayed cuffs from the box of clothes. I replaced it with the new hunter green jacket that I had found on sale last week. I hoped the young woman in the picture would love it as much as I did.

Elizabeth Cobb

Maya's Smile

Too often we underestimate the power of a touch, a smile, a kind word, a listening ear, an honest compliment, or the smallest act of caring, all of which have the potential to turn a life around.

Leo Buscaglia

Maya (pronounced *my-uh*) was named after my favorite author and poet, Maya Angelou. And like her namesake, Maya is wise—wiser than her six years. With her four front teeth missing, and eyes that sparkle like Fourth of July, she is a teeny, doll-like darling. Because she has had a lot of health problems, she is smaller than most girls her age, a fact that has made her self-conscious, but also more sensitive to others' feelings. She would often remark "Oh, poor him!" when she would see someone lonely or sick or in need.

Last year, Maya was in kindergarten. One day she came home from school, bubbling over with excitement. "Mama, guess what!" She hurled at me as she bounced in the front door. "Guess what—there's a new girl in my class, and she doesn't speak any English, and I'm her new best friend. I decided today!" she proclaimed jubilantly.

"Honey, slow down," I told her, laughing at her exuberance.

Maya does and says everything with exuberance. Finally she slowed down enough to tell me about a new girl who arrived from Mexico that day. Her name was Stephanie, and that was the extent of her English: her name. So Maya took it upon herself to become her best friend. It never occurred to her that Stephanie's Spanish and Maya's English might be a problem. To a five-year-old, communication is taken for granted. All Maya cared about was that this new little girl cried all day and had no one to talk to.

When it came time for the Halloween party, I met Stephanie.

She clung to Maya like spaghetti noodles cooked together, clearly scared and withdrawn. Never once smiling, she sat as the other kids played Halloween games, only watching the laughter and the fun, never even attempting to join in. Her teacher later told me that Maya was the *only* one Stephanie would sit with at lunch or play with at recess. She was afraid to speak and never participated in class. The really amazing thing was that Maya didn't know a word of Spanish.

The days flew by, and each day Maya came home from school babbling about her day, how it went, what Stephanie learned, etc. I usually mumbled, "That's nice, Honey," too busy to take the time to really listen to my daughter. I never realized what I was missing until the day her teacher called to ask me to teach the class sign language for the end-of-the-year kindergarten program. She also told me what a wonderful child Maya was, what a good friend and so on. I was pleased, but the impact of what she was saying didn't sink in until I went to teach.

Maya's desk was next to Stephanie's. That withdrawn,

paralyzed-with-fear little girl was now a radiant, confident, happy child. Her big brown eyes were as sparkly as Maya's. And she smiled! I couldn't believe the transformation! She still spoke very little English, but now she tried to participate, a change her teacher told me only recently took place. As the teacher and I talked, I watched Maya and Stephanie together. Most of their communication was pointing, helping, gesturing.

And smiling.

Maya would look into her little friend's eyes and smile the sweetest, widest smile that would melt your heart. And Stephanie would smile right back, a shy, priceless smile.

Her teacher told me of the gradual transformation that had taken place. She told me how day after day, Maya sacrificed her free time to sit patiently with her scared little friend, often defending her to other kids, always kind. She never, ever gave up on Stephanie. My eyes filled with tears as she described my little teeny girl's tremendous heart and selflessness.

When Maya and I were alone that night, I told her how proud I was of her, how she was a true friend. I admitted that I could learn a thing or two from her beautiful example of friendship. Then I asked her how she did it—how she created this amazing friendship without a word of language. My blue-eyed angel looked up at me and said, "I smiled."

She told me how every time Stephanie cried or looked sad, she would just do her best to reassure her with a smile, sticking close to her, always letting her know she had a friend, and that friend was for keeps.

Maya and Stephanie had first-grade class together this year, and next year will again be in the same class for second grade. Every time I see her, I remember the scared little girl and how my own little girl was a true friend.

She is my hero.

Susan Farr-Fahncke

I'm Not Your Slave

Children reinvent your world for you.

Susan Sarandon

During the course of the day, I assume many different roles: Laurie Laundress, Clara Cook, Ella Entertainer, Betty Book-Reader, even Nellie Nag. On one particularly trying morning, I seemed to be Polly Put-It-Away more than usual. After depositing my son's pajamas in his drawer one too many days in a row, I turned to him and said, "You need to put your own pajamas away. I'm not your slave!"

"What's a slave?" he asked. "A slave," I explained, "is someone who has to work but doesn't get paid for it." This simplistic answer seemed to satisfy his curiosity while summing up my own feelings.

The rest of the morning I worked like a slave—or at least I felt like one. I cleared off the breakfast table and grumbled. I loaded the dishwasher, wiped the counters and swept the floor. Even while dressing my daughter and changing her diaper I remained mopey. I think the only thing I took pleasure in that morning was my shower. And that was interrupted halfway through by both kids pounding on the bathroom door. They were thirsty.

After putting my daughter down for her afternoon nap and quietly slipping out of her room, I turned around. There in the hall was my son, holding a handful of coins, pennies mostly, that he'd collected from his grandparents. "Here," he said, giving them to me. "Now you're not a slave."

I thought about it for a minute and decided he was right. For a total of thirteen cents, he bought my freedom.

Reviewing the morning's activities, I realized that my feelings of self-pity had affected more than just my attitude. By considering myself a slave, I had unwittingly cast my children as the loathsome taskmasters. How much of my resentment for my workload had been carried over to them? Not much, I hope.

So now that I'm emancipated, how do I go about my day? The reality is that I still have all of the same jobs to do. How do I keep from feeling like a slave?

For starters, I've begun to think of myself as a volunteer. Together with my husband, I made a conscious decision to have a family. You could say that I volunteered to be a mother. On days when motherhood is a bit more than I bargained for, I find it helpful to remind myself that I chose this lifestyle.

Another way to feel liberated hinges upon service. Who has the time to ladle soup at the local soup kitchen? We all do. Only we have to stop thinking of the soup kitchen in strictly traditional terms. Why not think of it as our own homes? The very things that can make us feel like a slave— doing laundry, cleaning toilets, picking up toys—when viewed from another perspective, can be acts of service.

Of course now that I'm beginning to get the hang of home-based volunteerism, my son has other ideas for me.

Just the other night as I was sorting the last pair of socks, he approached, more coins in hand. "Take these," he urged. Once I was holding them he said, "Now come with me. I need help picking up my room."

Christie A. Hansen

Reprinted by permission of The Compleat Mother.

The Millionaire

While driving home from work one day
My total wealth I did survey
My mortgaged home and ancient car
A bank account not up to par
Furniture from which I fear
We may not get another year
The TV set with stamp-size screen
Carpets with that well-worn sheen
Two suits of clothes not quite threadbare
"All-purpose" shoes that need repair
Sadly then I saw my plight
After twenty years of toil and flight
My Treasure Chest was somewhat small
With house and car and clothes and all
On I drove trance-like I fear
When suddenly my house was near
"Your daddy's home!" I heard her cry
As nine pairs of feet went rushing by
And smothered in arms and curly hair
I knew that I was a Millionaire!

William G. Wood
Submitted by Jane Madison

Teen Wisdom

As teenagers, our children didn't always come right out and tell us where we, their parents, were going wrong. Instead, they had tricky little ways of reminding us that they were capable of outgrowing childhood.

For instance, when Tom was seventeen, he got a job at the cemetery, which required him to get up at four o'clock in the morning in order to meet his watering schedule. I felt guilty for not being up to get his breakfast, but he insisted he didn't want me to. I think it was a relief for him not to have me breathing on him that early in the day.

One night my conscience prodded me into making cinnamon rolls for his breakfast. I put the rolls in a plastic container and left it in a prominent place on the counter. Later in bed I began to wonder if he would notice the container, and if he did, would he have enough sense to know what was in it. So I shuffled downstairs, made a label that said "Sweet rolls" and put it on top of the container. The next morning when I got up, there was a label on the stove that said "Stove."

Shuffling through childhood mementos the other day, I found a note left over from our two older daughters'

teen years—a subtle reminder of the process of their
"growingupness."

My husband and I had made the heavy decision to go
out of town for the weekend, leaving the two older girls in
charge of their grade-school brother and sister.

Naturally I left a long list of reminders about heating TV
dinners, turning off the oven, persuading Tom to wear
clean clothes to Sunday school, not to have friends in
while we were gone, etc., etc.

When we returned from our trip the following Monday
morning, the kids were at school, but they had left a note
on the refrigerator that read:

Dear Mom,

Unpack your suitcase.
Have supper ready for us at six.
Call the cleaner.
Have clean clothes for Tom to wear to school tomorrow.
*Keep Sam Hill off Corbins' lawn. [Sam Hill was our
  dog; the Corbins, our neighbors.]*
Make us some cookies, but not with coconut.
Change the bedding. (It's Monday, you know.)
*Don't spend too much time on the phone. We might be
  trying to call you to bring us something we forgot.*
Don't wash Kathy's T-shirt. She prefers it the way it is.
Write a check for Gerry's music lesson.
*If a stranger comes to the door, let him in. The dish-
  washer broke, and someone will need to fix it.*

Love, Gerry and Kathy

I like to think our kids grew up to be reasonably normal
on account of us, their parents. Still, they just might have
made it anyway.

Margaret Hill

What Parents Say/
What Parents Actually Mean

To clear up any confusion:

Make up your bed	Learn good habits
Clean up your room	Have order in your life
Be careful	You're precious to us
Don't drive fast	We couldn't bear to live without you
Get off the phone	**Get off the phone**
Do your homework	Learn everything you can
Don't spend it all	Always keep some for emergencies
It's late	Get the rest you need
Pick up your clothes	**Pick up your clothes**
Good job in the play	You make us so proud

Feed the dog	Care for people and things other than yourself
Turn the lights off when you leave	Be responsible
Finish your project	Use your gifts and talents to their fullest
You're growing so tall	You're getting close to leaving home
Take out the garbage	**Take out the garbage**
College is important	Being prepared for life is important
Wear a tie	Look good, feel good, be good

And one that should never be confused:

We love you   **We love you**

Andy Skidmore

The Naked Patient

It is tough. If you just want a wonderful little creature to love, you can get a puppy.

Barbara Walters

A reader of Dr. Dobson's column wrote asking for his advice: "My three-year-old daughter, Nancy, plays unpleasant games with me in grocery stores. She runs when I call her and makes demands for candy and gum and cupcakes. When I refuse, she throws the most embarrassing temper tantrums you can imagine. I don't want to punish her in front of all those people, and she knows it. What should I do?"

Here is Dr. Dobson's response:

If there are sanctuaries where the usual rules and restrictions do not apply, then your children will behave differently in those protected zones than elsewhere. I would suggest that you have a talk with Nancy on the next trip to the market. Tell her exactly what you expect, and make it clear that you mean business. Then when the same behavior occurs, take her to the car or behind the building and do what you would have done at home. She'll get the message.

In the absence of this kind of away-from-home parental leadership, some children become extremely obnoxious and defiant, especially in public places. Perhaps the best example was a ten-year-old boy named Robert who was a patient of my good friend, Dr. William Slonecker. Dr. Slonecker said his pediatric staff dreaded the days when Robert was scheduled for an office visit. He literally attacked the clinic, grabbing instruments and files and telephones. His passive mother could do little more than shake her head in bewilderment.

During one physical examination, Dr. Slonecker observed severe cavities in Robert's teeth and knew that the boy must be referred to a local dentist. But who would be given the honor? A referral like Robert could mean the end of a professional friendship. Dr. Slonecker eventually decided to send him to an older dentist who reportedly understood children. The confrontation that followed now stands as one of the classic moments in the history of human conflict. Robert arrived in the dentist's office, prepared for battle. "Get into the chair, young man," said the doctor. "No chance!" replied the boy.

"Son, I told you to climb onto the chair, and that's what I intend for you to do," said the dentist.

Robert stared at his opponent for a moment and then replied, "If you make me get in that chair, I will take off all my clothes." The dentist calmly said, "Son, take 'em off." The boy forthwith removed his shirt, undershirt, shoes and socks, and then looked up in defiance. "All right, son," said the dentist. "Now get on the chair." "You didn't hear me," sputtered Robert. "I said if you make me get on that chair I will take off all my clothes." "Son, take 'em off," replied the man. Robert proceeded to remove his pants and shorts, finally standing totally naked before the dentist and his assistant. "Now, son, get into the chair," said the doctor. Robert did as he was told, and sat cooperatively through the entire procedure. When the cavities were drilled and filled, he was instructed to step down from the chair. "Give me my clothes now," said the boy. "I'm sorry," replied the dentist. "Tell your mother that we're going to keep your clothes tonight. She can pick them up tomorrow."

Can you comprehend the shock Robert's mother received when the door to the waiting room opened, and there stood her pink son, as naked as the day he was born? The room was filled with patients, but Robert and his mom walked past them and into the hall. They went down a public elevator and into the parking lot, ignoring the snickers of onlookers.

The next day, Robert's mother returned to retrieve his clothes, and asked to have a word with the dentist. However, she did not come to protest. These were her sentiments: "You don't know how much I appreciate what happened here yesterday. You see, Robert has been black-mailing me about his clothes for years. Whenever we are in a public place, such as a grocery store, he makes unreasonable demands of me. If I don't immediately buy him what he wants, he threatens to take off all his clothes. You are the first person who has called his bluff, Doctor, and the impact on Robert has been incredible!"

James Dobson, Ph.D.
Excerpted from Dr. Dobson Answers Your Questions

Man Plans and God Laughs

To become a father is not hard, to be a father is, however.

Wilhelm Busch

As a single parent with full custody of two little children, my life was busy—sometimes beyond management. I would teach at the university, come home and then have to cook, clean, do the wash, read stories and play with my little ones. As a man, I had to learn to do what many women had already been doing.

On top of that, my career as a trainer and public speaker was taking off like a rocket. Invitations to speak were coming in and opportunities abounded. Juggling all of these responsibilities was more than merely stressful. After all, I had made a commitment to myself to be the best. The best teacher, the best speaker, and most importantly, the best daddy.

Responsibilities at work weighed heavily upon me, and financial constraints made it very difficult for me to refuse any and all offers to lecture. Whether it was to speak for some company, a school district or an association, I just couldn't afford to pass up the additional income. In short, I found myself running at full speed every day.

It was a typical Cleveland winter morning—gray, blustery and very cold. Besides getting the children ready for nursery school and making sure the nanny would show, I had to pack for a trip and catch a plane. Frenzy ensued. The children, sensing my tension as keenly as a shark smells blood, began whining, fighting and clawing for my attention, making it virtually impossible for me to get anything done. Finally, I had had enough. I lost control and shouted at them. There I stood, red-faced and screaming. The nanny looked away, embarrassed. My daughter and my son began to cry. Through their tears, I tried to kiss them goodbye. My daughter pushed me away and my son stood, rigid and furious. Frustrated, I shrugged and headed for the airport, driving through snow and freezing rain.

Filled with anger and nervous about getting to my flight on time, I began to rationalize my behavior. *I work so hard for those kids! Do they appreciate me? No!* In my righteous indignation, I was full of self-pity.

I parked the car, maneuvered my luggage to check-in, headed for the gate and boarded the plane. The bleakness of the day only contributed to my mood. I vacillated between anger, justification and guilt.

To boot, the plane I was flying on was an older plane. We took off into a growing ice storm, leaving Cleveland for Detroit where I was to do a workshop. As we rose through the clouds and the plane bumped and twisted in the unsettled air, my pangs of guilt grew. How could I leave my children like that?

The flight attendant walked down the aisle with a tray of soft drinks, when suddenly there was a loud *bang!* The air in the cabin seemed to whoosh down the aisle like a hurricane. The oxygen masks popped out of their overhead compartments and dangled in front of us like the finger of death itself. A hatch had blown off the plane and we were in "explosive decompression." The plane was at about eleven thousand feet over frozen Lake Erie.

The flight attendant, in her surprise and shock, threw her tray of drinks in the air! People screamed. One row behind me, a man in his seventies who had just survived cardiac bypass surgery began shouting in a thick European accent, "For this God saved me? For THIS God saved me?!"

The plane banked sharply and started descending rapidly. I looked out the window to see the frozen surface of Lake Erie as we plummeted down toward it. I was sure we were going to die. I looked up to see the flight attendants trying to open the cockpit door, but it was bent in by the force of the outrushing air. Their intercom phone to the cockpit wasn't functioning either. They seemed in a panic. *This is it,* I thought, *I'm going to die.*

At that moment, my whole life did *not* pass before my eyes. Instead, only two thoughts came to mind. First, because I had not prepared a will, according to Ohio's laws my children would lose half of their inheritance. And second, the last memory my children would have of their father would be of this red-faced, screaming maniac finding fault with them. I was filled with regret. *How could I have left them that way?* I thought, deeply chagrined.

I began to pray, even as the plane descended further toward the lake. "Dear Lord," I prayed, "if only you will save us all, just this time, I promise that I will never leave the house in an angry manner. I promise to let my children always know how much I value and cherish them."

I don't know how much time elapsed from the moment the hatch blew off until the plane suddenly righted itself—it seemed like forever—but it happened just as I ended my prayer. I could have spoken that prayer twenty times or maybe only once, but I believe it was answered.

Our plane turned around and flew back to Cleveland.

We all got off and boarded an identical plane, which did little for our confidence. But we finally made it to Detroit, where I did my workshop. Ironically, the topic of my talk was "Stress Management." Sigmund Freud used to say that we teach best what we most need to learn. This was certainly true that day.

The postscript of this story is this—I have kept my promise. When I returned to Cleveland, the first thing I did was apologize to my children and hug them very, very tightly. Then I went to a lawyer and drafted a will. And I have always left my home, even just to go to work, with an affirmation of love to my kids. When I would leave for a big trip, I'd stand them by the door and say something like, "I want you to know that I love you, and I've always loved you. I've always been proud and delighted to be your dad. I may sometimes be mad at you for something you've done, but nothing can ever make me stop loving you!" Oh, after a while, they'd roll their eyes and sigh as if to say, "Oh, do we have to listen to this stuff again?" Sometimes they'd parody me in a whiny, droning voice, "Yes, yes, you know I love you and I've always loved you...." But I could tell that they really liked hearing it. One day, I did forget to say it and they called me on my car phone and said, "Dad, tell us that stuff about you loving us!"

That day on the plane taught me never to take my life, or the people in it, for granted. I know how precious and delicate life is, and you never really know what tomorrow will bring.

As my late dear mother used to say, "Man proposes and God disposes." But she much preferred the more pungent Yiddish proverb, "Man plans and God laughs."

Hanoch McCarty

Message from a Guardian Angel

Some time ago, I was invited to do a speaking tour in several cities across Canada. The program was to end on a Thursday evening in Vancouver, so I decided to bring along my son, who was fourteen at the time. We would then have a long weekend together white-water rafting and exploring.

The trip got off to a rocky start. Several flights were cancelled. We ended up having to charter a private plane to fly us to Chicago, where we could catch a Canadian Airlines flight to Toronto. This was on the other side of Canada from where we needed to be, but we could make a connection back to Edmonton with barely thirty minutes to spare.

No problem, I thought. *I'll walk onto the stage just in time.*

Then we got hung up in customs in Toronto and missed our flight. The people at Canadian Airlines were wonderful and did everything possible to help. They even arranged for a limo to be waiting with the engine running in Edmonton. Still, the fact remained that I was going to arrive two hours late—for a speaker a sin second only to finishing two hours late!

I showed up at 10:00 P.M. for my 8:00 P.M. talk. Never before have I received a standing ovation just for showing up! I spoke until after midnight and answered questions for another hour. As the crowd dwindled, I noticed one man standing in the back corner, apparently waiting to see me. After years of speaking about Never Fear, Never Quit, I've learned that the last person to leave is often the person I was "meant" to be there for.

The man walked over and asked me if there was any significance to the eagle on my necktie. I explained that the eagle represented the Never Fear, Never Quit attitude. "Eagles are important to me also," he replied, and then told me his story.

A number of years earlier, his eleven-year-old son was diagnosed with leukemia. The boy loved eagles and the family adopted the great bird as their mascot of faith and hope. They had eagle pictures, statues and feathers all about their home. Ultimately, his son lost the battle. Some time later, the family took a vacation and was on a boat with some friends out on a lake. Despite the sun shining and the beauty around them, for them it was a melancholy day.

Suddenly, a big eagle flew down from the mountains and began soaring and gliding around their boat, doing loops and dives like they'd never seen an eagle do before or since. It stayed near their boat for about an hour. "We just knew," he said, "that our boy had come back to us in the only way he could to tell us we could let go now—that everything was okay. And ever since, it's been easier. We still feel grief, but now it's different, because our son came back for that one moment to reassure us."

What could I possibly have said to this man whom I'd assumed I was "meant" to be there for? I was at a complete loss for words. Then he did something that let me know I had the roles reversed—he was meant to be there for me, not me for him.

Turning to my son Doug, he unhooked his belt and

removed a small black canvas pouch that had been hanging from it. He said, "My son had a collection of very fine titanium knives. I've never given one of them away before, but I want you to have this one." He handed the knife to Doug, then turned to me. I'll never forget the way he looked at me, as though looking right into my soul. He simply said, "Pay attention, Dad. These years go by really fast."

There is no way he could have known this, but at the time my wife and I were about to send our seventeen-year-old daughter off on an Outward Bound course for troubled teens in the Boundary Waters between Minnesota and Canada. Part of the program included having the parents arrive in Duluth two days before the kids returned, so we could be prepared for the likely changes.

I wasn't going to go. I had a big Never Fear, Never Quit conference coming up, planes to catch and bills to pay. So I was going to have my wife go up early for the conference, then at the last minute I would race up to pick up the two women in my life. I would, I assumed, get the executive summary on the way home.

And in the middle of the night, in the middle of Canada, this man was brought into my life to tell me that I was about to make a grievous mistake.

Wake up, Dad, and pay attention. What is really important? When Doug and I got back home, I changed my plans so I could be in Duluth for the parent orientation. When Annie came running off the bus with a big hug for Mom and Dad, I felt hope that the miracle we'd prayed for had occurred. And I said a silent prayer of thanksgiving for that guardian angel who had stayed up so late to help a confused father get straight about his real priorities in life.

Joe Tye

Daddy's Day

Her hair up in a pony tail, her favorite dress tied with a
  bow
Today was Daddy's Day at school, and she couldn't wait
  to go
But her mommy tried to tell her, that she probably should
  stay home
Why the kids might not understand, if she went to school
  alone
But she was not afraid; she knew just what to say
What to tell her classmates, on this Daddy's Day
But still her mother worried, for her to face this day alone
And that was why once again, she tried to keep her
  daughter home
But the little girl went to school, eager to tell them all
About a dad she never sees, a dad who never calls

There were daddies along the wall in back, for everyone
  to meet
Children squirming impatiently, anxious in their seats
One by one the teacher called, a student from the class
To introduce their daddy, as seconds slowly passed

At last the teacher called her name, every child turned to
  stare
Each of them were searching, for a man who wasn't there
"Where's her daddy at?" she heard a boy call out
"She probably doesn't have one," another student dared
  to shout
And from somewhere near the back, she heard a daddy
  say
"Looks like another deadbeat dad, too busy to waste his
  day."

The words did not offend her, as she smiled at her friends
And looked back at her teacher, who told her to begin
And with hands behind her back, slowly she began to
  speak
And out from the mouth of a child, came words incredibly
  unique
"My Daddy couldn't be here, because he lives so far away
But I know he wishes he could be with me on this day
And though you cannot meet him, I wanted you to know
All about my daddy, and how much he loves me so
He loved to tell me stories, he taught me to ride my bike
He surprised me with pink roses, and taught me to fly a
  kite
We used to share fudge sundaes and ice cream in a cone
And though you cannot see him, I'm not standing all
  alone
'Cause my daddy's always with me, even though we are
  apart
I know because he told me, he'll forever be here in my
  heart."

With that her little hand reached up, and lay across her
  chest
Feeling her own heartbeat, beneath her favorite dress

And from somewhere in the crowd of dads, her mother
    stood in tears
Proudly watching her daughter, who was wise beyond
    her years
For she stood up for the love of a man not in her life
Doing what was best for her, doing what was right
And when she dropped her hand back down, staring
    straight into the crowd
She finished with a voice so soft, but its message clear and
    loud

"I love my daddy very much, he's my shining star
And if he could he'd be here, but heaven's just too far
But sometimes when I close my eyes, it's like he never
    went away."
And then she closed her eyes, and saw him there that day
And to her mother's amazement, she witnessed with surprise
A room full of daddies and children, all starting to close
    their eyes
Who knows what they saw before them, who knows what
    they felt inside
Perhaps for merely a second, they saw him at her side.

"I know you're with me Daddy," to the silence she called
    out
And what happened next made believers, of those once
    filled with doubt
Not one in that room could explain it, for each of their
    eyes had been closed
But there placed on her desktop, was a beautiful fragrant
    pink rose
And a child was blessed, if only a moment, by the love of
    her shining bright star
And given the gift of believing, that heaven is never too far.

Cheryl Costello-Forshey

I Believe in Angels

Nothing in life is to be feared. It is only to be understood.

Madame Curie

This is the story of my miracle. This is my story of how, at the lowest and most difficult time in my life as a parent, two young girls taught me to believe and have hope.

My daughter Kathleen is a beautiful, talented, seventeen-year-old now, but when she was five years old, a tragedy struck our family. Kathleen's best friend, my brother's daughter Sara, died of cancer one week after her seventh birthday. Sara and Kathleen, though nearly two years apart in age, were as close as two little girls could be. I remember that between them, they had more than fifty My Little Ponies. When Sara came for the weekend, we would shampoo all of them, put them on the picnic table to dry, and they would spend the rest of the weekend brushing and styling the hair, and making up fantasy lands for their ponies to live in. I would watch them, my heart full, knowing how limited their time together was.

When Sara was diagnosed with cancer, she was just

three. After a long operation to remove the tumor, the doctor adopted a wait-and-see attitude. My mind was in such turmoil. I would yell at God for letting Sara become so ill, but shamefully thank him that it was not Kathleen who was sick. I remember when I apologized to my brother for my feelings, he simply said, "Don't you think I yell at God and wish it was reversed?" We understood each other.

Sara's cancer came back when she was five and Kathleen had just turned four. They were young enough that we decided not to mention Sara's illness to Kathleen, and to let them have as much carefree time together as possible. My brother and his wife did not say anything to Sara and forbade the doctor to mention anything around her, wanting her to go to school and be "normal" with the other kids in her kindergarten class.

The first "hint" that all had not gone as planned was when Sara and her class were discussing with their teacher what they wanted to be when they grew up. Sara's teacher of course knew the situation but was stunned when Sara's turn came to speak. She stated simply and matter-of-factly, "I'm not going to grow up, so I don't have to think about it." When we all heard this had happened, we assumed that she had heard someone talking about her somewhere.

Kathleen and Sara continued to spend weekends together both at her house and ours, and as far as we knew, the subject never came up and Kathleen didn't even know Sara was sick.

I was heartsick at this time. How was I going to tell my little innocent girl that her best friend and cousin was going to die? How could I wreck her innocence and beauty and belief that life was forever wonderful?

Eventually, Sara was coming for the weekend quite ill, and because of medications and precautions we would have to take, we could put off telling Kathleen no longer. I called her in and we went up to her bedroom and "snuggled" in. I will never forget how I felt, looking at her gorgeous little face, looking so completely trusting at me. I plunged in. "Kathleen honey, there is something you need to know before Sara gets here today. Something I don't want to have to tell you, but have to."

"I already know she is going to heaven, Mommy," Kathleen said matter-of-factly, hugging her Smurf, named Murphy, to her.

"How do you know that, Honey?" My tears were flowing now, and I couldn't believe what I was hearing.

"Sara and I talk about it all the time. When we spend the night together, we lie in bed and talk about it. She is going to be in heaven, and not be sick, and she is going to be able to take her betty [blanket] with her. It's okay, Mommy. Don't cry."

Hugging Kathleen to me and getting us both soaked with my tears, I asked her how Sara knew all of this.

"Angels told her, Mommy. They talked to her and she talked to me. I'm going to go and wait for Sara to get here, okay?" And with that, *she* comforted *me* with a mighty hug and kiss and ran downstairs to wait for her friend.

I sat stunned for I don't know how long. My thoughts of death were so dark and lonely, and here I was hearing from a five-year-old about light and happiness and angels. How could I not believe all was well?

Sara went into the hospital for the last time shortly after that visit. We had her seventh birthday party there and Kathleen took her a My Little Pony and a homemade card. We lived far enough away that I knew that day there was a good chance we would not see her again. We kept our visit light and gay, and it turns out that this last party is one of Kathleen's only clear memories of being with Sara. That evening, after visiting my parents, I went to the hospital alone, helped my sister-in-law make Sara comfortable and kissed her goodnight. One week later to the day, Sara passed peacefully away, surrounded by ponies, with a picture of her little brother under her pillow.

Kathleen, when told, had a good cry with me and then, as children do, put it behind her. As I watched her in the days ahead, she lightened my heart. Sara was in heaven with her "betty" and was not sick anymore. An angel had told her so, and I believed.

Wendy Ann Lowden

7

OVERCOMING OBSTACLES

I am not afraid of storms, for I am learning how to sail my ship.

Louisa May Alcott

The Light at the End of the Tunnel

Who is it that loves me and will love me forever with an affection which no chance, no misery, no crime of mine can do away? It is you, my mother.

Thomas Carlyle

It was early in the morning, and the challenge of the day left a dull ache in my heart. Our beautiful daughter Lara had been depressed for months, and her behavior had become more and more radical. She wore all black, worshipped death-rock, and had white face-makeup and purple eyeshadow with black lips and nail polish. She was angry all the time and hurtful to her father and me. Her brother couldn't stand being in the same room with her. A pattern had established during the past few years and what we thought was a passing stage had become a nightmare. I used to think all I had to do was "kiss it and make it better," but now I couldn't and I felt like a failure.

Our home was no longer a home but a camp under siege. Forget about schoolwork. I started helping Lara so that she could graduate. Eventually I did her homework for her. It became my responsibility. I couldn't help myself as I became more and more codependent to my dysfunctional and troubled young child. Lara continually lashed out to punish and hurt us for the hopelessness she felt. I was afraid for her life, worried that one day I would come home from work and find her lifeless alongside an empty bottle of sleeping pills.

After a last-ditch attempt at a hospital stay, my husband and I had to make plans for her future that did not include bringing her home. A light in my long dark tunnel had been turned on by a psychiatric consultant in the hospital when he said, "Your daughter needs long-term care. She is depressed and suicidal. May I suggest a wonderful and nurturing environment for her called Rocky Mountain Academy in northern Idaho? It's part of a facility called The CEDU Family of Services. They have good results with teens in the condition your daughter is in."

After much deliberation, my husband and I felt we had no choice but to send her there. Her anger and frustration were destroying our marriage and the happiness of our son. Our daughter was becoming more and more unreachable, isolated from us and from life itself.

Now, my day of challenge lay before me. I had gotten up early. Lara knew she would be going away—for a rest from us and her environment, she thought. I couldn't tell her how long she would be there. I had to have help to get her to Bonners Ferry, Idaho, as it was a long trip. Would she attempt to run? I couldn't be sure, so I hired a gentleman from the hospital to accompany us. She wouldn't speak with me all the way to Idaho, but she did enjoy the company of her temporary companion. At least it gave me a rest.

Finally, the entrance to Rocky Mountain Academy was visible. What a beautiful and serene place! The children's faces were warm and friendly. The counselors who greeted us were like a warm blanket on a cold day. The venomous words that spewed from Lara's mouth I couldn't repeat. They cut me to my heart. I began to sob and the school staff took over. "I never want to see your face again. I will spit on your grave" were Lara's parting words. The desolation, the self-doubt, the guilt began to take over. I spent the night at the local motel, as depressed and despondent as one could be. *How did it all come to this?* I thought. *What did I do wrong? How could I raise a child to be so hateful?*

I returned home with my heart aching, constantly on the verge of tears. We had to rely on the school from here on in to accomplish what we had been unable to do.

For five months her father and I did not hear from Lara—not a card, not a call, nothing. I called Rocky Mountain Academy almost every day. How is she? Is she okay? What is she doing? Why won't she speak to me? A parent's worst nightmare was becoming a reality. Had I lost her forever? Did we do the right thing?

Finally, a sign. A letter arrived from Lara thanking me and her father for her new clothes, written, I'm sure, at the behest of one of the counselors. For whatever reason, I was thrilled to have that contact. Gradually the communication got better, and that led to our first visit. She cried, I cried and my husband cried. We had so much relationship repairing to do. Rocky Mountain was beginning to work its magic, reducing the "onion" to a mere bud and then building slowly, layer upon layer, accomplishment upon accomplishment. Each time we came for a visit, we saw more improvement in our daughter.

Lara expressed herself first through beautiful and sad poetry published in the monthly paper the children put out. The love and nurturing of the staff was beginning to pay off. I could see her face softening, the anger and the hardness were gone. Devoid of all the heavy makeup, her girlish face was beautiful and soft, warm and caring. At the same time, Lara discovered she had a beautiful voice. With encouragement, she began to sing every chance she got. The more she sang, the more validated she felt. As she found her voice, she slowly began to love herself. My heart also began to sing.

During these many months of hard work and self-discovery, my husband and I rediscovered what had attracted us so much to each other years ago. Because of Lara's dysfunction, we had become separate people, spiritually and physically alienated, and had lost our ability to communicate. The CEDU program, through its quarterly seminars for parents, began to bring us together again— no, not the same as before, but with a renewed appreciation and understanding of one another. It became even better than it was before Lara's six-year decline. We became a couple again, lovers again, friends again.

Perhaps things happen for a reason. Two and a half years flew by as Lara bloomed like a rose, my husband and I became one again, our son became happy and self-confident. I think we were meant to go through all this pain, for only when one experiences such pain can one experience such joy.

Lara's graduation from Rocky Mountain Academy was a time of pride and love. Lara wore a dress she knitted herself. It took her seven months to complete it, but it was a labor of love and commitment. It was a new beginning for all of us. Her grandmother, her father, brother and I proudly watched as she made her graduation speech.

Now where are we? Lara truly found her voice. She graduated from U.C. Irvine with honors, earning a bachelor's degree in music and vocal performance. Then she did her last year of graduate school at the San Francisco Conservatory of Music, which she paid for herself. In March 1999, she was accepted as the youngest member of the San Francisco Opera Company—her dream (and ours for her) come true. A wonderful and gifted soul has emerged from her cocoon, with the voice of an angel as well as great ambition, drive and the will to make things happen.

For those struggling with children with problems, *don't give up.* There is a light at the end of the tunnel. We know. We have been there.

Bobbi Bisserier

My Son, My Grandson

Trouble is a part of life, and if you don't share it, you don't give the person who loves you a chance to love you enough.

Dinah Shore

I drove home from work that day wholly unprepared for what was awaiting me at home. As I came through the door, I was greeted with the usual "What's for supper?" from my husband and sons. But then Corey, my oldest at twenty-one, followed me into the kitchen, and as I turned to give him one of my looks, I saw the nervousness in his eyes. He looked like a terrified little boy who was turning to his mommy to make things all better.

As soon as he asked, "Mom, can I talk to you?" I got that sick feeling in the pit of my stomach. He anxiously shuffled me into his bedroom and shut the door. He didn't have to say anything; I just knew.

"Who's pregnant, Corey?" I asked.

He lowered his head and said softly, "Deanna."

I sat there, my mind racing and the blood seemingly draining out of my body. I felt weak. In a strained voice, all I was able to mutter was, "What are you going to do?"

My mind became clouded with thoughts and questions—*How many times had I warned him about needing to use protection? How did this happen?! How far along is she? Is she okay? Has she been examined? I'm too young to be a grandmother—* but I was able to collect my thoughts to be the mother that my son so desperately needed. Corey looked visibly relieved that I didn't react strongly, and we were able to sit and talk about it without overreacting.

Compounding a difficult situation was the awkward reality of Corey and Deanna's breakup—only a month earlier. Deanna was three months pregnant and I knew that the next six months would be an emotional roller coaster for Corey. My heart ached for my son as I watched him grapple with confusing emotions and the responsibility of decisions to be made. At times, the fear and sadness were overwhelming for Corey and he would hug me and cry, his body shaking with anguish. The unconditional love and support I felt for him over those months seemed to fill both our hearts. In those moments spent with Corey, I forgot about the stress of my job or the state of my faltering marriage. I prayed that everything would work out for the best and that they would make the right decision for them.

Corey and Deanna finally told me they had decided on adoption. As much as they yearned to be able to parent their child themselves, they knew they were not ready. They made their decision in the best interests of the baby, and I was very proud of them for that.

They went through a private adoption agency and interviewed several couples. The questions they asked the prospective parents were well thought-out and showed that they cared deeply about the future of their unborn child. They decided on a couple who already had one adopted daughter at home. The couple agreed to give

Corey and Deanna updates on the baby's progress through the years. They felt strongly that the baby would be loved and nurtured by this family.

On July 17, 1995, at 3:18 A.M. a baby boy was kissed by angels and given life. Corey called me from the hospital emotionally drained and in tears. I would get to see the baby and meet the adoptive parents later that day. I was surprised at how strongly mixed my emotions were. I was filled with love and excitement one moment, sadness and loss the next. I arrived at the hospital and met Corey with tears in my eyes and a loving hug. I was so proud of him, and yet my heart was breaking for him as well.

I had bought a ceramic cherub for my grandson, a guardian angel to watch over him since we wouldn't be able to ourselves. I handed it to his new parents and asked if they would keep it in his nursery at home. They said they would. They were wonderful people with whom I felt an instant connection. I sensed a strong bond of love between them. They could hardly wait to get their new baby home to meet the rest of their family. I knew they would be wonderful parents to my grandson.

Corey took me into a small room beside the nursery. The nurse brought in this tiny angel wrapped in blue and placed him gently in Corey's arms. I immediately started to cry. I will never forget those precious moments when I held my grandson. It hurt so much to know that I would never see him again. As I watched this tiny soul sleeping, I remembered the first time I had held Corey. I silently said a prayer to my grandson, "May your guardian angel walk your every step, kiss your every breath and always protect you. I will always love you no matter where you are." When the nurse came back to take the baby, I gave Corey a hug, told him I loved him and quietly left. I was overwhelmed with emotions. I silently gave thanks for a healthy baby and to the loving couple who would be his new parents.

It has been three years now and my grandson, Tye, is doing wonderfully with his adoptive parents. He is a happy, well-adjusted little boy. Corey and Deanna have moved on from each other and have found new loves. Although I have never seen Tye again, I think of him every day. I carry his photo in my wallet to remind myself of both my precious grandson and my incredible, loving son.

Debbie Rikley

Tough Love Wins the Day

There are times when parenthood seems like nothing but feeding the mouth that bites you.

Peter DeVries

I sat in my car crying for fifteen minutes before I finally found the courage to climb out and walk inside the high school. Thirty-five friendly faces were already there to greet me. It was my first meeting of Tough Love International, and I didn't know what to expect.

Before the meeting began one of the leaders took me and two other first-timers aside and told us about the program. "It took your child a long time to get where he's at today, and the problems can't be fixed overnight," she explained. "It's not going to be easy, but we can help you get your child back again."

A tiny flutter of hope rose inside my heart. But I was also plagued with doubts. Over the years, I'd tried counseling, meetings with teachers and even medications. I'd followed the advice of every parenting expert who'd ever written a book. Nothing worked. My teenage son Kevin was completely out of control, and I was at the frazzled end of my rope.

Kevin had always been a problem child. At school, he refused to listen or turn in any homework. At home, he argued with his dad and picked fights with his older brother, Keith.

"You need to discipline him more," my husband, Kenny, insisted, but I couldn't handle my son. I could barely talk to him without being sassed and the two of us winding up in a shouting match.

When he entered high school, Kevin dropped all his old friends and started hanging out with a tougher, sleazier crowd. He went to their drinking parties and didn't stagger home until well past midnight.

"Kevin, why are you doing this to yourself?" I pleaded with my son, but his only reply was a bedroom door slammed in my face.

In the morning, I literally had to drag Kevin out of bed and dress him for school. It was all I could do to get him into the car and drop him off in time for class. Often as not, Kevin would walk in the building's front door and then straight out the back door with his friends. Other days, I'd get a call at work telling me to come pick up my son because he'd been suspended for fighting or smoking in the boys' room.

My son kept my life in a constant state of crisis. My marriage was floundering, and I felt so alone and ashamed.

My guilt was a black cloud that hovered above me always. *I'm such a terrible mother*, I blamed myself. *Somehow I've failed Kevin. Why can't I be a better mom and make him change?*

Then one day the school called to tell me Kevin had been picked up at one of his friend's houses during school hours, drunk and high on pot.

Dear God, please tell me what to do! I cried myself to sleep that night. *If I can't help Kevin change his ways, sooner or later I'll be visiting him in jail . . . or in a cemetery.*

"My sister told me about Tough Love International," I told the group during one of the very first meetings I attended. "I carried around the phone number for almost a year before I finally made the call. I kept telling myself, 'Things aren't that bad. I can handle Kevin's problems myself.'" I swallowed my pride, then continued. "That wasn't the truth. The real reason I didn't call was because I knew this was my very last hope. I was so terrified it wouldn't work, and then I'd have no hope left at all."

I attended group meetings faithfully every week. The more I got to know the other parents and listened to their stories, so much like my own, the better I began to feel. These people loved their children and would have done anything to help them. They didn't fail their kids. They weren't bad parents, and just maybe, neither was I.

One of the most important things I learned at Tough Love International was that I couldn't change Kevin's behavior. I could only make positive changes in my own life and the ways I interacted with my son.

I learned to recognize when Kevin was manipulating me and how to stop enabling his bad decisions. He could be so sweet when he wanted me to lift his grounding because there was this concert he simply had to attend, and I used to fall for it every time. But not anymore. And when I'd try to lay down the law and he'd argue, "You never treated Keith this way!" Before, I might have caved in. But now I knew just what to say.

"You're right. I never treated Keith this way. I never had to. Your brother never misbehaved like you do."

No longer did I spend all morning trying to get Kevin ready for school. "I'm leaving at eight o'clock tomorrow morning, and if you're not in the car, I'm leaving without you," I explained to him. The next morning Kevin was still sleeping when I drove off to work, but the morning after that he was dressed and in the car waiting for me.

The people at Tough Love International also taught me that Kevin was never going to change as long as I was always there to rescue him from the consequences of his actions. The next time I got a call from his school I told them I would no longer drop everything and come running to fetch him whenever he got into trouble. "I'll be there after work," I told his principal. "Tell him to sit there and wait for me."

The next time Kevin got into trouble with drugs I searched his room and collected all of his paraphernalia. I had the support of the entire Tough Love Parents Group. Fifteen other parents arrived at my home to help me deal with this situation. They unbolted his bedroom door and took it away. "You've lost the right to privacy in this house," he was told. "You'll get it back when you can prove to us that you deserve it. And that's when you can stay clean and sober for eight full weeks."

Slowly, Kevin's behavior began to improve. But a few months later he failed a court-ordered urine test and was sentenced to thirty days of juvenile detention. It was the toughest thing my husband and I have ever done in our lives, but during the entire thirty days we never visited Kevin once. I knew that if we did he'd spend the whole visit complaining and playing on our sympathies, and then he'd learn absolutely nothing about consequences.

We were there at the end of the sentence when Kevin had to face the judge. He looked wan and haggard, but for Kevin the experience proved to be a turning point.

Facing the judge, Kevin said, "I'm sorry for all the trouble I've caused my parents. I've lied to them and stolen money from them for drugs. I'm glad they love me enough to be tough on me."

"Those were strong words you spoke in court," I told Kevin on the way home. "But now you're going to have to back them up with deeds."

Kevin did just that. He dropped his bad friends and found a job at a fast food place. He came straight home from work every evening, and actually talked to his father, brother and me without getting into arguments.

Kevin volunteered to attend an eight-week, outpatient drug program. At the end of the eight weeks, the fifteen Tough Love Parents returned to our home and rebolted his bedroom door in place. Then they congratulated him on meeting the requirements of staying clean and sober for eight full weeks. There were lots of hugs and tears all around, as the entire group celebrated Kevin's outstanding success. For the next two years, until he was eighteen, he never failed a single drug test.

One day Kevin gave me a hug and said, "You and Dad could have put me out on the streets for the way I used to act. But you never did. You loved me enough to be strong and make me find my own way out of trouble. You saved me, and for that I love you very much."

Today, Kevin is attending trade school to be a welder. His drug use is a thing of the past. I'm so proud of my son, I could cry.

I still attend Tough Love meetings, but nowadays I do so as a group coordinator. The organization gave me back my sanity, my marriage and my son. I figure the least I can do is try to help other parents who feel that there is no hope for their children.

Marina Tennyson
As told to Bill Holton

A Voice for Elizabeth

*The potential possibilities of any child are the
most intriguing and stimulating in all creation.*

Ray Lyman Wilbur

Sometimes, the way you learn a word sticks with you.
Such as the word *naches,* a Yiddish word for joy. It is a special kind of joy, a joy combining pleasure and pride that
only parents can get from their children.

I won't forget its meaning soon, because I heard it after
a long, uphill struggle on the part of my daughter
Elizabeth. She's a pretty twenty-year-old with an engaging smile. But her life has not been like that of most other
girls.

Elizabeth has cerebral palsy, a birth-related condition
that has fouled up her nervous system and confines her to
a wheelchair. It has left her with poor balance and legs
that cannot bear her weight—even though she is barely
ninety pounds. But her biggest problem is speech.
Cerebral palsy has left her with poor tongue control. She
can pronounce only a few words clearly.

Most of us will never know how frustrating it is not to

be able to speak. Talking opens windows. Elizabeth's windows are closed. She understands all that is said, but cannot hold up her end of a conversation.

It was not until she became a teenager that full awareness of her affliction really became apparent to her. Gradually, the dirty deal that life gave her began to prey on her mind. She disobeyed her teacher in class, pulled children's hair on the school bus. At home, she upset furniture, scratched her face. At the darkest hour, we had to hospitalize her to calm her. With the help of a family therapist, Don-David Lusterman, things began to improve. But there was always that undercurrent of despair.

Then one day, Elizabeth's school speech therapist, Elaine Glaser, let her try a voice synthesizer, an electronic "talking box" that works something like a typewriter. Instead of letter keys, it has word and phrase keys that are sounded when you strike them. You can put together almost 400 words. The voice is a bit toneless, something like HAL, the spaceship computer in the movie *2001: A Space Odyssey.* But you can say a wide variety of things, and if you master the keys of the phonetic alphabet, you can say anything.

Elizabeth brightened right away. She began to make progress with the synthesizer. But with her poor hand control, it was slow going. Other children were learning on the same machine, so she could use it only a few hours a week. Dr. Lusterman thought it might make a big difference if she had a voice box of her own to use all the time. He felt her emotional problems all stemmed from her inability to communicate.

The synthesizer cost three thousand dollars, an amount way beyond our means. Elaine suggested we ask the school board of Elizabeth's school district to buy one for her, pointing out that it was essential for her educational progress.

It was sure worth a try. The first step was to present Elizabeth's case before the district's Committee on the Handicapped.

On the day the committee met, Elizabeth, in her wheelchair, went before the group to demonstrate her ability with the machine. "Well, Elizabeth," said Fred Zellinger, a school psychologist and the committee's chairman, "let's see what you can do." His voice was encouraging. But everyone knew three thousand dollars was a big investment in these financially tight times.

Using the machine, Elizabeth said, "Hello." Then the committee members began asking questions. "How old are you?" Elizabeth struggled to find the right keys. But there was no seventeen. She was trying to figure out how to put together the "one" and "seven" keys. Before she could find them, the committee went on to another question. "Why do you need your own voice box?" Elizabeth's mind was still trying to work out a solution to the first question. Now she was confused.

The sweat started forming on my brow. "What is your name?" a committee member asked. Her name wasn't programmed into the system. She would have to use the phonetic keys, and Elizabeth had not learned them. She looked up. Her big brown eyes held mine for an instant, seemingly asking why couldn't she respond, what was wrong?

I had to fight back the emotions that started to well up inside me. It was clear she wasn't going to make it. But I didn't want her to go down without a fight. "I know Elizabeth could do better with a little more time," I said, sounding like an adolescent boy whose voice was cracking. "If she could only practice a bit more, I know she could do it."

There was a silence. A week later, a letter came from the school board turning her down. They felt she had not proved she could master the machine. At the behest of the Committee on the Handicapped, however, they did agree to rent a machine for her for the summer. They were willing to see what progress she could make.

We hired Liz McMahon, a young nurse, to work with Elizabeth. Her speech teacher mapped out the program and worked out the daily exercises that Liz would carry out.

That summer, for two hours each day, they practiced together. From behind the closed bedroom door, I could hear Liz asking questions and Elizabeth responding with her computer voice, "I am hungry . . . I want bathroom . . . I am sleepy." They never missed a day. At night, instead of television, I heard the voice box: "How are you . . . I'm fine . . . I'm speaking with an artificial voice."

In October, the big day came. Elizabeth appeared before the committee again. The district superintendent took the unusual step of attending. There was a lot of money riding on the board's decision and a possible precedent in the making, too.

There was a tenseness in the air, similar to a pianist taking the stage for a debut. Elizabeth sat at the end of a long table. The committee members lined each side.

"How are you feeling, Elizabeth?" a committee member asked.

"Fine, thank you," she said with her electronic voice. "How are you?"

"Do you know where you are and what today is?"

"I'm at school, and today is Friday, October 1-2 [12th]."

So far, Elizabeth had answered every question. And her fingers had gone to the right keys without any delay.

"Why do you need a voice box?"

"To say: 'I'm hungry. I'm sleepy. I want bathroom.' To talk like you do."

Then came the toughest part. Could she use phonetics?

Fred Zellinger asked if Elizabeth could say his name. I knew she had learned to say her own name. But I wasn't sure if she could use phonetics to say a new word. Slowly, using the phonetic alphabet, Elizabeth made the machine say "ZUH-LUH-EN-GER." Heads turned.

Two weeks passed. We heard that the committee had recommended something to the school board, but we were told not to be too optimistic. Funds were low. It was, at best, a 50/50 chance. A month passed. Then one day, the phone rang. My wife, Sara, had taken the call. I held my breath. Suppose the answer was "no." How would Elizabeth react? Would it take away her determination to achieve other goals in years to come? Had it been right to put her in a vulnerable position?

Then, I looked at my wife, and knew the answer even before she hung up. She was crying tears of joy.

For the next two weeks, congratulations poured in— from friends, teachers, neighbors. A smile stretched across Elizabeth's face all week.

In the four years since, we have seen that Elizabeth's acting-out problems have not entirely disappeared, but they have diminished significantly. She has found that she can set a goal, work toward it and achieve it. She has learned that, just as able-bodied people can get self-esteem and satisfaction from a job well-done, so can she.

And so can her parents. I heard nice things from many friends. But the one I remember best came from Dr. Lusterman, a gentleman who likes to sprinkle his conversation with Yiddish. He captured my feelings perfectly with a word for which there is no precise English counterpart. He told me, "You've got *naches*."

David Zinman

My Daughter's Smile

Mother love is the fuel that enables a normal human being to do the impossible.

Marion C. Garretty

One night, as I stood brushing my daughter Chelsey's hair, I noticed her studying our two images in the bathroom mirror.

Watching me carefully she said, "Mom, I want to have that surgery on my face."

"Why?" I asked her, catching my breath, a lump instantly forming in my throat.

"So I can smile like you," she replied, her gaze holding mine.

Somehow I found my voice, and managed to reply, "I'll see what I can find out about it, honey."

Chelsey was born with a rare condition called Moebius Syndrome. She was asking me about the special technique of reconstructive surgery that would help overcome the mask-like quality of her face that resulted from this condition. We had heard it had been successful with other children, and now Chelsey was determined to have it for herself.

Chelsey's birth had been uneventful and the delivery a breeze. But within moments of her birth I became aware from the look on my husband's face there was a problem, and I was suddenly frightened. During the next few hours, it was uncertain if Chelsey would make it. My only thoughts were, *I don't care what I have to deal with—just let her live.*

The following day, when I finally got a close look at her, she looked so tiny and fragile that I was scared I might hurt her. When I picked her up for the first time, I saw immediately that the fingers on her right hand were fused together, and only partially formed on her left. Her jaw was small and recessed, and I noticed the mask-like appearance of her face. One of the nurses suggested she might be retarded. I was devastated.

As I tenderly stroked her silken cheek, I wondered, *Are you there? Do you know how much I love you?*

We were released from the hospital when Chelsey was just ten days old after the doctors determined that nothing more could be done. Once home, her weight dropped rapidly. After a frightening episode in which she choked and stopped breathing, we had Chelsey examined by a pediatrician and geneticist. He immediately recognized the rare Moebius Syndrome, and his tests were conclusive. She was missing two important cranial nerves, one that governs lateral eye movement and the other which activates facial expressions. Chelsey's mask-like expression was the result of these two missing nerves.

What did the future hold for my daughter? Would I ever get to experience her smile?

Dr. Bass explained to us that Chelsey would never be able to smile, move her eyes from side to side or squint. Although her hands would be weak, surgery could easily separate the fingers on her webbed hand. The nerves that controlled her ability to smile also controlled her ability to chew, swallow and speak. We learned that all of these would present challenges for her.

In spite of my shock, learning the exact truth was a relief, and helped me to take better care of her. I was also encouraged to react and interact with her more, something I had not been doing much of because of her apparent lack of response. She did much better after that—and so did I. We learned how to work on the problems we knew were ahead: feeding, swallowing, and because of her lack of facial expression, getting her feelings across to others.

But Chelsey had a very determined nature and because of this her development was much faster than predicted. She learned to crawl by propping herself up on her fists. When told by the occupational therapist not to expect Chelsey to walk until she was two, I thought, *You don't know my daughter.*

Seeing her older brothers tear through the house gave her extra motivation, and it wasn't hard to see where it would lead. Only six days after her first birthday, Chelsey took her first steps.

When she was eighteen months old, the doctors tested Chelsey's intelligence. By now I knew she was smart, but the doctors were uncertain. The pediatric specialist placed several split peas on the table and asked her to drop them into a bottle placed a short distance away. I was miffed at the seeming unfairness because of her fused fingers.

Again Chelsey did the unexpected. She studied the peas and the bottle, licked her fingertips, touched them to a pea and reaching forward, drew her fingertips back across the rim. When I heard the pea ring in the glass I almost burst out laughing.

With a satisfied smile, I asked, "So, does she pass?"

Chelsey beat the odds in several other ways by learning to swallow finely diced foods and then to speak. I hoped that speech therapy would improve her ability to communicate and socialize, but as time passed it became clear that things were getting worse.

When the children at school began to tease her more and more, I decided it was time to explore the new reconstructive-surgery technique I'd heard about. Skeptically, I made an appointment with Dr. Donald M. Zucker at Toronto's Hospital for Sick Children.

Even after I heard other children had been receiving surgery for this condition, I was loath to put my daughter through more trauma. *What if it only repaired half her face?* I wondered. *What if she is left with an expression that is artificial and is unhappy with the outcome?*

I began doing research and discovered that Dr. Zucker transplanted muscles from a child's thigh and placed them where they would create the most natural expression. The procedure required two operations, one for each side of the face.

We saw Dr. Zucker and we were told that Chelsey was an excellent candidate. I still wasn't 100 percent convinced it was the right thing. My little girl was still only six years old. Then a very disturbing incident helped me make up my mind.

One day while we were shopping, I noticed Chelsey hiding behind a rack of sweaters. When I asked her why, she pointed out two children who stood by giggling. "They're talking about me," she answered. I thought she was imagining this but when I asked her why she thought their laughter was directed at her she said, "Because they're whispering and pointing at me. I hate it, Mom."

I'd never seen Chelsey that low before.

Then, I met a child who'd undergone Dr. Zucker's

operation. At first I thought she looked just like Chelsey, but when she gave me a brilliant, natural smile, my heart lifted. I knew then I must give this same gift to Chelsey.

In December 1995, Dr. Zucker performed the twelve-hour procedure on Chelsey at a clinic in California. When he announced, "Everything went well," I was relieved and overjoyed.

Dr. Zucker had explained it would take time and practice for the new expression to become more natural. Seven weeks later Chelsey came to me and said, "Mom, I think I feel something!" I pulled my daughter closer and studied the right corner of her mouth. There was the unmistakable first faint twitch. In that moment, I knew for sure the operation was a success!

Then to Chelsey's great joy, in about a month the tiny twitch had formed into a resounding half-smile.

In April, Dr. Zucker operated on the right side of Chelsey's face. The wait to see if both sides of the operation were successful was almost unbearable. Six weeks later that muscle began to show signs of movement. Chelsey would stand in front of the mirror, and as soon as she saw or felt her face twitch for the first time, she'd run to me saying, "Look how much it moved!" When both sides of her face were finally working together, I breathed a huge sigh of relief, encouraging Chelsey to smile as much as possible. She was absolutely delighted and never tired of practicing her smile. She couldn't wait to show it to everyone!

Interest was growing with the media, and we began receiving invitations to show Chelsey's miraculous new smile. On June 29, the day Chelsey turned eight, Disneyland gave her a celebration, and it seemed to us the whole world was there. Friends, relatives, doctors and media all turned out to help her celebrate her birthday— and her new smile. Chelsey had a great time but the best present of all was the one she gave to all of us. Chelsey smiled her first full, beautiful, symmetrical smile that day. It was a moment I'll never forget, a moment frozen in time.

A few weeks later, Chelsey and I were traveling on another media tour. I was very tired, and glad to be able to relax in our motel room. I began recalling the events that had led to this moment, my fears and hesitancy over the risk of the operation. Chelsey was curled up on a chair across the room. Our eyes met in a silent exchange of love. For a moment, I was back in the hospital when I'd asked the questions: *Are you there? Do you know I love you?*

As if she'd read my thoughts, the corners of Chelsey's mouth slowly began to turn up and then she gave me the biggest brightest smile I'd ever seen. Long after I'd stopped wishing for such a gift, I found myself basking in the soul-deep warmth of my daughter's first smile.

Lori Thomas
As told to Darlene Montgomery

A Heart in the Shadows

Each child carries his own blessing into the world.

Proverb

I was so engrossed in watching the ultrasound monitor that at first the obstetrician's questions seemed merely annoying, not alarming.

"Does anyone in your family have a short neck?"

"Short neck?" I echoed. I was more interested in the liquid-like appendage on the shadowy screen—a leg or maybe a folded arm.

"How old are you?"

"Thirty-four," I answered, noticing the blurry orb—quite possibly the face.

"Does your husband have short legs?"

Then I heard the doctor whisper something about a "left ventricle" too.

"What's the matter?" I snapped.

"You probably need a more powerful ultrasound. We can't make out part of the heart," she said, her offhand tone sounding a bit tinny.

"So, what was the result of your alpha-fetoprotein test?" This blood test, I knew, screened for congenital disabilities.

"I didn't take it," I said. "I didn't want to know."

"I'm with you," she quipped. "Congratulations," she added. "It's a girl."

I tried to look happy arriving home from the ultrasound visit, as my three-year-old twin boys dashed to greet me at the door. When I handed them a souvenir ultrasound picture, they jumped, twirled and yelled, "We have a sister!"

We went into the kitchen and hung the shadowy picture labeled nineteen weeks on the refrigerator. "Isn't she pretty?" I asked. Now she had a face, and even a name. My husband, Joel, and I had decided a girl would be named "Ronit," Hebrew for *my joy*.

I stood back, trying to picture a future for Ronit that was pleasurable and routine. But, instead, the doctor's remarks replayed in my mind—the heart and the neck. The taking what God gives me. I certainly knew what that meant.

I fought back my fears until my appointment with Hannah, the obstetrician who had seen me through my twin pregnancy. We began that exam with small talk about our children while she reached for the ultrasound report.

Scanning the page, her face froze into a startled look. It was a while before she could speak.

The next morning, Joel and I went to the hospital for a higher-intensity ultrasound. This time, Ronit's face and body appeared larger than life. I lay on my back, eyes fixed to the monitor as a cardiologist zoomed in on the heart. With the volume turned up, Ronit's "flub-dub" filled the room.

When the screen went blank, the cardiologist gave us the news. Our baby had a heart condition called atrioventricular canal defect. Coupled with her distinctive body type, the heart findings made the diagnosis of Down syndrome a near certainty.

Her heart might fail soon, he said, and she would be stillborn. If she survived to birth, heart failure would soon follow. By age six months she would require open-heart surgery. If she survived that, as most babies did, she would likely be given a good prognosis.

My knees almost buckled as Joel and I were led around the corner to the geneticist's office. But the moment the doctor walked in, I surprised myself by blurting, "If I don't want an abortion, why am I talking to you?"

The doctor rolled his eyes. "I don't want you to go into this naively," he said. "Not all children with Down syndrome are healthy and high functioning and sweet, like Corky on *Life Goes On.*"

We spent the next half-hour reading chromosome charts, after which he recommended amniocentesis to confirm the diagnosis.

During the weeks surrounding the amnio, Joel and I couldn't discuss the future without feeling ill and drained. Every possible scenario ahead seemed bleak, and caring for our boys was already challenging. When the results came back positive, I couldn't stop asking, *Why us? Why her?* Every time I saw friends romping with their bright-faced children, I had to fight back tears.

Most of the specialists I saw urged abortion, sometimes subtly, sometimes not. I was asked, "Do you really want this baby?" I was reminded of "the deadline"; told "the fetus will be viable soon"; asked, "What if she just never came to be?" One doctor advised that if I passed the deadline for abortion in Ohio, I could still "have it done" in another state.

But was "it" really an option? How could I still a heart that I had seen in bold color, a heart I felt I knew and even loved? In the kitchen, I often found myself blowing kisses at Ronit's picture on the refrigerator. I always kept one of Joel's old stethoscopes nearby and whenever Ronit's kicking subsided, I listened, aching to hear the rhythmic beat.

I didn't want Ronit to die inside me. I just didn't want her coming into this world to suffer.

One day in my sixth month, Joel drove me home from a doctor's visit with *The Phantom of the Opera* playing in the tape deck. When we heard the phantom blare, "Past the point of no return," our eyes met, knowing that we, too, had passed that point. Perhaps we had known all along that for us there could be no "return." But on that day, for the first time, the realization didn't bring pain, only hope.

Joel and I began reading books about Down syndrome. We contacted the local chapter of The Upside of Downs and researched congenital heart programs. A month before my due date, we told relatives and friends that our third baby would be "special." The news brought tears, and I was glad that they were being shed while Ronit was still inside. At birth, I wanted her to be greeted with joy.

Which she was.

"Six pounds, thirteen ounces," a nurse announced from the gurney in the corner of the delivery room. There, a team of neonatologists and nurses huddled so closely around Ronit that I couldn't even catch a glimpse from my bed. Finally a doctor wheeled Ronit toward me and placed her on my chest.

She had the widest, bluest and most vulnerable-looking eyes I had ever seen. The most perfect hands. "Isn't she gorgeous?" Joel asked. I kissed her forehead, and, in a matter of seconds, the doctor scooped her up again and hurried off to get her chest X ray.

As soon as they were out the door, I noticed that the very pregnant medical resident sitting beside me was crying softly. "Don't worry," I said, smiling. "It's going to be okay."

Today, Ronit is a joyful and engaging four-year-old with a mended heart, who attends preschool and loves to play with her big brothers. Recently, one of her brothers was rifling through a drawer when he came across a long slick sheet filled with shadows and lights. "What's this thing?" he asked.

Studying it for a moment, I recalled how this barely discernible collection of shadows that once hung on my refrigerator had brought me first to despair, and then to love and treasure a life even more.

"It's a picture of your sister before she was born," I said. "She was beautiful even then, wasn't she?"

Sharon Peerless

8

SURVIVING LOSS

In the midst of winter I discovered that there was in me an invincible summer.

Albert Camus

Erin's Legacy of Love

Love is the only thing that we can carry with us when we go, and it makes the end so easy.

Louisa May Alcott

We were like so many people, just forging ahead, working hard and not really being sensitive to the lack of balance in our lives.

My wife Erin and I were what you would call type A business executives. We were on the fast track. I had just started a retail business unit for a wireless messaging company. Erin had established herself as one of the leading venture capitalists in the Southwest. We had our beautiful two-year-old daughter Peyton, a wonderful family and a great network of friends.

But from time to time we sensed we were missing a balance in our lives, and we felt a spiritual void. Often we would lay in bed at night and talk about how we were feeling, but we were moving so fast and driving so hard that we never took the time to address those issues.

Business was going so well and we were so successful that there was no motivation to change. Why would God make us so successful in what were doing if he wanted us to change?

Then, in January of 1994, Erin was diagnosed with cancer. This sudden turn of events really shocked us into re-evaluating our priorities. Our mortality hit home for the first time. At first everything went on very much as it had been. Erin managed to keep working, while she began receiving treatments.

Suddenly, two years later, Erin became so ill from an infection that the doctor told me she might die very soon, probably within twenty-four hours. She was placed in an isolation bubble room where she remained barely conscious for the next three weeks. Her parents and I stayed by her side day and night, preparing for her to die.

While her body fought for life, her spirit was in another place, and she began a spiritual journey. During her experience, Erin later told us, she came in contact with a white light and was told her real purpose in life. She became aware that her life's simple purpose was just to let God's love flow through her.

One evening while Erin was getting some X rays done, I sat out in the hallway preparing myself for the fact she might go any minute. I thought of our daughter, Peyton, soon to be without a mother. Suddenly a thought came to my mind: *What happens if Peyton asks me, "What's Mom's favorite color? What's Mom's favorite food or movie?"*

These were basic questions about her mother, and I couldn't come up with the answers to most of them. I started to panic, thinking, *Oh my gosh, if I don't know the answers to these questions, who will?*

I started to reach out to God for the first time. It was on Easter morning when Erin's white blood counts finally rose and she slowly began to come back to us.

When she was released, we got focused very quickly. We had a new attitude toward our future which we called "living with the end in mind." An important part of that was "parenting with the end in mind."

Erin's experience in the bubble room had changed her to a person who was now very focused on love. She wanted to instill as much of this as possible into our daughter, Peyton, before she died, so Erin quit her job and made parenting her full-time occupation.

We had a lot to discuss about Peyton's future. A friend offered us a condo at the foot of Mount Crestabute in Colorado, so we flew there for a few days to reflect.

While there, we thought about how we envisioned Peyton as a twenty-five-year-old woman and asked ourselves, *What are the things we can do to help her be the best person she can be?* We realized we wanted to empower our daughter to grow the character traits we thought would be most helpful to her self-esteem, confidence and decision-making capabilities. Up until that point, we hadn't really empowered her. We realized we had controlled her more than anything.

We came up with a plan to leave a legacy for Peyton— a legacy of Erin's love. We made it a project to gather as many ways as possible to nurture her all the way through her life. Erin wanted to make sure that as Peyton was growing up, she would continue to have the love and guidance of both her mother and her father, even though Erin would not be physically present.

Erin began making videotapes of herself, each one about a specific subject geared to some age or time of Peyton's life. Sometimes this was very hard for her, and she would often cry before she could get a word out. But then she would think about the love she had for Peyton and how these recordings would help her in her future and she'd find the courage to start the tape. On one tape, Erin talked to her daughter about boys and dating. On another, she shared with her some tips on makeup techniques. There was another on the basics of cooking, and they went on from there, covering many of the subjects on which a young girl needs her mother's wisdom and advice. I made tapes for Peyton as well, giving her the dad's perspective on many of these topics.

We gently started to introduce Peyton to the concept of death and our mortality. Because it wasn't a morbid concept to us anymore, why should it be a morbid concept with Peyton? So we used different opportunities to explain the subject.

One day Peyton brought an empty cicada shell into the house. Erin used that as an opportunity to explain the separation of spirit and body. She showed her how the shell was empty and the body that was in there had just left the shell behind. She explained that when we die, only the shell of our bodies are left. Our spirit leaves and travels to its true home in heaven. Erin told Peyton how her great-grandmother was there and her great-great-grandmother, as well as all the relatives who had died. Erin explained, "Peyton, you'll be part of the great circle of life as well," and Peyton understood.

Over four years had passed since the original diagnosis, and Erin had outlived all of the doctor's predictions. But now as Erin started declining, we brought a hospital bed into our home, and put it in the den next to a big picture window.

One evening in early October when she was resting, I was with her and holding her hand. After a long rest, she opened her eyes and said that she had seen the white light again. This was the same white light that she had seen in the bubble room and she knew that God was coming for her. We knew that she didn't have much time, and we realized that we were going to have to talk to Peyton very soon.

On October 30, Erin woke up at 6:30 P.M. from a nap with a brightness and clarity that she hadn't had. I knew it was time to get Peyton. I got a piece of paper and jotted down some notes. The very first thing I wrote down was, cicada shell, the next was circle of life and the next was angel.

It took all my strength to focus as I walked up the stairs towards Peyton's bedroom. It was the hardest thing I've ever had to do in my life. Even with all the planning and preparation, my heart was pounding.

I gently pushed open Peyton's bedroom door and told her we needed to go and see Mom. As we entered the den, Peyton jumped up in bed with Erin and began to snuggle. The two of them were smiling and cuddling though Erin wasn't strong enough to do a lot of talking.

I asked Peyton if she remembered the cicada shell and she did. We began to talk about some of the things we'd discussed over the years about the cicada shell, angels in heaven and the circle of life. Then it was time to tell her: "Mom's getting ready to go to heaven. It's her time very soon." You could see in Peyton's eyes that she understood. She nodded her head and said, "I understand." She cried and Erin and I cried but we knew that she understood. This fact was so important to both Erin and me.

Erin passed away Halloween morning at 4:00 A.M.

That Sunday passed in a flurry of phone calls and preparations for the memorial service.

The next morning I woke up to a voice that said, "God's love, God's love, God's love." I felt this great force of light and love flowing into me so strongly that I could hardly take it. The next moment it stopped and then suddenly I felt Erin there with me as if she had walked up behind and put her arms around me. Again I felt a surge of energy and love from her, and then it gently subsided.

To this day, I still feel Erin with me. Although I have experienced sadness and grief, the intensity of those emotions have been greatly softened knowing that Erin is right here with me.

I remember the first night after Erin died. Peyton was praying and she said, "Mom, I know you're up in heaven and you're having a great time. We thank you for Halloween because it's going to be a double holiday from now on. It's going to be a day that we always get candy and it's a day that we'll get to celebrate you getting to heaven."

It's been a year now since Erin passed away. Today, Peyton is a happy, well-developed little girl.

One day I happened to say, "You know what Peyton, I really missed Mom today."

Peyton looked at me and said, "Why Dad? She's been with us all day long."

And you know what? She was right.

Douglas Kramp
As told to Darlene Montgomery

My Message

Death is the veil which those who live call life:
They sleep, and it is lifted.

Percy Bysshe Shelley

I'll never forget the message that I received that winter day, three years ago. It was from my daughter, who had been married just a little over two months by then. She had just come back from a doctor's appointment and had something to tell me. "Could you come over?" *Could I come over?* I was in the car faster than my answering machine could rewind the message. My newly-wed daughter wanted to see me. What else could it be but news of a baby on the way? I found myself getting very excited over the prospect. My husband and I were in our late forties. We would be young grandparents with a great deal to offer our daughter and son-in-law.

By the time I arrived at my daughter's house, I had the baby shower completely planned in my head. I pulled into the driveway and found my daughter outside waiting for me. No sooner did I get out of my car when she ran into my arms. "Oh, Mom!" She was crying. *Hormones kicking in already,* I thought. *Pretty cute. My little girl is going to be a mother.* "Mom, I'm sick." Like a needle scratching to a halt through an old record, my world stopped.

Several specialists later the diagnosis was confirmed, my daughter had myelocytic leukemia—cancer of the blood. Over the next few months, I learned much more than I ever wanted to know about the disease. But we were determined to beat this thing. The entire family rallied together. My husband and son-in-law were so supportive and loving, and our thirteen-year-old daughter became her sister's champion. She would sit and read to her for hours, any and all material that she thought was funny. She heard that laughter was good for the immune system. They also watched funny movies, and I would hear peals of laughter coming from the upstairs bedroom. We became so close as a family, and other issues or disagreements we previously might have had seemed to melt away in the face of this tragedy.

None of us ever wanted to entertain any other scenario than restored health. With that intention in hand, we prepared for a bone marrow transplant. We were all tested to see if any of us would be a compatible donor. We were told that finding a relative that matches reduces the chances of rejection. Bingo! My younger daughter was a perfect match. We were so lucky.

The City of Hope in Duarte, California, is a most incredible place. The staff is amazing. I had previously thought that a bone marrow transplant just consisted of removing cells from the donor and injecting them into the patient. I was in for a rude awakening. Before they do the transplant, the patient has to be given massive amounts of chemotherapy. They literally try to suppress the immune system so it won't reject the new cells. But in doing so, they nearly killed my daughter. My sweet little girl had lost all of her beautiful hair, and she couldn't eat either. She was wasting away before my very eyes. Because her immune system was so fragile, she had to be kept in a sterile environment for weeks before and after the treatment. When we entered her room, we had to wash, and put on gowns, gloves and surgical masks. Her husband and I took turns holding her until she fell asleep. Tears would stream down our faces as we rocked her tiny little frame.

Miraculously, she recovered and the new cells thrived. Slowly but surely she came back to normal, and for an entire year we enjoyed, reveled in and appreciated the gift of health. But almost a year to the day later, the return of abnormal cells sent us back to the City of Hope. Since these bone marrow procedures are so hard on the body, they don't like to perform too many on one patient. This would be our second chance.

I was so proud of the way my daughter handled herself. Because she was a veteran to the procedure, she would walk around the ward, wheeling her IV, and visit the other patients to offer words of encouragement. She would say, "It helps me more than it helps them." There was a definite bond that formed between patients, families and the staff.

Four years and three bone marrow transplants later, after pushing beyond medical, as well as my own daughter's, limits, I knew there was nothing more that could be done. My daughter's tiny body had had enough, and she knew it. A mother should never, ever have to bury a child, but I knew that any mothering I had done up to that point would be in vain if I couldn't help deliver my daughter into the hands of the angels. I was there when she came into this world, and I was going to be there if she had to leave it.

I took her home, made her as comfortable as possible and we talked, read and learned everything we could about death. We weren't going to dance around it like it wasn't there, and that seemed to bring great comfort to my child. The whole family had a chance to talk, laugh and cry about it with each other. We shared the most precious moments together. We were all getting our chances to say good-bye.

The analogy my daughter and I liked the best about this fragile thing we call life and death was something we saw in a movie. They explained that life is eternal and when you come into this world it's like putting your hand into a glove; and when you leave, all you're doing is simply removing your hand.

My oldest child died peacefully and in her sleep, with her husband right there beside her. The expression on her face was almost angelic. I knew I had done my job. Her suffering was over, and I had to keep that in mind, especially when my grief would become more than I thought I could bear.

Two years later I went to visit my daughter's grave. As always, I would put fresh flowers on it and sit and talk to her. She would always be alive and well in my heart. On that particular day when I arrived at the cemetery, I was wondering about all the talks my daughter and I had about life continuing after death. I wondered if she was well and happy. One could really never know, I guess. When I got to her grave, I was shocked to see that there was a glove draped gently over her headstone. I picked it up and I started to cry. A groundskeeper rushed over to me and sincerely apologized for leaving his glove there, "his mistake." Suddenly a warm feeling of peace and well-being welled up inside of me, feelings I had not felt since my daughter's death. And at that moment I knew . . . there had been no mistake.

M. Schneider
As told to Zan Gaudioso

Forgiveness

If I could bear your pain, I would. If money could buy solutions or my comfort solve the worst hurts, then they would be there for you. It hurts me not to help, and it hurts me to know that all my kindnesses would be inhibiting to your growth. I'll always be there for you. I hope you know, but you are free—you must grow away.

Helen M. Exley

My husband of eighteen years, the father of my three daughters, was diagnosed with congestive heart failure at age forty-six. His only hope for survival was a transplant. While waiting, our only hope for survival as a family was to create as much normalcy as possible. Webster's definition of bravery must contain a summary of my husband during this time, as he made our friendship each day a priority and hid from his children the extreme pain of his condition. Despite our resolve, it was not easy.

One trying day, my closest friend stopped by to pick up her youngest daughter, my daughter's best friend. One look and she knew, as close friends will, that I was having a tough time. She hugged me and I said, "Sometimes, widowhood doesn't look so bad."

"I know," she said, both knowing and not knowing. It was a horrible thing to say. I didn't mean it. It certainly wasn't funny. It *was* human. Strange as it may seem, though, I never thought of it again. I never felt guilty about it, nor, as we women are so prone to do, did I ever feel guilty about not feeling guilty. It was simply a passing comment.

Several weeks later, my oldest daughter Melanie and I had an argument over something she required and I denied. I don't remember what, simply that it was one of many typical arguments in which my independent sixteen-year-old and I engaged as an exercise of our roles. Her father backed me up. However, when it escalated into a shouting match, I approached her privately in her room and cautioned her to give up the argument. "I will not have you upsetting your father. I will not risk him dying over this silliness."

Melanie flew out of her room in a rage and screamed, "I don't care! I wish he *was* dead!"

The next day he was.

Melanie had not caused her father to die. It simply happened. Nothing I could say, however, would convince my daughter that what seemed to her an obvious cause and effect was not evidence of her guilt. The mother in me wanted to take the moment away that caused her so much heartache. The mother in me also wanted her to learn everything she could from this unfortunate life experience.

Melanie sang Jim Croce's "Time in a Bottle" at her father's memorial service. She made it through the entire song without faltering while hundreds of guests cried. It was her apology to him. Somehow, she did not hear his whispered forgiveness.

She joined a peer counseling group in school for troubled teens. I sent her for private professional counseling. The wound kept closing, opening, festering, closing and reopening. I could not brush it off and kiss it better.

As her eighteenth birthday approached, I had no idea what to give her. Money was tight. Nothing seemed appropriate. A walk in a children's section of a local department store jogged a buried memory, and suddenly I knew what to do. When my new adult child walked in the house from school that day I gave her these three things: a bag of party balloons, a set of darts and the board game Life. As she opened them, I explained, "The balloons are for the ups and downs in your life. The darts are to throw at my picture, which will hurt much less than my heart. The game is so that you will learn that Life is not a game, until you are old enough to discover that it really is." To add to her confusion, I handed her an essay describing the passing comments I had made to my friend that day nearly two years before. For some reason, I had suddenly remembered it in the department store. Bitterness and anger edged her voice when she finished reading it. "What is the tone of this, Mother? What are you trying to say to me?"

"The tone is that you never did anything that I had not done already. The tone is that I never had anything to forgive you for."

My new adult child suddenly melted in my arms, sobbing. "Thank you for forgiving me, Mommy."

I am a firm believer in the concept that everything happens for a reason. I said what I did on that day to a friend, not so that I would be able to forgive my daughter, but so that she would be able to forgive herself.

Mary-Ann Joustra Borstad

Held in Our Hearts Forever

If at times we are somewhat stunned by the tempest, never fear; let us take breath, and go on afresh.

Francis de Sales

"C'mon, Jordie," I offered. "Let's read a story."

I sank heavily against the wall, lowering my pregnant torso gently to the floor. My young son picked a favorite book, fully memorized from many bedtime readings. His blond head cocked with suspicion as he sat next to me. "Are you okay, Mommy?" he asked.

I placed his hand on my belly which, as if on cue, grew tight with a contraction. Jordie's eyes widened. "Oh, you are in labor," he whispered. Our precocious son had celebrated his third birthday just two weeks previously. And now, as he snuggled up against me, I thought back to the peaceful days we spent awaiting his birth. My husband Harry and I had experienced the miscarriages of three planned and wanted babies, so that by the time Jordie arrived, he did so into very welcoming arms. And we held fast this new life, determined that nothing would part us.

When insistent nurses wanted to take the baby to the nursery I held him tighter and told them that they would need a crowbar.

I couldn't keep my eyes off our son. The word "precious" kept springing to my lips, for now there was justification for this addition to my vocabulary. Yet somehow we felt that we really didn't have a newborn. This child was born with the look of an already experienced adult. Even friends with babies of their own would look into his eyes and say, "This kid is spooky! It's like he knows. . . ."

Jordie started talking, clearly and distinctly, at the age of nine months. When barely two years old he could carry on an adult conversation. I remember listening to him tell a friend, "You know, there's this theory of where the moon came from. See, there is a hole in the Pacific Ocean. . . ."

And now, this little boy who knew was silent.

That night was a blur of pain, doctors, nurses, hospital smells, sharing decisions with Harry, and laughing between contractions with my friend and midwife, Linda. Finally I was pushing out tiny feet, and the obstetrician whom I had only met the day before was asking, "Is there a possibility of twins here?"

Suddenly this joyous event became one of sheer terror: pushing twins that were wedged together, that could not be born; the doctor pushing back, unlocking them, catching two little boys.

Joshua died first. His little heart beat only briefly. Cole stayed with us for almost three hours; long enough to squeeze his daddy's finger, to let me hold his hand as he struggled to breathe. We waited for the flying squad to arrive from Children's Hospital. They finally appeared as Cole's heart beat its last. Later we were to discover that both boys were born without kidneys. They had no chance of survival.

Shock and grief filled the room. The head nurse bathed

Cole at my bedside, her tears splashing into the water. As a physically and emotionally traumatized mother was handed her still babies, doctors and cleaning staff alike dabbed at their eyes. Children are not supposed to die.

Harry and I kept our babies for hours, forcing the coroner to wait. We had them footprinted, saved locks of hair, took photos and loved their physical beings for as long as we could.

At home, Jordie had not been told anything. My mother bundled him up and brought him to the hospital. The incredulous nurses tried to stop her from taking him in.

My mother put aside her own grief long enough to gather her courage and insist, "Diane wants him there, and he is going in!"

Jordie walked in quietly, obviously worried about his very pale mother. He crawled up beside me. "Jordie, something very sad has happened. You had two little brothers, but they both died."

"Oh. That's too bad." In reverence, his voice was hushed.

"Would you like to see them?"

He nodded.

His grandmother picked Jordie up and took him over to the bassinet where Josh and Cole lay. He looked in and cooed, "Aww. They're so beautiful. May I touch them?"

"Yes," I replied. "But you have to remember, they died. They are cold and they won't move."

"That's okay," he assured me, reaching out and gently stroking their cheeks. "They are so soft . . . ," he sighed.

Jordie taught the hospital staff priceless lessons about grieving and about not underestimating children. He continued his teaching during the difficult days, weeks and months ahead. Once, during one of my particularly intense crying sessions, I heard him answer, "No, I'm sorry. She can't come to the phone now. She's crying because our babies died." Death and grief were now subjects worth exploring for our surviving son. And he did so with confidence, and with a new understanding that death is an integral part of this continuum we call life and is not to be avoided or feared.

Several years later Harry and I felt that it was time to try for another baby. That pregnancy ended in another miscarriage, this time of a little girl. Friends and family expected that we would remain a one-child family, but I had a strong feeling that there was another child waiting for us. I convinced my husband that we should try one last time and that however it concluded, it would be our last attempt.

When the pregnancy developed complications at thirteen weeks, Harry shook his head, "Here we go again."

"No," I was emphatic. "This baby is fine."

That August, with my husband, my mother and Linda in attendance, I gave birth to a nine-pound, five-ounce boy. Harry held his breath until our baby took one of his own. Benjamin was healthy, beautiful and a custom-fit for the void in our arms. Again, there wasn't a dry eye in the room, but this time the tears were those of joy.

Although Benjie's birth allowed our hearts to heal, Josh and Cole remain part of our lives. Jordie, now a young man who prefers the name Jordan, remembers little of his time with them. And Benjie knows the twins only from stories and from looking through their scrapbook. But they both understand why I light two candles every year in September. And they have both visited the grave and know the meaning of the headstone that reads: Our Twins. Held in Our Arms for Hours; Held in Our Hearts Forever.

Diane C. Nicholson

A Dolphin Wish Fulfilled

They that love beyond the world cannot be separated by it. Death is but crossing the world, as friends do the seas; they live in one another still.

William Pen

Lee Katherine had a bright future ahead of her. At the age of fifteen, she had already charted her path in life and was determined to become a marine biologist. She had always felt a close connection to the sea, and told her parents, Robert and Ruth, that her love of marine life would help thousands of animals one day. In her back pocket she carried a book written by her hero, Jacques Cousteau, and the tattered pages only further illustrated her conviction to become a famous marine biologist.

It was during this time that Robert and Ruth were dealt the devastating blow of having their daughter diagnosed with a terminal illness. After doctors delivered the news that she had cancer of the nasal cavity, all of their dreams for Lee Katherine came crashing down. Although her parents did everything they could to help her fight her illness, including seeing her through a rigorous round of chemotherapy, Lee Katherine's medical team soon realized that she was losing her battle. They told Robert and Ruth to take her home and keep her comfortable; there was nothing else they could do.

As they left the doctor's office that day, Robert and Ruth were in a state of shock; they couldn't believe that their beloved daughter was going to lose her battle. Still reeling from the sting of what they had just learned, they were unprepared for what Lee Katherine told them next. Leaving the office, she turned to her mother and said, "Mom, there is one thing I want to do before I die. I want to swim with dolphins." Shocked, Ruth nodded, but was shattered inside, believing that she had nowhere to turn to for help. Despair turned to desperation as she struggled with the realization that she would not be able to fulfill her daughter's last request.

It was only a few days later when Ruth ran into a friend at the supermarket, who happened to be a volunteer for Children's Wish Foundation. The friend asked about Lee Katherine and Ruth repeated her daughter's wish, saying, "It's the only thing she wants to do and I don't know how to do it." Her friend gave her the phone number to Children's Wish Foundation International.

Ruth called the foundation's headquarters and explained Lee Katherine's situation. She told the foundation that her daughter would not live to see her dream of becoming a marine biologist come to fruition, but that she clung to the hope that she would experience the magic of swimming with the beautiful dolphins that had always captivated her.

That very day, Children's Wish sent an overnight package containing all of the paperwork the family needed to sign along with instructions for Ruth to overnight the signed papers back. Calls were placed to Lee Katherine's medical team immediately to inquire about any special provisions that should be made for a child in her condition. These doctors knew that Lee Katherine could pass away at almost any time, but with Lee Katherine's determination to swim with dolphins so strong, they approved her for traveling and signed off on the medical forms. They also provided guidelines that needed to be followed carefully for the young girl's comfort and safety.

Too frail to travel by air, the foundation rented a special RV to transport Lee Katherine from her home in North Carolina to the Florida Keys. To help alleviate the pain, doctors had her receiving round-the-clock morphine treatments through an IV, and it was necessary to equip the RV with padding to provide Lee Katherine comfort as she traveled.

It was obvious to all who saw Lee Katherine that her illness had taken its toll, and most of all to Ruth and Robert. But as the RV drew closer and closer to the dolphin center, her entire spirit changed. Memories of her illness and thoughts of what lay ahead were replaced with a renewed excitement of finally having her wish fulfilled.

Before she could enter the water, the IV administering the morphine had to be removed. There were concerns about how she would manage the pain but Lee Katherine was determined. Ruth placed a life vest over her daughter to keep her afloat, then stood by and watched as a team of volunteers carefully lowered Lee Katherine into the water, where two beautiful dolphins awaited her.

What happened next was a miracle to all who were present. The two dolphins, Nat and Tursi, seemed to instinctively sense Lee Katherine's fragile condition. They nudged her neck, gave her soft dolphin kisses, provided gentle piggyback rides, and delighted her with leaps over her head. Throughout her swim, despite her fragile appearance, it was hard to believe that she was sick at all. As the sun sparkled across the water, Ruth and Robert watched their terminally ill daughter beaming with happiness as her lifetime dream was fulfilled

After her swim, Lee Katherine told her parents, "I'm not afraid to die anymore." She explained how she felt that the communication with the dolphins was her "bridge to the other side" and she now felt totally peaceful. Miraculously, for Lee Katherine and her parents, she never needed another drop of morphine.

Just thirty-six hours after her swim, Lee Katherine passed away. In the midst of their enormous grief, Ruth and Robert felt their daughter had given them a priceless gift they never expected. Through her courage, grace and determination, Lee Katherine taught them that even in the most tragic of circumstances and regardless of how short is the life that was lived, dreams can come true. The images of her laughing and swimming with the dolphins remain forever etched in her parents' hearts as a reminder of the gift of Lee Katherine to her family.

In order to fulfill their daughter's final wish, Ruth and Robert returned once again to the Florida Keys. There, they scattered her ashes amongst the same school of dolphins that had brought their daughter so much joy and peace. They had indeed been her "bridge to the other side."

Christy Chappelear Andrews

I Miss You Most at Christmas

*Into the nebulous, ongoing mystery of life I wel-
come as if through an open door, the continuing
spirit of the one I have loved.*

Martha Whitmore Hickman

Jay was always aware of the telltale signs before I was.
Shortly after Thanksgiving I would become distracted,
my normally easygoing disposition tinged with gloom,
tears ever close to the surface.

"You get like this every year," my husband said last
November, exasperation in his voice. He sat on the edge
of the bed where I lay teary-eyed. "I do everything I can
think of to help you feel better, but nothing works. It's no fun
for either of us anymore. Is it always going to be this way?"

When I didn't reply, he left the room. *He simply doesn't
understand,* I thought miserably—though if anyone understood, it was Jay.

But he couldn't make Christmas okay for me. No one
could. In 1986, our ten-year-old son was hit by a car and
killed. I had hated the holidays ever since. I missed Ben
every day, but his loss was intensified at Christmas. For

years after his death, I went through the motions of a family Christmas for our two daughters, keeping a happy face for them and grieving in private. Now that they were in their twenties and lived away from home, my holiday depression had resurfaced with a vengeance.

I wanted Christmas past. I wanted my little boy back so we could experience the wonder and joy of Christmas again, the way it was before our family was plunged into grief. I lay there wrestling with my feelings. I didn't want to ruin another holiday season for Jay. I owed him more than that. He had his own grief issues, but they did not intensify at this time of year as mine did. *Could I ever feel the spirit of Christmas again? Did I even have that capacity within me?*

One evening several days later, I talked to one of my daughters on the phone. She had recently moved to a different state and, like her sister, could not be home for Christmas. I mentioned how much Ben was on my mind. For a moment there was silence, and then, "I've been thinking about him, too," she said, her voice breaking. "Ever since he died, I've just wanted to get Christmas over with."

Her words jolted me. All those years I thought she and her sister were having a good time, were they just putting on an act? Had they, like me, become incapable of enjoying what I knew in my heart could be the happiest, best time of year?

I had thought that somehow, over time, I would naturally begin to enjoy Christmas again. Now I realized that time couldn't make this happen, for Ben would always be missing, and we would feel his loss most acutely at Christmas. If I could acknowledge my grief and honor my son's memory at Christmas, perhaps I could enjoy the holidays again—which meant my husband could as well. In turn, we might be able to help our daughters do the same.

I thought long and hard, then I talked to Jay. I told him I wanted this year to be different, that I didn't want to spend December under a cloud of gloom. I could see the relief in his eyes as he offered to do whatever he could to help.

We discussed every issue and came up with three things we would both try. First, we would work at finding pleasure in all that was magical and wonderful about the holidays. Second, we would speak of Ben whenever he came to mind—no holding back for fear of depressing ourselves or others. Finally, we would do one special thing to commemorate how much we missed our son at Christmas. All three, it turned out, were important.

To fulfill the first goal of finding pleasure, I concentrated on engaging my senses to the fullest. In the past, I had shut them down, numbing myself to twinkling lights, the sound of carols, the smell of evergreen, and the tastes of mint, almond and ginger. Now I embraced them.

I also gave more thought to each holiday task, from wrapping presents to mailing cards, appreciating them as time-honored rituals instead of just things to get done.

I unpacked several paper and paste ornaments Ben had made in first grade, including a primitive little yarn frame with his school picture in it. I closed my eyes and ran my fingers over the aging yarn and the small color photo of Ben with his happy, gap-toothed grin. In the past I hadn't been able to bear looking at it and had kept it put away, along with his other ornament creations. But our son had made these for us. I hung them on the tree. From now on I would bring them out and touch them and allow them to touch me.

We said we would speak openly of Ben. Several weeks before Christmas I lunched with a friend I had not seen in many months, and she dwelt at length on how much she hated the holidays—too expensive, too much rich food, too many expectations. She also lamented that her newly married son would be spending the holidays with his wife's family and that she felt "deserted."

The old me would have inwardly screamed at her, *At least you have your son. Look at me—your pain is nothing compared to mine!* Instead, I took a deep breath and forced myself to sympathize with her. Then, measuring my words very carefully, I told her how hard I was trying to enjoy the holidays in spite of how much I still missed Ben.

She looked startled and for a moment I regretted my words. Then she put her hand on my arm. Her eyes were moist. "I think this is the first time since Ben's death that you've mentioned him to me. Whenever I started to speak about him, I could tell you didn't want to, so I assumed you must be over your grief. But now I know . . . ." Her words caught in her throat. "You've just given me a special gift. I'm going to be grateful for what I have and stop complaining."

I would have given anything to be sitting there commiserating together about our adult sons, but at least I had finally spoken. In breaking my silence at long last, I let my friend draw me close. No longer would I repress my speech when Ben was in my thoughts.

A few days later while out shopping, Jay and I stopped at a busy coffee shop. Something reminded me of a Christmas past when Ben had the flu and we had spent the day caring for him. As I spoke of this, tears welled in Jay's eyes, then in mine. "I miss him so much," Jay whispered.

There, amid the bustle of holiday shoppers, we held hands under the table and let our tears fall and managed to smile at each other, enriched by our shared remembrance and our love.

To achieve our third goal, that of commemoration, we were thinking about attending a special Christmas concert. Then we saw a notice in our newspaper about a new "Service of Remembrance: In Memory of Those We Miss the Most at Christmas." The evening service was in a church of a religion different from our own, but no matter. We gathered with a hundred other bereaved souls, and in a lovely, quiet service, we listened to beautiful music and comforting words, then lit candles as we put the names of those we had loved and lost in a special basket on the altar.

My tears felt especially healing that night, and I entered the busy final week before Christmas with a sense of peace that had eluded me in years past.

Jay and I talked to both daughters on the phone, openly sharing our feelings and offering heartfelt support as they expressed their own grief for their brother. When we wished them a Merry Christmas, I felt as though attaining this was finally possible for all of us.

On December 25, Jay and I toasted our families and Ben's memory at my brother's home in Nashville. When January 2 rolled around, I realized that for the first time since 1986 I had actually enjoyed Christmas. It could not be what it once was, but I now knew it could still be good, and somehow I felt Ben would be pleased by that.

This year, with the holidays approaching, I am aware once again of my sadness for what cannot be, but I am focusing on what I still have and what is worth celebrating. For the bereaved, whether our losses be new or old, our challenge is to be happy in the moment, to see the star, to celebrate the magic of the season and to remember in cherished memory our beloved dead.

Andrea Warren

The Day My Daughter Died

May I honor—and trust—the processes of grief and healing, knowing that, in time, a new day will come.

Martha Whitmore Hickman

The day my daughter, Mary Jo, died, she slept until ten because she and her sister, Emily, had been up until the wee hours of the morning making plans about their futures. Emily was home for the weekend, taking a break from her studies at the University of Toronto. Mary Jo thought that she might want to be a travel agent. She wanted to attend college in Toronto and share a place with Emily.

The day my daughter died, we had breakfast together. She had been shopping with her sister, Kate, the night before, and was excited about the gift they had bought. "Mum," she exclaimed. "I can hardly wait until Christmas! You're going to love the gift Kate and I got you!"

The day my daughter died, our whole family did housework together. For once, we didn't bicker about who should do what job, or whether someone was not doing their work adequately. We finished hanging the decorations on the Christmas tree, and laughed about some of the ornaments that had been made by the children when they were very young. Pictures of John and Mary Jo hung in felt ornaments they had glued together in preschool. Mary Jo thought they looked funny; I remembered what beautiful little children they had been.

The day my daughter died, Mary Jo asked Kate and me to play Monopoly with her.

I really wanted to finish vacuuming the carpet, which was covered with bits of tinsel and Christmas tree, but I said "Sure!" I thought, *How often does a sixteen-year-old girl ask her mum to play Monopoly with her?* We laughed together as the three of us played Monopoly all afternoon.

The day my daughter died, I wanted to pick up Swiss Chalet Chicken for the kids to have at supper time, as my husband Al and I were going to a staff Christmas party. But the girls said, "Why don't you give us some money, and we can go and eat in the restaurant? It will be more fun!" So we gave them the money, and they went and had a wonderful time together.

The day my daughter died, we dropped her off at her friend's house. She took a bottle of Coke and a bag of chips to share with her friends. From the car, we watched as she waved good-bye happily.

That was the last time we saw her alive. She died in a car accident at 10:35 P.M. that night.

A prayer has been hanging in our family room for years. It reads:

> *Bless our home,*
> *Father that we*
> *cherish the bread*
> *before there is none,*
> *discover each other*

before we leave,
and enjoy each
other for what
we are while
we have time.*

The day my daughter died, I learned what it meant.

Marguerite Annen

---

*Prayer by Richard Wuong. ©1981 Abbey Press, St. Meinrad, Indiana. Used with permission.

Cori's Beads

*Spirituality is that place where the utterly inti-
mate and the vastly infinite meet.*

Rick Fields

I believe in miracles, some as subtle as a butterfly kiss,
some so bold that the air seems to leave the room. My
miracle is my daughter, Cori. Although she is gone, she
brought me back to life.

Cori was born July 10, 1975. As I held her in my arms
that first time I knew immediately there was something
different and special about her. Her handmade birth
announcement read: "A miracle, and we thought all babies
were alike." I didn't understand the prophecy behind
those words until years later.

Cori grew into a beautiful child, adapting well to all the
changes in life's rich pageant. But our family had its
struggles, and when Cori was six, her father and I
divorced. Not long afterward, I fell into a life of addiction.
As Cori grew, it broke her heart to see her own mother
increasingly drawn into the insidious world of drugs, cons
and welfare. Sickness was all I could offer her at that time,

yet she never wavered in her love for me. And through her own strength she rose above the mire of my life and walked her own path. At the age of sixteen, she was amazing—she was a cheerleading instructor, an excellent student and dreamed of becoming a lawyer. Even in my drug-induced fog, I was fiercely proud of her.

I believe God doesn't take anyone until their life's work is completed. Cori died on her birthday. She was one of eight teenagers who died on a sparkling summer day of horsing around in the sunshine. A head-on collision killed them all on their way back home. The accident was so brutal that I was the only mother who was allowed to see her child one last time, lying there in the coroner's office.

A frostbitten numbness descended on me and followed me throughout her funeral. I sat alone with her coffin, and my tears seemed to fall through eternity. Lost in pain, I wanted desperately to pray. But after years of hard living, I had forgotten how.

It would be a neat and tidy story to say that Cori's death sobered me up. But that is not what happened. When the numbness of shock started to wear off, I redoubled my drug taking, seeking to deaden my feelings the best way I knew how. My life continued in a downward spiral. There were several more years of addiction before I finally sought treatment.

But seek treatment I did, and with each day away from drugs my head cleared and I walked a little closer to both reality and spirituality. And in this healing environment "things" started to happen for me, little miracles that orbited around my daughter, Cori.

After graduating from Crutchers Serenity House, I stayed on to work with other addicts. I was terrified of this new role, but I had begun to turn to God for direction.

The more my spirituality grew, the more I evolved. I had begun my journey.

One of the stops on my journey was the very coroner's office in which I'd last seen Cori. As I worked to undo the damage I'd left in the wake of my addiction, I sought to give back in some small way through community service. The coroner's office was the last place Cori had been, and I was both sickened and compelled by the place. But God had sent me here so that I might be better prepared to counsel others in the same position I had been in many years before—a distraught parent facing the ultimate loss.

When the coroner gently explained that he had been there when they brought Cori in, I knew why I was there. I learned everything about how she died. That she died quickly was important for me to know. That she had not been drinking meant a great deal to me. It bolstered my deep desire to have her be proud of me, too. I prayed that, wherever she was, she could see me.

Wanting so much to feel her presence again, I went to visit the accident site. The spot on the road had been marked with eight crosses, each one dedicated to the special life that was now gone. I stood frozen at the sight that greeted me—after all these years, Cori's cross was the only one still standing. This vision struck me deeply and I started to pray. I prayed for some kind of connection, any kind of connection, with my lost daughter. My heart ached as I prayed, reliving those last moments in the coroner's office with her lifeless body. Surely her soul had soared free at this very place as her body had died. Where was that soul now?

As I stood quietly praying, my body swayed slightly. I spread my feet quickly to regain my balance and I heard a faint crunch from under one foot. I looked down at the ground. There was something sticking out of the dirt. I bent down for a closer look and brushed away the dirt to reveal a faded string of rosary beads. Cori's rosary beads.

Filled with awe and gratitude at God's compassionate sign, I began to cry. Cori was with me. She was watching over me then, and she continues to show herself to me now. Cori appears in the faces of the troubled young women I counsel, in that moment when I see their eyes light up with hope and promise. She comes to me when my spirit is low and breathes a warm glow into my heart. She brings me the people who were a part of her life— friends in trouble who mercifully cross my path. She is all around me, and the most important miracle is that, today, I finally know that.

Chris Lloyd

Rachel's Gift

*You give but little when you give of your posses-
sions. It is when you give of yourself that you
truly give.*

Kahlil Gibran

The rousing aroma of freshly brewed coffee washed
across Cheryl Parker's face as she settled down at the
kitchen table to read her Sunday newspaper. Downstairs
shuffled eight-year-old daughter Rachel Davidson, on
that crisp November morning, wiping sleep away from
her ever-sparkling, big brown eyes.

As Mom scoured the *Sunday Sun* headlines, Rachel
suddenly noticed and inquired about the front-page
photograph of a little boy in a hospital bed, hooked up to
a myriad of tubes and monitors but braving a smile.
Cheryl explained to her only daughter that the boy had
been saved by a double lung transplant. Another child
had died tragically. But his family had authorized
doctors to harvest the vital, viable organs for transplant
into other children desperately awaiting life-saving
operations.

"Mommy, I want to do that. I want to donate my organs when I die," said Rachel, always wise beyond her years.

Rachel lovingly embraced the spirit of giving. Just a few months earlier, when Grandma Audrey Parker shaved her head bald to raise money for cancer research as a show of support for a cancer-stricken colleague at the office, Rachel had chipped in her allowance for the cause. One day when her mom visited the bank, Rachel quizzed the branch manager about a poster for the United Way, then asked how could she donate her allowance. If there was a food or clothing drive for people less fortunate, Rachel wanted to be part of the effort, for sure.

Rachel worshipped God and the Spice Girls, believed in heaven and humor. They called her Rachey, Pumpkin or Princess.

On the playground at school, Rachel and her pals Kristen, Samantha, Sarah and Haileigh were known as the Spice Girls. Rachel, who adored Ginger Spice, dazzled with her jazz routines and vocal strains that made her a popular member of their church choir.

A wicked flu bug invaded the school in late November. First to be struck was Rachel's six-year-old brother, Shawn, who spent a week in bed. He passed it on to Mom. Then came Rachel's turn. But Christmas was drawing near, and she was determined that sickness wouldn't dampen her enthusiasm.

Christmas, after all, was her favorite time of year. She had been thrilled the previous year to play Mary in the church pageant. And she was overjoyed, that same year, to unwrap a children's version of the Holy Bible. Cheryl remembered how the Bible fascinated her daughter and how she read the book from cover to cover.

Despite a runny nose and mild chest congestion, on a Saturday in late November, Rachel gladly accompanied her mom and brother to a Christmas party in Toronto and then to the annual Santa Claus parade in Port Perry. That night, she slept over at the home of her grandparents.

"I can't wait to go back to school on Monday," she said excitedly. "My friends will be glad to see me."

The following day, family gathered at Cheryl's to decorate the house, trim the Christmas tree and share their warmth with a cup of thick eggnog. The brightest smile belonged to Rachel.

After dinner, at the table where they'd discussed organ donation a few weeks earlier, Cheryl and Rachel laughed their fool heads off as they colored silly pictures.

Just before midnight, as Cheryl crept gingerly upstairs, she was drawn aside by a whimper coming from her daughter's bedroom. She rolled back the comforter to find her little girl shivering and her body tense. Figuring she was simply cold, Cheryl climbed in beside her, cradled her head and shared a mother's warmth.

It took Rachel an hour to relax. Two hours later, she ran from her bed to the bathroom and vomited. Cheryl guessed that the nagging flu had returned. There would be no school tomorrow.

Rachel spent Monday at her grandparents' house. Her grandmother noticed the tyke was still feverish and her stomach was hard. She called Cheryl at work and asked her to meet them at the hospital.

Blood tests taken that night showed Rachel had a low platelet count: a condition usually associated with a virus. Doctors worked to pinpoint the illness. Less than twenty-four hours later the platelet count plummeted, and Rachel was whisked by paramedics through rush-hour traffic to the world-renowned Hospital For Sick Children in downtown Toronto.

Rachel only wanted to sleep. Doctors and nurses would check her frequently, but she would again drift off.

Physicians warned Cheryl that a dangerously low

platelet count might trigger internal hemorrhaging; medication would be required to prevent it.

Suddenly, out of a seemingly deep slumber, Rachel sat straight up in her bed and stared at her mom. Her pupils were dilated. Cheryl could sense a cry for help coming from within her daughter, but the mind and body were being held hostage by illness. Her left side went weak as if she'd suffered a stroke. Her eyes glazed over, she became agitated and her limbs stiffened. She tried to talk, but her mouth wouldn't open.

Cheryl understood: She was crying for Mommy.

Doctors swarmed to her bedside and immediately rushed her to the neurology unit for a CT scan. The test confirmed bleeding on the brain. Early next morning, Rachel was rushed into the operating room.

It was too late.

The look on the doctor's face told Cheryl everything.

Rachel's brain had swollen so much there was no chance to save her. But her gentle heart was still beating like a lion.

An eerie silence enveloped the room where Rachel lay, peacefully, draped by banks of modern medical machinery sustaining life in her vital organs.

Cheryl and her family gathered quietly at Rachel's side, and through their tears and heartache, said good-bye.

The angel took flight.

Rachel's pledge to donate her organs—that generous gesture made a few weeks earlier—was communicated to coordinators of the Multiple Organ Retrieval and Exchange (MORE) program at Sick Children's hospital.

Just a few hours after Rachel was removed from life-support systems, her heart was used to save the life of an eight-year-old girl. Doctors flew in from the United States to procure her lungs for a thirteen-year-old girl who'd undergone a double lung transplant in 1991 but now required new ones. And her corneas opened up a bright new world for two young strangers—a two-year-old boy blinded by surgical complications and an infant born blind with opaque corneas.

In the true spirit of Christmas, which she so richly believed in, Rachel's last wish had been fulfilled.

In the days after Rachel's passing, her third-grade classmates composed a book of memories about the tiny friend who always stuck up for others or went out of her way to share a treat or a laugh with them. Their pure and heartfelt thoughts were framed by sketches of angels. The book was presented to her family.

In their eulogy, her teachers said: "Rachel touched the lives of many in her eight short years. She made us laugh, she made us cry, she made us think. She made us look at ourselves, and she made us accountable. What Rachel represented is giving."

Cheryl shared her own memory: "She just loved to give and give and give. No matter how much she gave, she didn't think it was enough. When she was six years old, Rachel said she wanted to be an angel when she grew up, so she could help people. She was always intrigued by heaven and meeting God. She wondered what she would wear."

In a classroom at Meadowcrest Public School, there now hangs a star with the words: "I wish that nobody in my family gets sick and dies at a young age."

And, in the school hallway once filled with Rachel's laughter and exuberant spirit, there is a paper cross onto which is sketched Rachel's likeness. It bears the handwritten message: "I will miss you. Good-bye, Rachel."

And may God bless you, Angel Spice.

Kevin Hann

9

LETTING GO

There are only two lasting bequests we can hope to give our children: One of these is roots, the other is wings.

Hodding Carter

"I think it's time to NUDGE our LITTLE BIRDIE
from the NEST."

Reprinted by permission of Joan Wiberg.

Watching Me Go

What feeling is so nice as a child's hand in yours? So small, so soft and warm, like a kitten huddling in the shelter of your clasp.

Marjorie Holmes

The crayoned picture shows a first-grade boy with shoebox arms, stovepipe legs and tears squirting like melon seeds. The carefully printed caption reads, "I am so sad." It is my son Brendan's drawing–journal entry for September 19. Brendan cried his first day of school, dissolving at his classroom door like a human bouillon cube. The classroom jiggled with small faces, wet-combed hair, white Nikes and new backpacks. Something furry scuttled around in a big wire cage. Garden flowers rested on Mrs. Phillips's desk. Mrs. Phillips has halo status at our school. She is a kind, soft-spoken master of the six-year-old mind. But even she could not coax Brendan to a seat. Most kids sat eagerly awaiting Dick and Jane and two plus two. Not my Brendan. His eyes streamed, his nose ran and he clung to me like a snail on a strawberry. I plucked him off and escaped.

It wasn't that Brendan didn't like school. He was the kid at the preschool Christmas concert who knew everyone's part and who performed "Jingle Bells" with operatic passion. Brendan just didn't like being apart from me. We'd had some good times, he and I, in those preschool years. We played at the pool. We skated on quiet morning ice. We sampled half the treat tray at weekly neighborhood coffee parties. Our time together wasn't exactly material for a picture book, but it was time together. And time moves differently for a child.

Now in first grade, Brendan was faced with five hours of wondering what I was doing with my day. Brendan always came home for lunch, the only one of his class not to eat at his desk. But once home, fed and hugged, a faraway look of longing would crease his gentle brow—he wanted to go back to school to play! So I walked him back, waited with him until he spotted someone he knew, then left. He told me once that he watched me until he couldn't see me anymore, so I always walked fast and never looked back. One day when I took Brendan back after lunch, he spied a friend, kissed me good-bye and scampered right off. I went, feeling pleased for him, celebrating his new independence, his entry into the first-grade social loop. And I felt pleased for myself, a sense of well-being and accomplishment that I, too, had entered the mystic circle of parents whose children separated easily.

Then—I don't know why—I glanced back. And there he was. The playground buzzed all around him, kids everywhere, and he stood, his chin tucked close, his body held small, his face intent but not sad, blowing me kisses. So brave, so unashamed, so completely loving, Brendan was watching me go.

No book on mothering could have prepared me for that quick, raw glimpse into my child's soul. My mind leaped fifteen years ahead to him packing boxes and his dog grown old and him saying, "Dry up, Mom. It's not like I'm leaving the country." In my mind, I tore up the card every mother signs saying she'll let her child go when he's ready. I looked at my Brendan, his shirt tucked in, every button done up, his toes just turned in a bit, and I thought, *Okay, you're six for me forever. Just try to grow up, I dare you.* With a smile I had to really dig for, I blew him a kiss, turned and walked away.

Diane Tullson

The Video of Life

One Sunday afternoon as my family settled in to watch television, my six-year-old daughter queried from the video closet, "Mommy, where are my Barney videos?" I reminded her that a few months ago she had let friends of ours borrow the videos for their recently adopted young child. (It was no longer "cool" for her to watch the big, purple guy once she entered second grade!)

Remembering the loan, she returned disappointed to the video closet to make an alternate decision. She came to my side two minutes later and with big, brown-eyed child wisdom said, "Don't you just sometimes wish you could rewind life?"

Yes, Taylor Jae, there are some special moments and milestones that I would love to relive, choices I would make differently and embarrassing moments I would gladly rescind. But as you stand beside me as a continuous source of pride and great joy, and evolve each day into a beautiful young lady, both inside and out, I want to reach for the VCR of Life and put you on pause!

Beverley Bolger Gordon

"That's far enough for this year."

The Parting

The day, it started early
That cool September morn,
She stood waiting by my bedside
A little before dawn.
Her clothes were starched and ready.
All plans were carefully made.
She knew the day had finally come
And she was not afraid.
I, too, had known this day would come
Those six short years ago,
When first we met, I held her close
My heart was all aglow.
And so, I treasured every day
We had to share together.
But time just seemed to float away
As quickly as a feather.
And now she waits impatiently,
All smiles, so glad to leave.
Our parting doesn't make her sad
Or cause her heart to grieve.
I hold her close just one more time
And feel her body strain.

Her shuffling feet, now finally free
Go skipping down the lane.
One last swift glance, a hasty wave
And now she's out of sight,
And I am standing all alone
To ponder my sad plight.
I look ahead with sadness
At the long impending week,
And tho' I swore I wouldn't,
A tear slides down my cheek.
My husband hugs and smiles at me,
This sentimental fool,
And yet I know he feels sad, too,
On our child's first day of school.

Doreen S. Austman

Dancing in the Street

Parenthood: The state of being better chaperoned than you were before marriage.

Marcelene Cox

It happened on a bright morning, early in September, some years ago as I came out the front door of my home on my way to work. As I headed for my car, I saw her, out there in the middle of the road. *Dancing.* My neighbor. A mother. A wife. Otherwise, quite mature. Nevertheless, dancing in her pajamas and robe, and wearing her giant furry-dog bedroom slippers. Sipping on coffee, dancing. Curlers in her hair. And all alone, to the tune of some music only she could hear, my neighbor was dancing!

I was stopped dead in my tracks. Staring. She saw me and laughed, and giggled and danced some more. And then, by way of an explanation, she called out to me: "I have four children, and this morning, my youngest just went off to her first day of school. I'M FREEEEEE!" And she kept on dancing!

Raymond Aaron

The End of Childhood

Truly, it is allowed to weep. By weeping, we disperse our wrath; and tears go through the heart even like a stream.

Ovid

On a summer day in late August, my eldest son cleaned his room without prompting. While normally I'd have been thrilled by his spate of cleanliness, the spotless "Parade of Homes" look was a flashing red light, signaling he was leaving the next day for college . . . an event I'd been dreading.

His final twenty-four hours as a full-time resident in our home went by too quickly for me, but not fast enough for him. Biding time until his farewell dinner, he perched on a kitchen stool in front of the counter television and watched an ancient episode of *Star Trek.* Reaching over his shoulder to open a cabinet, I spontaneously hugged him from behind. As I inhaled his familiar odor—a funky mixture of sweat and cologne, a roller coaster filled with sadness appeared out of nowhere and careened through my heart. My nose brushed against the back of his hair, and I felt myself drowning in a flood of maternal memories. Mesmerized by Captain Kirk, my son didn't notice that my tightened hug was all that prevented me from falling to my knees and begging time to stand still, or at the very least, for his college to relocate in our backyard.

The thirty-five-minute drive to the airport took five seconds, ample time to acknowledge that for all my intellectualizing, no way was I prepared for this most terrible of days. As a family not given to the emotional displays often witnessed at airports, our farewell was short and to the point. With our youngest son sandwiched between us, my husband and I waved our firstborn on his way. Eager to begin his adventure, his return gesture more closely resembled "good riddance" than "until we meet again." My feelings weren't hurt; I imagined Mrs. Polo and Mrs. Columbus received a similar sentiment from their sons.

We drove home a different family. No longer a quartet, we were like a wobbly, three-legged table. Within an hour of pulling into the driveway, our youngest informed us he hated being an only child, and, "No way am I living in this house with you guys for two years by myself." Learning to balance was going to take time.

As the first day without him ended, I visited my eldest's room. I thought I'd find comfort surrounded by his things, but order had replaced chaos, and the personality I sought was two thousand miles away. Seated at his desk, I visually searched the room for what I was missing. As my eyes grazed his collection of awards, I smiled at the sight of a stuffed bear occupying the cup of a sports trophy.

A favorite from birth, "Fred" always smelled like the river of drool he'd absorbed. As my little boy's constant companion, the bare spots on Fred's fur were proof he'd been an able weapon against nightmare monsters, his frayed ears testament to the comfort he'd provided his young owner.

The juxtaposition of Fred in the high school trophy was serendipitous. Studying the symbols of the child and the young man, I recognized my eighteen-year-old's inevitable departure from home had nothing to do with the roller coaster riding my heart. The sadness was about the loss of my son's childhood. At that moment of revelation, I wanted the impossible: to have the curly-haired little boy back. Contrary to my husband's jovial acceptance of our son's adult status, I mourned for his boyhood. When nonstop crying brought me no comfort, I realized I needed a mechanism to help me accept the loss.

I remembered a widowed friend telling me about her search for solace after her beloved husband died and her description of the comfort she experienced through observing the Jewish death ritual. "It's worked for two thousand years," she'd told me, "and it worked for me." I decided to try it.

In accordance with traditional Jewish law, I was to bury the deceased within twenty-four hours of death or as soon as practicable. With Fred now absorbing my tears, I said a final good-bye to the childhood that had brought so much joy to my life as a mother. The next morning, I began the week-long ritual of grieving, called *sitting shiva*. Adapting the principle to my needs, I watched old home movies, looked through the earliest photo albums, read my little boy's favorite bedtime story books, unfolded and refolded the baby undershirts I'd embroidered with teensy hearts and flowers and wept for seven days. On the eighth day, I followed Judaic precedent and began formally acknowledging my grief twice a day. But rather than visiting a synagogue and reciting the mourner's kaddish, I set aside sunrise and sunset to reflect on my son's childhood and to thank God for giving me the opportunity to be his mama.

While the traditional ritual of Jewish grieving is a year in length, I came to terms with my loss much sooner. After several weeks, I found myself thinking less about the boy and more about the man that he had become. My friend was right—the sages knew what they were talking about when they devised a ritual for dealing with this inevitable human situation and all its emotions.

In utilizing ritual to effect my own emotional recovery, I realized that every parental crisis doesn't require reinventing the wheel. The old ways, I'd learned, may hold answers for parents of the New Age.

Ellyn L. Geisel

A Gift from Brandon

While my twenty-one-year-old son Brandon is in college, we talk a couple of times a week. A senior at Linfield College in Oregon, he's studying to be an elementary education teacher. We always had great conversations, but on this particular day it was very special!

When I picked up the phone he told me, "Mom, I had my first teaching experience today." The rest of what he told me went something like this:

I was pretty apprehensive, not knowing what to expect, but Mr. Schindler, the older teacher in the classroom assigned to help me get started in the world of teaching, assigned me to several young boys to help them with their math.

I didn't know it, but Mr. Schindler had told them before I entered the classroom that I was a football player for the college. When I entered the room, the little guys began asking me for my autograph. It made me laugh, but obviously, it made me feel great too; and the way they acted you would have thought I was one of the 49ers or something. I enjoyed the moment and signed some autographs, and then we got down to work.

I started working with this particular young fellow who was around eight years old. He was having some difficulty getting a grasp on the math problem and he sadly looked up at me and said, "I'm so stupid, aren't I?" I told him he wasn't stupid at all and that math hadn't been my favorite subject either. He was really struggling, but he smiled at my comment and we carried on.

Several hours zoomed by and then I heard Mr. Schindler say, "Well, it's time to have some lunch." He called out, "Brandon, let's get ready to go." When he called out to Brandon, I immediately came to attention, and turning around saw Mr. Schindler coming towards me with a wheelchair. He brought it up to the little guy I was working with. I had no idea that this young boy had special needs; no one had mentioned it. We proceeded to move Brandon from his desk to his wheelchair. I was hiding it, but my heart was feeling very heavy at the moment. Mr. Schindler looked up at me and said, "Brandon, why don't you and this Brandon have some lunch." Mr. Schindler reached down and gave little Brandon two peanuts, a little treat he gave out when they worked hard. Those treats were really special to them, because they had received Mr. Schindler's approval.

Rolling down the hallway, Brandon looked over his shoulder at me and said, "Wow, I have your name!" Mom, he seemed to be so proud that we shared the same name. By the time we reached the cafeteria, he had a million questions, but one that stayed with me was, "How's it feel to run and catch a football?" Little Brandon told me he had never been able to walk, so all he knew was that wheelchair.

The slammer came when we reached the cafeteria door and little Brandon called out, "Wait, Mr. Flood!" Believe me, I was still adjusting to being called Mr. Flood so I said, "That's my Dad's name, not mine." The wheelchair stopped, and little Brandon wiggled around so he could look me in the eyes. Then he reached up, and opening his small hand, he handed me his two peanuts and said, "I want you to have these for helping me so much today." It stopped me in my tracks, and I must have glued my eyes to those two peanuts, as I felt the lump in my throat growing. I could hardly look at little Brandon at that moment.

Here was a little boy who had never felt his feet touch the ground, who had never had the use of his legs, never experienced so many of the things in his young life that I had. And, yet, his heart was filled with so much kindness that he handed me his two special peanuts. Mom, he had no idea the impact he had on me—my first day of teaching. All I could say was, "Thanks, Brandon!"

Listening to my son tell his story, as I was going through a box of tissues, I realized that my son, my *own* Brandon had grown up! On that day, I experienced him for the first time as a man, and I found my heart bursting with love and pride. I had no doubts whatsoever, after that conversation, what a wonderful, caring TEACHER he would become.

Myrna Flood

Words That Bind

*I know fame and power are for the birds. But
then suddenly life comes into focus for me. And,
ah, there stand my kids. I love them.*

Lee Iacocca

In the doorway of my home, I looked closely at the face
of my twenty-three-year-old son, Daniel, his backpack by
his side. We were saying good-bye. In a few hours, he
would be flying to Europe. He would be staying in France
for at least a year to learn another language and experience life in a different country. I wanted to make this parting one that he would remember, one that would become
fixed in his memory.

It was a transitional time in his life, a passage, a step
from college into the adult world. I wanted to leave him
with some words that would have some meaning, some
significance beyond the moment. Perhaps he, too, would
one day stand before his own son or daughter at a key
moment in their life, and he would remember how he had
felt when his own father had taken him aside.

Nothing came from my lips. No sound broke the

stillness of my Long Island home at the ocean. Outside, I could hear the shrill cries of seagulls as they circled the ever-changing surf. Inside, I stood frozen and quiet, looking into the searching green eyes of my son.

What made the moment more difficult was the fact that I knew that this was not the first time I had let a moment pass. When Daniel was five years old, I took him to the school bus stop on his first day of kindergarten. That was his first passage, a transition from his life at home to the school world. I felt the tension in his hand holding mine as the bus turned the corner. I saw color flush in his cheeks as the bus pulled up. His eyes looked up then—as they did now.

What is it going to be like, Dad? Can I do it? Will I be okay? And then he walked up the steps of the bus and disappeared inside. The bus drove away and I said nothing.

A decade later, a similar scene played itself out. With his mother, I drove him to the College of William and Mary in Virginia. I helped carry his things into his dorm room. That night, he went drinking with his new schoolmates, and when he met us the next morning he was sick.

He was coming down with mononucleosis, but we could not know that then. We thought he had a hangover.

In his room, Daniel lay stretched out on his bed. As I started to leave for the return trip back home, I tried to think of something to say to give him some courage and confidence as he started his new phase of life.

Again, words failed me. I mumbled something like, "Hope you feel better, Dan. Good luck." And I left.

Now, as I stood before him, grown into a man, I thought of these lost opportunities. How many times have we all let such moments pass? A parent dies, and instead of giving a eulogy ourselves, we let a clergyman speak. A child asks if Santa Claus is real, or where babies come from and, embarrassed, we slough it off. When a daughter graduates

or a son is married, we go through the motions of the ceremony, but we do not seek out our children and find a
quiet, private moment to tell them what they have meant
to us. Or what they might expect to face in the years
ahead.

How fast the years had passed. Daniel was born in New
Orleans, slow to walk and talk and small of stature. He
was the tiniest in his class, but he developed an outgoing
nature. With a friendly face and ready smile, he was popular with his peers.

Baseball gave him his earliest challenge. He was an outstanding pitcher in Little League, hoping to make it big in
high school. It didn't work out that way. The coach
passed him over as a sophomore, then as a junior. Finally,
as a senior, he made the varsity team, winning half the
games. The coach named him the team's most valuable
player.

His finest hour came at a science fair. He entered an
exhibit showing how the circulatory system works. He
had sketched it on cardboard. It was primitive and crude
compared to the computerized, blinking-light models
entered by other students. My wife felt embarrassed for
him.

It turned out that the other kids had not done their
own work. Their parents had made their exhibits. But the
judges found that these kids couldn't answer their questions. Daniel answered every one. When the judges
awarded the Albert Einstein Plaque for the best exhibit,
they gave it to Daniel.

By the time Daniel had left for college, he had a growth
spurt. He stood six feet tall and weighed one hundred
seventy pounds. He never did pitch another inning of
baseball, though. He found that he could not combine
academics and athletics. He gave up baseball for English
literature. I was proud that he made such a mature

decision. He graduated with a "B" average.

One day, I told Daniel that the great failing in my life had come when I did not take a year or two off after college to go to Europe. I believed this was the best way to broaden and develop a larger perspective on life. Once I had married and begun working, I found that the dream of living in another culture had vanished.

Daniel thought about this. His friends said that he would be insane to put his career on hold. But he decided it wasn't so crazy. After graduation, he worked as a waiter, a bike messenger and a house painter. With the money he earned, he had enough to go to Paris.

The night before he was to leave, I tossed in bed. I was trying to figure out something to say. Nothing came to mind. Maybe, I thought, it wasn't necessary to say anything.

What does it matter in the course of a lifetime if a father never tells a son what he really thinks of him? But as I stood before Daniel, I knew that it *does* matter. My father and I loved each other, yet I always regretted never hearing him put his feelings into words and never having the memory of that moment. Now, I could feel my palms sweat and my throat tighten. Why is it so hard to tell a son something from the heart? My mouth turned dry and I knew I would only be able to get a few words out clearly.

"Daniel," I said, "if I could have picked, I would have picked you."

That's all I could say. I wasn't sure he understood what I meant. Then he came toward me and threw his arms around me. For a moment, the world vanished, and there was just Daniel and I in our home.

He was saying something, but my eyes misted over and I couldn't understand him. All I was aware of was the stubble on his chin as his face pressed against mine. Then the moment ended.

Daniel left for Europe. I think about him when I walk along the beach. Thousands of miles away, somewhere out past the ocean waves breaking on the deserted shore, he might be scurrying across Boulevard Saint Germain, strolling through a musty hallway of the Louvre or sipping coffee in a Left Bank café.

What I had said to Daniel was clumsy and trite. It was nothing. And yet, it was everything.

David Zinman

Mapping Life's Journey on the Refrigerator Door

A child enters your home and for the next twenty years makes so much noise you can hardly stand it. The child departs, leaving the house so silent you think you are going mad.

John Andrew Holmes

There is a Polaroid picture of my oldest boy on the refrigerator door.

He is wearing a surgical mask and gown, his eyes look intense as he studies a doctor's hands doing their healing work.

Watching surgery is like going to Mars, my boy tells me. It is beyond a miracle. It is why he's going to be a doctor. When he graduates from college next week, he will begin his own long journey through medical school to Mars.

But the Polaroid on the refrigerator reminds me of the journey he has traveled before this moment. For it is on this door that his life has been recorded. It is here that his big moments and small ones have been displayed in a kaleidoscope of changing scenes—grade-school report cards, dental appointment reminders, letters, vacation photos, prom pictures.

And even as he continues his journey away from me, it is the scenes from this refrigerator door that I linger over.

October 1974: The boy's kindergarten class has done a footprint project, each child walking through paint, then stepping on paper. For some reason, there are five tiny blue feet on my boy's paper displayed on the refrigerator door. The teacher has written "Sean's feet" in the upper left-hand corner.

November 1975: A note from the boy's first-grade teacher is on the door: "Doesn't always finish his work because he talks constantly. Needs to practice blending sounds and spelling."

April 1976: The boy, seven, leaves a note on the door after a bully has picked on him: "Mom, Mikel lost my bays bol on purpis, and he maide me sit in a mud puddel and I am cryen. P.S. My durdy cloths are in the garbij."

He still needs to practice spelling.

May 1977: The boy, now eight, has written a "baseball report card" for his three-year-old brother and displays it on the door for him: "Brendan's First Report Card on Baseball," it says on the homemade cover. Inside it says: "He hussels very good for his age. He is smart. He is a good pitcher for his age, too."

July 1978: The boy has done something bad. He draws a red heart and leaves it on the door. Inside, it says: "To Mom. I'm sorry."

March 1981: The boy, now twelve, has written and illustrated a story, which hangs from the door. "The Curse of Herowista," it is called. In it, a slime man eats the main characters, Peter and Suzanne. The pictures are disgusting.

November 1982: A photo montage depicting "Who I Am" is on the door. The boy, now in eighth grade, has used these pictures from magazines in his montage: a skier, a football player, a dog, a book, a beautiful woman and a slogan that says, "I don't have herpes."

March 1983: A letter from the boy, who has gone to ski camp in Colorado, is on the door: "Dear Mom," it begins. "I'm sitting in an airplane in Atlanta right now. Hold on. I'm taking off. I'm in the air now. The takeoff was fine except I got sick. Luckily, I grabbed the bag on time."

March 1985: A high-school disciplinary report is on the door. Under "Infraction," it says, "Kissing in the halls with Beth DePuy." Under "Disposition," it says, "Two administrative detentions."

October 1986: A newspaper clipping from the sports pages is on the door. A paragraph in the story about a high school football game is highlighted in yellow marker: "Passing on the first down, Mike Zigross hoisted a rainbow. Sean Mullally gathered it in. On his way down the right sideline for a TD, Mullally broke four tackles and dragged three Crusaders with him."

June 1988: A list of things to pack for college is on the door: "Iron, ace bandages, James Thurber book, pillow" are the first four items on the list.

The final item is "refrigerator magnets." He is, apparently, planning to hang things on his own refrigerator door when he gets to where he's going.

Perhaps he is too old, now, for the refrigerator door. Perhaps the Polaroid picture is the last sign of this growing up that will appear here.

I don't know.

What I do know is this: There will always be something of the little boy who was cryen in a mud puddel on this door. Always. No matter how far his journey toward Mars takes him.

Beth Mullally

"Please excuse my mother. This is my first interview."

10

ACROSS THE GENERATIONS

Walking, I am listening to a deeper way.
Suddenly all my ancestors are behind me.
Be still, they say. Watch and listen. You are
the result of the love of thousands.

Linda Hogan
Native American writer

"Before you start yelling, you ought to know that I had a long, nostalgic talk with Grandma today."

Bedtime Stories Across the Miles

I stood in the airport, my eyes so full of tears that I could barely see my six-month-old grandson's face as I bent to kiss him one last time. My son, an air force career man, was being sent to Turkey, and he was taking his wife and baby with him. "He won't know me when you get back to the States," I said brokenly.

"Now, Mom," my son tried to comfort me. "It won't take you long to get reacquainted."

"How?" I wailed. "He won't even be able to understand a thing I say." I was referring to my heavy southern accent, which would be almost like a foreign language to little Damon when they returned in three years.

As the weeks passed, my self-pity turned into fierce determination. I would find a way to make a bond between me and my little grandson, no matter how many miles or how many oceans might stand between us. I bought a children's picture book, a blank cassette tape and a disposable camera. I popped the blank cassette into the recorder and read the picture book aloud, using the same tone of voice and accents I would use if reading to a child. When I finished the story, I spoke a few words to Damon, ending with, "Always remember that Grandma loves you very much." I had some friends take some snapshots of me doing routine, grandmotherly things such as baking and working in my flower beds. It was a friend who came up with the brilliant idea of including a picture of me reading the book in front of the recorder. When the pictures were developed, I sent the best ones, along with the book and the cassette, to my son and his wife. I asked them to play the recording to Damon while they turned the pages of the book for him. I also asked them to show him the pictures of Grandma whenever they read this particular book to him.

A couple of months later, I bought another book, another blank cassette, another disposable camera and repeated the process. Every few months Damon would receive a new story package from Grandma. By the time he was a toddler, my son reported, at bedtime he would often demand a story "from Grandma across the ocean."

It was an inexpensive way to keep Damon familiar with my face and my southern drawl. And it created a wondrous, strong bond between us even though there were many miles and months separating us.

Almost three years later, I stood nervously in the airport, waiting for my son and his family to disembark. Would Damon recognize his Grandma in the flesh and blood? Thus far, I had merely been a funny voice on a cassette tape and a face in a snapshot. They came through the gate, Damon clutching his mother's hand. He saw me first. Breaking away from my daughter-in-law, he ran toward me, crying out exuberantly, "It's Grandma!" I stooped to catch him in my arms. He looked up at me, little face beaming. "You're my Grandma!" he exclaimed. He grabbed my hand and began to pull me toward his parents. "It's Grandma! Grandma! Grandma!"

The word tugged at my heart and warmed my soul. I would never, ever tire of hearing it.

Ruth Ayers

Miriam's Umbrella

*Love is the immortal flow of energy that nour-
ishes, extends and preserves. Its eternal goal is life.*

Smiley Blanton

Miriam looked out the big front window. The maple
trees were bare; the sky was a low ceiling of gray. A strong
breeze couldn't move the rain-soaked leaves. Her father
knelt on the ground, his back to the house. His dark blue
jacket contrasted with his drab surroundings; his hair
fluttered in the wind. He lifted something above his head,
then drove it down into the earth and worked at the sod.

A fine, gentle rain slowly dotted the veranda floor in
front of Miriam's window. She ran for her raincoat and
boots. She took her tiny umbrella onto the porch, her little
hands working to open it, without help, like a big girl. It
finally spread out above her, protecting her.

"What are you doing, Daddy?" Without looking up, he
answered, "Working." His voice sounded tired. He should
have known better; a one-word answer simply invited the
inevitable next question.

"Digging a hole?"

He sighed. "Not really. It's a garden."

Miriam looked at the flower beds along the front of the house. She peered into the backyard, where her mother's roses bloomed in the summer and her father planted tomatoes and beans.

"We have lots of gardens," she said.

"This one is special," her father said quietly, still not looking up. "It's for Grandma."

Miriam paused. "Because she died."

"Yes."

"Did Grandma's cancerd make her die?" she asked.

"Can-*cer*, honey. Yes, it did."

She looked at the dark brown dirt. "Why does she need a garden?" Her father finally stopped digging. "She doesn't *need* a garden, Miriam," he said, smiling slightly. "But we'll think of Grandma when we see it." He sunk his spade into the newly turned earth. "And we'll plant a mock orange bush in Grandma's garden as a memorial to her." He anticipated her next question. "A memorial reminds us of someone who's gone."

He went on, telling Miriam more about Grandma; that she'd say, "Mmm, smell the mock orange" every summer at her own home. He told of Grandma's love of flowers and music, reading and cats; that she always spent time with each family member, making them feel special; of her happy smile and her wonderful laugh.

At last, Miriam asked, "Do you miss her?"

He began digging again. "More than I ever thought I could." He was quiet for a moment. "Even after I grew up, Grandma could always make everything alright again; she made me feel protected."

Miriam couldn't remember a time when Grandma wasn't sick. When she'd rest on the couch from her illness, Miriam would "tuck her in" with the living room quilt. She'd try on some of Grandma's many hats and be rewarded with

Grandma's laugh. She'd sit on Grandma's lap, listening to her read in her slow, warm voice. And when it was time for bedtime hugs, Grandma always told her, "I love you, Miriam." Miriam looked at the small, transparent raindrops in her father's hair.

"Who'll protect you now, Daddy?" she asked.

When he raised his head she saw that, even in the rain, his face was dry except for a wet streak down each cheek. "Mommy, I guess. And Grandpa." He shut his eyes tightly, as though sealing them would stop the tears. "And you," he whispered.

Miriam's mother looked out the big front window. The fine mist had turned the veranda floor a dark slate color. Across the lawn, she saw two figures in the gloom. One knelt, digging a new garden. The other stood silently to one side, covering her father with her tiny umbrella.

Bill Petch

Grandma Meyer's Gift

Where there is great love, there are always miracles.

Willa Cather

The day my second son, Nicholas, was born, I felt like the luckiest woman on Earth. "He's beautiful," I told my husband Steve as I nursed my new baby for the very first time. A while later, my mom and dad came by with my eldest son, Nathaniel. Nathaniel looked so cute, sitting in the rocking chair beside my bed holding his new baby brother in his arms.

But then, a few minutes after everyone left, Nicholas's pediatrician came into my room and sat wearily in that same rocking chair. "I have some bad news, Paula," he began. "Nicholas is showing signs of Down syndrome. I'm almost certain he has it, but I've ordered a blood test to be sure."

I felt like I was having an out-of-body experience. I could hear the doctor's words; I understood everything he said. But it was as if he was relating the terrible news to some other mother. He couldn't possibly be talking to me.

After the doctor left, the news finally sank in. I burst into tears and cried for what seemed like hours. And later, when a nurse brought Nicholas into my room again, Steve and I spotted the little telltale signs we'd overlooked before. The single crease line across Nicholas's left palm. The slight almond shape of his beautiful brown eyes.

"What kind of a life will our son have?" Steve and I asked one another. "Will he ever grow up to make his own way in the world and pursue a lifetime of dreams? Will he even have dreams to pursue?"

I called my mom and told her the devastating news. "Things couldn't get any worse," I sobbed. But then they did.

"Nicholas is turning blue," a nurse hurried into my room to tell me. "His blood oxygen level keeps dropping, only we don't understand why."

By the time they let me see Nicholas he was sleeping inside an oxygen tent. I couldn't hold him or let him nurse. I felt so helpless. I'd been so worried about how my baby would live with Down syndrome. Now I didn't know if he was even going to live.

I left the hospital the next day, my eyes swollen red from crying. Nicholas stayed behind in the baby nursery as doctors ran one test after another in a frantic search for the cause of his low oxygen levels.

"Will Nicholas ever walk?" Steve's dad asked me, and I had to admit, "I honestly don't know." There was so much about Down syndrome I didn't know, but I was determined to find out.

Steve and I read every book on the subject we could find, and contacted the Down Syndrome Guild in Dallas for information and support. Meanwhile, every three hours for the next ten days, I left Nathaniel with my folks and went to the hospital to bottle feed Nicholas the breast milk I insisted he get because I knew it would help keep his immune system strong. My baby had so many strikes against him, already—I didn't want him to get sick with some bug, too.

After ten days Nicholas was transferred to another hospital, where they finally discovered what was wrong. "Your son has sleep apnea," a doctor explained. When Nicholas slept, his tongue and throat muscles grew so relaxed, they fell back and blocked his air passage. The good news was that with a supply of oxygen and an oximeter (a device to measure the amount of oxygen in his blood), we could take Nicholas home that very afternoon.

I was relieved to learn that Nicholas would likely outgrow his sleep apnea. But I knew my baby would never outgrow his Down syndrome, which the blood test had confirmed.

What will his life be like? I worried as I bathed my son and then reattached the monitor that sounded an alarm whenever his oxygen level dropped. *Will he be able to go to school and learn? Will he make friends, or will the other kids tease him and call him ugly names?*

Nicholas was such a quiet baby, I had to guess when he was hungry or needed a change. My heart ached whenever I held him in my arms. "I love you so much," I told him, but I wondered when he grew up, would he find someone to love him and share his life with? I tried to be strong, but every night as I settled Nicholas into his cradle at the foot of my bed, tears stung my cheeks.

One night around midnight, I was awakened by a strange noise at the foot of the bed. Opening my eyes, I was startled to discover my Grandma Meyer standing beside Nicholas's cradle. I was thrilled to see her. Grandma Meyer always knew just the right thing to say, and how to fix all of my problems.

But Grandma Meyer had died six years ago from cancer. "This can't be!" I gasped as my grandmother reached into Nicholas's cradle and lifted him into her arms. He looked so peaceful snuggled against her, and my grandmother's smile all but lit up the room with kindness.

I was about to shake Steve awake when Grandma Meyer looked me straight in the eye and softly spoke, "Everything is going to be just fine." Then, in a blink of my eyes, Nicholas was back in his cradle and my grandmother was gone.

When I awoke the next morning at first I thought it must all have been a dream. But then I picked up Nicholas, and for the very first time since I learned he had Down syndrome, my heart didn't ache. All of my fears had vanished—just like Grandma Meyer the night before.

Giving Nicholas a big kiss, I told him, "Everything is going to be just fine, because you and I have a very special guardian angel watching over us."

Two weeks later tests revealed that Nicholas's sleep apnea had completely disappeared. Somehow, Grandma Meyer knew this would happen.

Today, Nicholas is a vibrant, happy three-year-old who loves playing with his big brother, Nathaniel, and with his new baby brother, Hayden. At school he understands everything any other three-year-old understands, and he has a vocabulary of more than fifty words.

Just the other night Nicholas strung three of these words together in his very first sentence. "I love you," he told me. It was the happiest day of my life.

My grandmother gave me the strength and the confidence to believe that not only will Nicholas have dreams, but that somehow they will all come true. I know my child has a future. He'll get a job and live a happy and productive life. He'll get married. And best of all, Nicholas will always have his very own guardian angel watching down on him from heaven above.

Paula Mathers
As told to Bill Holton

From Mother to Daughter to Mother

In youth we learn; in age we understand.

Marie von Ebner-Eschenbach

Sweltering in the humid heat of a Kansas August, my daughter Sony sighed, her face flushed, her belly swollen. "I'm ready to have the baby, Mom," she said. "I don't know what's holding up the show."

"Babies come when they're ready," I replied.

"I know, but you need to go see Grammy."

"Hey, your grandmother said she can wait."

Sony patted her belly. "Well, I wish our little Whozit would get a move on."

Little Whozit.

In a flash these two words stirred my memory back to July 1960. I'm laughing and very pregnant, and along with my husband John, I'm running for cover from a North Carolina downpour. Several hours later, at 2:00 A.M., we're on our way to the hospital.

"It's the rain that did it," he says with certainty. "Finally jogged our little Whozit along."

He'd held my hand. I'd squeezed back, wincing

because of the labor pain. I was just twenty years old. I felt like a little girl instead of a mother-to-be, and I was scared. I desperately wanted my mother, who was far away in Europe.

Shaking off the memory, I kissed Sony goodbye. "I'm heading back home," I told my daughter, "Call me if something happens."

As soon as I was home, I reached for the phone and called my own mother in California. It seemed like an eternity before she picked up the phone.

"Mom? It's Barb. Sony's not in labor yet. Do you think you'll be able to hold on for another day?"

I strained to hear her answer. My mother, who had always been strong and capable, spoke in a voice so wispy and tinged with fear that I felt goose bumps. How could I associate being frightened with Mom? She had never been afraid of anything. But things were different now. Daddy was gone, she was sixty-eight and cancer was growing inside her. I grasped the phone more tightly.

"Stay with Sony," Mom said. "She needs her mother." Then her voice dropped. "But come as soon as you can, Barbara."

It was a simple imperative sentence, yet it filled me with dread. I used to wish that Mom would tell me what she wanted, so I wouldn't have to guess. Now I wished she hadn't.

I realized my fingers were trembling. *Should I go today? Leave my daughter?* Sony wouldn't complain. She was like her grandmother in that respect. Besides, her husband Kevin would be at her side. *I didn't have that when she was born,* I told myself, a thought that transported me back in time again.

I could see the windshield wipers flicking steadily back and forth, as John and I sped through the back roads of California. I was scared, and I talked nonstop. "Is this really it, Honey? Am I really going to have the baby?"

"You're ten days late, Barb," John said. "It has to be. You feel okay?"

"Sure," I answered. But inside, a voice whimpered: *No! What am I doing here? I don't know anything about babies. I'm frightened. What's going to happen? Where's my mommy?*

As we entered the hospital at the naval station, a nurse spoke briskly: "Wait over there, Lieutenant. Barbara, you come with me." John gave me a thumbs-up as I was whisked into an elevator. Navy regulations did not allow a husband to stay with his wife during labor.

The nurse escorted me into a small room on the fifth floor with a bed and little else.

"I really don't know what to expect," I blurted. "We just moved here, and well, no one has told me what you do when you have a baby."

The nurse smiled. "Nature will take its course," she replied. "Now take off your clothes, put on this gown and a corpsman will be in to prep you in just a few minutes."

"A corps*man*?"

"Honey, believe me, he's seen plenty of women."

I put on the short scratchy gown and lay on the bed, feeling vulnerable and exposed. My belly clenched and I cried out, suddenly wanting someone—anyone—to come. No one had explained the birth process to me. I guess they thought I knew, but everything had happened so fast: getting married, learning I was pregnant three months later, the Navy moving us just weeks before my due date.

"I wish you'd waited to start your family," my mother had written from Germany, where she and my Air Force colonel father had been transferred three weeks after my wedding.

If Mom were here, I'd feel so much better, I thought. She'd take charge of everything. I pictured her giving the baby instructions: "Hurry up, now, we don't have all night."

But Mom wasn't with me. Nor was John. Nor anyone.

Then I remembered something. I managed to pull myself out of bed, and waddled over to the closet to retrieve my purse. I felt around inside, and my fingers closed over the nubbly string of beads. A rosary. The one my Catholic mother had given me to carry at my wedding.

These tiny white beads made me feel less alone. Clutching the strand, I whispered the prayers over and over as the pains grew more intense. Then the corpsman returned and moments later, I blinked beneath the bright lights of the delivery room.

"Push," commanded the voice of a doctor I'd never seen before. "Push." So I did. I'd never heard of breathing, panting or going with the flow. But I prayed in rhythm with the pain and the pushing. And then, a final push and a squall. The doctor placed my baby girl, still sticky and slippery, right on my stomach. Instantly, I loved her. I went to sleep and the rosary fell from my hand.

The sharp crack of thunder brought me back to the present. Lightning flared, and raindrops pelted the ground.

Having a baby will be different for Sony, I thought again. *She and her husband will do it together.* But hadn't she said she was glad I was going to be there?

I burst into tears, for I knew the answer to my question all too well. And then I thought of my own mother. I still needed her. But she was leaving me. She was bound for a place unknown, and I didn't want her to go. I didn't want her to die.

The next day I called her. "Still no baby," I announced.

Her voice sounded faint but matter-of-fact. "Tell Sony to get a move on," she said. "Say I said so. And let her know I want a girl."

"Kevin wants a boy," I said.

"Men always say that, but then they go crazy over their daughters. Besides, it's Sony I'm thinking about. I want

Sony to know the joy"—her voice faded, then rose—"the joy I've known in having a daughter."

"Why Mom!" I exclaimed, genuinely touched. "Thank you. You've never said that before."

"Well, come as soon as you can."

But three more days passed before Kevin called me at 4:00 A.M. "It's happening," he said. I threw on my clothes and sped through dark silent streets to the hospital. Kevin soon appeared wearing surgical greens, and grinning widely. "Meet your grandson," he said, as he held out a bundle wrapped in white. The baby's mouth opened in a tiny yawn. *Child of my child!* I thought to myself, suddenly giddy. Gently, I carried him into the room where my daughter lay in bed, her hair matted with sweat, her skin still flushed.

"Thanks for staying, Mom," she said, clasping my hand. "I'm not exactly sure why it mattered so much, but it did."

"I know, Honey."

"Will you go out to be with Grammy now?"

"I'll catch a flight this afternoon."

"Tell her about the baby, Mom,"

"Don't worry, Honey, I will."

When the airport limo dropped me off at my mother's and she opened the front door, I swallowed hard. In the pale California light, she seemed so old. Her cheeks were gaunt, and her eyes had a yellowish cast. Her belly was bloated with the tumor. I realized suddenly how heroic she had been to whisper to me, day after day, "Stay with your daughter 'til she has her baby."

I dropped my suitcase. "Mom, you look so ill. I had no idea. Here, let me help you."

She uttered no protest as I led her—this independent mother who hated being told what to do—into her bedroom. As I lowered her to the bed, she gasped.

"Mom, are you in pain?"

"A little." Her lips whitened. "It comes and goes."

Her hand felt dry, like paper that flutters in the wind and disintegrates. I pulled up the comforter.

"I brought you something," I said. Her eyes, which were half-closed, opened a little. I pulled from my suit pocket the gift I'd been saving for her. "Mom, do you remember this?"

Small white beads. "My rosary? The one I gave you? I thought you'd lost it."

"I almost did once. A hospital corpsman found it for me."

"After all these years," she whispered, amazed.

I gently wrapped the rosary around her fingers. She closed her eyes, but when I tiptoed to the door and looked back, she was still holding the rosary tight.

I leaned my head against the cool glass of my mother's patio door. As if glimpsing a reflection, I saw my daughter, cradling my new grandson. Behind her, I could see myself, carrying my infant daughter. In the shadows was my mother holding me. And then I seemed to discern, like a strand of beads stretching on forever, an endless procession of mothers with their babies. And for an instant, before the tears came, I clung to the image and smiled.

Barbara Bartocci

More Chicken Soup?

Many of the stories and poems you have read in this book were submitted by readers like you who had read earlier *Chicken Soup for the Soul* books. We are planning to publish five or six *Chicken Soup for the Soul* books every year. We invite you to contribute a story to one of these future volumes.

Stories may be up to 1,200 words and must uplift or inspire. You may submit an original piece, something you have read or your favorite quotation on your refrigerator door.

To obtain a copy of our submission guidelines and a listing of upcoming *Chicken Soup* books, please write, fax or check one of our Web sites.

Chicken Soup for the *(Specify Which Edition)* **Soul**
P.O. Box 30880 • Santa Barbara, CA 93130
fax: 805-563-2945
To e-mail or visit our Web site:
www.chickensoup.com

You can also visit the *Chicken Soup for the Soul* site on America Online at keyword: chickensoup.

Just send a copy of your stories and other pieces, indicating which edition they are for, to any of the above addresses.

We will be sure that both you and the author are credited for your submission.

For information about speaking engagements, other books, audiotapes, workshops and training programs, please contact any of the authors directly.

Supporting Parents and Children of the World

In the spirit of supporting parents and children everywhere, the publisher and coauthors of *Chicken Soup for the Parent's Soul* will donate a portion of the proceeds from this book to:

Children's Wish Foundation International, Inc.
P.O. Box 28785
Atlanta, Georgia 30358
Phone: 800-323-WISH (9474)
Web site: *www.childrenswish.org*

Children's Wish Foundation International, Inc., is a nonprofit organization dedicated to fulfilling a favorite wish for children afflicted with a high-risk, life-threatening illness. Founded in 1985 by a mother who lost her eldest child to cancer, the foundation has been responsible for bringing a special moment of joy into the lives of thousands of children from thirty-two countries around the world. The immediate family is included in the wish fulfillment, so that the child and family can share in the experience and create happy memories together.

Information concerning Children's Wish Foundation International, Inc., may be obtained from the Web site or by writing to the above address. Please call to refer a child or make a donation.

Proceeds from this book will also be donated to:

**International Network for Children and Families
(INCAF) Foundation**
P.O. Box 357582
Gainesville, FL 32635
Phone: 904-377-2176
Fax: 904-388-3536
Web site: *www.redirectingbehavior.com*

The International Network for Children and Families (INCAF) Foundation provides scholarships to parents who cannot afford to take parenting classes and to professionals who want to start a career teaching parenting courses but lack funding. INCAF teaches courses to enrich the lives of children in families and schools. The Redirecting Children's Behavior parenting course gives parents the tools to empower their children to want to cooperate. Instead of yelling, bribing, threatening and punishing, parents learn more than one hundred practical skills for effectively dealing with everyday situations such as temper tantrums, power struggles, homework and chores. As a result of the course, children learn self-control, responsibility and how to be more self-directed. INCAF has 350 instructors in fifteen countries.

Reference Information

We are happy to include information on the following organizations for parents who need help or who want to help others. Please contact them directly for information, and support them with your time and money.

For Parents Who Need Help

Autism Research Institute (ARI), 4182 Adams Avenue, San Diego, CA 92116, Phone: 619-281-7165, Fax: 619-563-6840, Web site: *www.autism.com/ari.* ARI is the hub of a worldwide network of parents and professionals. It is a nonprofit organization that conducts and fosters scientific research designed to improve the methods of diagnosing, treating and preventing autism. ARI disseminates research findings worldwide to parents seeking help.

CEDU Family of Services, 110 Main Street, Sandpoint, Idaho 83864, Phone: 800-858-1933, Fax: 208-263-3461, Web site: *www.cedu.com.* CEDU Family of Services continues to be the leader in emotional-growth education for young people. Their boarding schools and therapeutic adventure programs offer struggling teenagers emotional growth, challenging academics and practical learning opportunities. They provide adolescents with the skills necessary to approach life with greater confidence and success. Programs are located in Idaho and California, and enrollment is accepted year-round, seven days a week.

*TOUGH*LOVE International, P.O. Box 1069, Doylestown, PA 18901, Phone: 800-333-1069, Fax: 215-348-9874, Web site: *www.toughlove.org. TOUGH*LOVE International is a nonprofit, self-help organization that provides education and ongoing support to families, empowering parents and young people to accept responsibility for their actions. Their network strives to make communities a safe place to live by empowering people through *TOUGH*LOVE community-based self-help programs. When requesting information, please include a #10 self-addressed stamped envelope.

National Down Syndrome Society (NDSS), 666 Broadway, New York, NY 10012, Phone: 212-460-9330, Web site: *www.ndss.org.* NDSS was established as a nonprofit organization in 1979 to ensure that all people with Down syndrome have the opportunity to achieve their full potential in community life. NDSS is now the largest nongovernmental supporter of Down syndrome research in the United States. NDSS works to increase public awareness about Down syndrome and discover its underlying causes through research, education and advocacy.

For Parents Who Want to Help

Local Foster Parents Associations, Web site: *www.fosterparents.com*. If you are concerned about family violence and have ever considered bringing a neglected child into your home, there is a child out there who desperately needs your love. Please contact the Foster Parents Association in your own community by checking the Web site, which provides links to Foster Parents Associations around the United States and Canada.

Foster Parents PLAN International, Web site: *www.plan-international.org*. If you would like to sponsor a deprived child from a developing country for a few dollars a month, PLAN International needs your help. Founded in 1937, PLAN is a nonprofit, humanitarian, child-focused development agency without religious, political or governmental affiliation. Child sponsorship is the basic foundation of the organization.

Organ Donations, Web site: *www.organdonation.org*. This public-information Web site will answer all your questions about the life-giving decision to become an organ donor. In the event of an emergency, your loss could mean a life saved somewhere else.

Other Resources

Web Sites for Parents

www.parentsoup.com
www.parentsplace.com
www.abcparenting.com
www.parentingteens.com
www.parentsworld.com

Suggested Reading

Coburn, Karen L. and Madge Lawrence Treeger. *Letting Go: A Parent's Guide to Understanding the College Years.* New York: HarperCollins Publishers, Inc., 1997.

Riera, Michael. *Uncommon Sense for Parents with Teenagers.* Berkeley, Calif.: Celestial Arts Publishing Co., 1995.

Who Is Jack Canfield?

Jack Canfield is a bestselling author with thirty-nine books published, including twenty-one *New York Times* bestsellers. In 1998 *USA Today* declared that Jack Canfield and his writing partner, Mark Victor Hansen, sold more books during the previous year than any other author in the United States. Jack and Mark also have a syndicated *Chicken Soup for the Soul* newspaper column through King Features and a weekly column in *Woman's World* magazine. He has appeared on numerous television shows including *Good Morning America*, *20/20*, *Eye to Eye*, CNN's *Talk Back Live*, PBS and the BBC.

Jack is the parent of three boys—twenty-five-year-old Oran, twenty-two-year-old Kyle and ten-year-old Christopher. He has also conducted seminars on Parenting for High Self-Esteem for tens of thousands of parents in the United States and Canada.

Jack conducts keynote speeches for about seventy-five groups each year. His clients have included schools and school districts in all fifty states, over one hundred education associations including the American School Counselors Association and Californians for a Drug Free Youth, plus corporate clients such as AT&T, Campbell Soup, Clairol, Domino's Pizza, GE, New England Telephone, Re/Max, Sunkist, Supercuts and Virgin Records.

Jack conducts an annual seven-day Training of Trainers program in the areas of building self-esteem and achieving peak performance in all areas of your life. The program attracts educators, counselors, parenting trainers, corporate trainers, professional speakers, ministers, youth workers and interested others.

To contact Jack for further information about his books, tapes and trainings, or to schedule him for a keynote speech, please contact:

P.O. Box 30880
Santa Barbara, CA 93130
Phone: 805-563-2935
Fax: 805-563-2945
To e-mail or visit our Web site: *www.chickensoup.com*

Who Is Mark Victor Hansen?

Mark Victor Hansen is a professional speaker who, in the last twenty years, has made over four thousand presentations to more than 2 million people in thirty-two countries. His presentations cover sales excellence and strategies; personal empowerment and development; and how to triple your income and double your time off.

Mark has spent a lifetime dedicated to his mission to make a profound and positive difference in people's lives. Throughout his career, he has inspired hundreds of thousands of people to create a more powerful and purposeful future for themselves while stimulating the sale of billions of dollars worth of goods and services.

Mark is a prolific writer and has authored *Future Diary, How to Achieve Total Prosperity* and *The Miracle of Tithing*. He is coauthor of the *Chicken Soup for the Soul* series, *Dare to Win* and *The Aladdin Factor* (all with Jack Canfield) and *The Master Motivator* (with Joe Batten).

Mark has also produced a complete library of personal empowerment audio- and videocassette programs that have enabled his listeners to recognize and use their innate abilities in their business and personal lives. His message has made him a popular television and radio personality, with appearances on ABC, NBC, CBS, HBO, PBS and CNN. He has also appeared on the cover of numerous magazines, including *Success, Entrepreneur* and *Changes*.

Mark is a big man with a heart and spirit to match—an inspiration to all who seek to better themselves.

For further information about Mark write:

P.O. Box 7665
Newport Beach, CA 92658
phone: 949-759-9304 or 800-433-2314
fax: 949-722-6912
Web site: *www.chickensoup.com*

Who Is Kimberly Kirberger?

Kimberly is the president and founder of Inspiration and Motivation for Teens, Inc. (I.A.M. 4 Teens, Inc.), a corporation formed entirely to work with and for teens. It is her strong belief that teens deserve recognition, a more positive image and better treatment within our society.

When she is not writing, Kimberly spends her time working for the empowerment of teenagers and the improvement of teen education. She provides a Web site that is designed as a safe and comfortable environment for teens to discuss complex issues, and give each other support and encouragement.

She reads the thousands of e-mails, letters and stories sent to her each month, and travels around the country speaking to high school students and parents, using humor and compassion to bridge the gap of miscommunication. She has appeared as a teen consultant on television and radio shows, including *Geraldo*, MSNBC, Fox Family Channel's *Parenting 101* and the *Terry Bradshaw Show*.

Kimberly created the *Teen Love* series in answer to the questions teens most often ask her, and to enable them to gain wisdom and choose more wisely when making decisions in love and relationships. The bestselling *Teen Love: On Relationships* and *Teen Love: A Journal on Relationships* are the first books in the series. *Teen Love: On Friendship* will be released in Fall 2000. She is coauthor of the *New York Times* bestseller *Chicken Soup for the Teenage Soul*, *New York Times* #1 bestsellers *Chicken Soup for the Teenage Soul II* and *Chicken Soup for the Teenage Soul III*, *Chicken Soup for the Teenage Soul Journal* and *Chicken Soup for the College Soul*.

Kimberly saw her utmost dream come to fruition when she cofounded the Teen Letter Project (T.L.P.) with donations from sales of her books. Under Kim's guidance, the staff of teenagers is responsible for answering the thousands of heartfelt letters received from other teenagers. Together they reach out to teens in trouble and let them know that there are those who care. They encourage them to seek outside help and support for their problems, and reassure them that they are not alone in these challenging years.

For further information about I.A.M. 4 Teens, Inc., please contact:

P.O. Box 936
Pacific Palisades, CA 90272
phone: 310-573-3655
fax: 310-573-3657
e-mail: *kim@IAM4Teens.com*
Web site: *www.IAM4Teens.com*

Who Is Raymond Aaron?

Raymond Aaron is a professional speaker and business coach. Over a career spanning two decades, he has mentored thousands of Americans and Canadians to achieve brilliant new heights of entrepreneurial and investment success using proven principles.

Raymond offers his wisdom in a worldwide coaching service called The Monthly Mentor which teaches you to double your income doing what you love. Thousands of his monthly clients have dramatically increased their net worth and income. Indeed, hundreds have become millionaires—in a surprisingly short time—following his guidance.

He has been on many major radio and TV talk shows, including *The Phil Donahue Show,* and has delivered more than four thousand seminars, inspiring and educating his audiences in his patented mentoring techniques for achieving outrageous success *"automagically."*

Raymond's speeches are powerful, enjoyable, educational, Contrarian, insightful and lots of fun. His commanding and entertaining style offers practical insights and unique business tools not available anywhere else.

His most popular audiotape program is *Double Your Income Doing What You Love,* a double-cassette package selling for $199. One of the unique benefits of this taped program is that you will learn how to eliminate all messes from your life. As a special bonus, you can listen to it free at *www.UnprecedentedProsperity.com,* or e-mail your credit card number and expiration date, and Raymond will mail it to you for $10 shipping. Also, see the Web site for other new offers.

Raymond's favorite motto is: *"Bite off more than you can chew, then chew like crazy!"*

To be mentored by Raymond, engage him as a speaker or obtain his audiotapes, please contact The Raymond Aaron Group at:

2-9225 Leslie Street
Richmond Hill, ON, Canada L4B 3H6
phone: 905-881-8995, ext. 1
fax: 905-881-8996
e-mail: *success@aaron.com*
Web site: *www.UnprecedentedProsperity.com*

Contributors

Alvin Abram is the author of several international award-winning trade papers on the graphics industry. In-house publications that he has designed have won international awards. He is the author of the non-fiction book, *The Light After the Dark*, published by Key Porter Books, and more than twenty short stories published over the past three years.

Christy Chappelear Andrews began working with Children's Wish Foundation International in 1991 and now serves as Vice President of Operations and Communications. In raising awareness for Children's Wish, she has appeared on several major talk shows and been published in various magazines. Christy lives in her hometown of Atlanta, Georgia, with her husband, Johnny, and her beloved dog, Bailey. Contact CWFI at 1-800-323-9474.

Marguerite Annen is a wife, mother and law school graduate. She is currently on the Board of the Ontario Association of Children's Aid Societies, as well as the Transitional Council for the Ontario College of Social Service. The Annen family struggles each day to cope with the loss of Mary Jo, who was the heart of their family, and are grateful for the unfailing support of friends and family.

Doreen S. Austman grew up on a farm in Saskatchewan, Canada. She started writing short stories and poems in her teen years, mainly for family events, but soon became busy with family and business. In 1987, she joined the Writers Alliance group in Saskatchewan, Canada. She now writes mainly for fun and has been published in local papers and magazines.

Ruth Ayers is a seventy-seven-year-old widow who spends quite a bit of her spare time languishing in fond memories and reliving poignant stories. "Bedtime Stories Across the Miles" is one of the many splendid 'rainbows' she carries in her heart.

Kathrine A. Barhydt lives in Bullhead, Arizona, and is the mother of three adult children: Susan, Gary Jr. and Sandra. She was a legal secretary most of her life and is presently a court clerk. This is her first entry into the world of writing. Her story was gleaned from her youngest daughter, Sandra; however, it is dedicated to all of her children.

Donna Barstow feels blessed to be a cartoonist. Her special drawings appear in over one hundred forty-five newspapers, books and magazines, including the *Los Angeles Times, The New Yorker,* and *Chicken Soup for the Soul* books. Write to her at *dbarstow@hotmail.com* or see more of her cartoons at *www.reuben.org/dbarstow.*

Barbara Bartocci is an award-winning author and speaker. Her latest books are *Midlife Awakenings: Discovering the Gifts Life Has Given Us* (Ave Maria Press, Notre Dame) and *Nobody's Child Anymore: Inspiration and Comfort When Your Parents Die* (Sorin Press). She is a keynote speaker at major women's conferences and for church groups throughout North America. She can be reached by e-mail at *BBartocci@aol.com.*

Martha Beck is a contributing editor to *Redbook, Mademoiselle* and *Real Simple* magazines. She is also a sociologist, with B.A., M.A. and Ph.D. degrees from Harvard University. Martha has written several books, including *Expecting Adam,* a memoir describing the birth of Adam, who has Down syndrome. She appears weekly as a "relationship expert" on the television program *Good Day Arizona.* Martha lives in Phoenix with her husband and three children.

Bobbi Bisserier lives with her husband in the San Francisco Bay area. Currently, Bobbi operates her own business in advertising specialty products. Her family is very close and Lara's difficult life has brought them even closer. She continues to bring great joy into all of their lives. Bobbi can be reached by e-mail at *bjb@pacbell.net.*

Bits & Pieces, the magazine that inspires the world, has motivated and amused millions for almost thirty years. For your free issue, call 1-800-526-2554. Available in English, Spanish and Japanese.

Mary-Ann Joustra Borstad, the daughter of Norwegian immigrants, grew up in New Jersey with her parents' construction business. A Florida resident, Mary-Ann began a part-time residential houseplan design service twenty years ago to supplement her family income. The mother of three daughters, she now works full time with her business, the sole source of income and pride for her family. Contact her at *k4m@bellsouth.net.*

Laurin Broadbent is an investigator for Child Protective Services with the Clark County Family and Youth Services and the mother of two daughters, Courtney and Carli. She and her husband, Kevin, live in Henderson, Nevada. She hopes to one day be a published fiction novelist.

Lori Broadfoot is an artist and writer. She lives in Winnipeg, Manitoba, Canada, with her husband and two children. Lori can be reached by e-mail at *lori@pathwayspublishing.com.*

Leo Buscaglia (1924-1998) was a well-loved author and lecturer focusing on the dynamics of human relations, especially the topic of love. His books have been bestsellers from Japan to Turkey, with five at once appearing on the American Best Sellers List in the 1980s. His Web site is *www.buscaglia.com.*

Dave Carpenter has been a full-time cartoonist since 1981. His cartoons have appeared in such publications as *Harvard Business Review, Barrons, Wall Street Journal, Forbes, Better Homes & Gardens, Saturday Evening Post, Good Housekeeping* and *Woman's World.* Dave can be reached at P.O. Box 520, Emmetsburg, IA 50536.

Judy E. Carter has been a high school English and French teacher for thirteen years. She has an Honors Degree in English, and currently teaches in the London, Ontario area. Married with four teenage stepchildren, she enjoys creative writing. She thanks her husband for his encouragement, and her family and stepkids for inspiring her stories. This is her first published work. Contact her at *teddyp@ican.net*.

A. W. Cobb is a fifty-four-year-old electrician, born and raised in rural Virginia, who now makes his home in Stoneville, North Carolina. His spelling is atrocious and his grammar is not much better, therefore he writes primarily to relieve stress and tension, and to ease his mind. He believes it's better than Prozac!

Elizabeth Cobb resides in North Carolina. Separated after almost thirty years of marriage, she writes in her spare time because it quiets her soul and calms her spirit. She works for Proctor and Gamble to keep the gas and electricity from being turned off. She is among the hordes in transition, drifting toward, she hopes, at least a brief interlude with happiness.

The Compleat Mother magazine, known affectionately to its fifteen thousand mother subscribers in fourteen countries as *The Mother,* is the radical voice of pregnancy, birth and breastfeeding. Founded in Canada in 1985, *The Mother* embraced stories of home birth, water birth and breastfeeding toddlers long before mainstream media found those subjects tolerable. For more information on *The Mother* go to their Web site at *www. compleatmother.com.*

David Cooney's cartoons and illustrations have been published in a variety of magazines including *USA Weekend, American Legion, Mutual Funds* and *The Chronicle of Higher Education.* His cartoons run in numerous newspapers under the title *Twisted View.* David lives with his wife, Marcia, and two children in the small Pennsylvania town of Mifflinburg. His Web site is *www.davidcooney.com* and he can be reached at *david@davidcooney.com.*

Cheryl Costello-Forshey is a poet whose work appears in four previous *Chicken Soup for the Soul* books, as well as *Stories for the Teen's Heart* and *Stories for a Faithful Heart.* Cheryl also writes commissioned pieces for individuals, and is currently searching for a publisher for her first book of poetry, *Heart Impressions.* She can be reached by phone or fax at 740-757-9217.

Elaine Decker lives in Vancouver with her cat, Franklin. She has always been a teacher and currently works in continuing education at a university. Although her children are now grown, they continue to teach her every day by asking difficult questions.

James Dobson, Ph.D., is founder and president of Focus on the Family. He is also the bestselling author of *The New Dare to Discipline, The Strong-Willed Child, Parenting Isn't for Cowards, Love for a Lifetime* and *Life on the Edge.* Dr. Dobson and his wife are the parents of two grown children.

Kittie Ellis is a proud, stay-at-home, full-time mother of four children. She volunteers within the school, promoting literacy among children and is involved with fundraising. She loves spending time with her family and friends, and enjoys being an active member of women's writing and craft groups.

Janie Emaus has been writing short stories and poems since she was a little girl. Her work has been published in magazines and newspapers across the country. She lives in Southern California with her loving husband, Rick, her creative daughter, Anna, and her devoted dog, Angel Boo Boo. Janie can be reached at *zarnt@aol.com*.

Elizabeth Enns is a retired nurse living in Manitoba, Canada. She has traveled with her husband to many parishes and mission stations around the world. She is proud to have six children, all with careers in caring professions, and loves living right next door to one set of children and grandchildren. She is deeply grateful to *Chicken Soup for the Soul* for its soul-lifting literature, something so essential for the world today.

Susan Farr-Fahncke is a freelance writer, wife and mother of four living in Kaysville, Utah. She runs a Web site of free daily inspirational stories, *www.2THEHEART.com*. She has written stories for other *Chicken Soup* books, *Stories for the Heart* series, *Whispers from Heaven, Wisdom* and other magazines. Contact Susan at *Susan@theheart.com* or 1325 North Highway 89, Suite 315, Farmington, Utah 84025.

Myrna Flood has been an Alaskan businesswoman for the past twenty-five years. An aspiring writer, she now resides in Bend, Oregon. Her story is dedicated to her one and only son, Brandon. She can be reached at *MyrnF@aol.com*.

Peter Fonda is as accomplished a director as he is an actor. From early movies including *Tammy and the Doctor* and *Dirty Mary, Crazy Larry*, to 1995's *Nadja*, Fonda has starred in and directed a wide range of films that have appealed to audiences of all types. He continues his work in independent filmmaking as an actor and director, and recently wrote his memoir, *Don't Tell Dad* (Hyperion, 1998).

Hunter S. Fulghum is a writer trapped in the body of a telecommunications engineer. He is married and the father of two very fine children. In his free time, he enjoys rock climbing and scuba diving. Hunter has authored "Like Father, Like Son," "Office Dirty Tricks," and "You're Not Getting Better, You're Getting Older," as well as numerous articles. He can be reached at *moab_98011@yahoo.com*.

Zan Gaudioso is a freelance writer whose stories have appeared in newspapers across the country. Zan has a degree in special education for the deaf and now teaches sign language, as well as teaching deaf children and adults. She is part of a landmark program, the first to utilize sign language to foster verbal language skills in autistic children. She currently lives with her fiancé and their dog, Delilah, in Pacific Palisades, California. She can be reached at *zannie1@aol.com*.

Ellyn L. Geisel resides in Pueblo, Colorado. Having raised her sons to be good citizens and excellent "husband material," she retired from her twenty-year career as a stay-at-home mom and is concentrating full-time on her writing.

Her guest columns in lifestyle commentary have appeared in several Colorado newspapers. Current projects include books for children and young readers, and a parenting book.

Eileen Goltz is a freelance writer living in Ft. Wayne, Indiana with her husband and two sons. She writes for a variety of newspapers and magazines and her first book is being published this summer.

Beverley Bolger Gordon is a high school teacher and counts her blessings every day (sometimes twice!). These include her husband Paul, daughter Taylor Jae, and her extended circle of loving and supportive family and friends. A "video of her life" outside the classroom would include folk-art painting, crafts, singing and enjoying Lake Temiskaming. She lives in Haileybury, Ontario, Canada.

Rabona Gordon is busy raising three of her five children, who are inspiration for much of her poetry. She lives in Marietta, Georgia, with Montana, an up-and-coming poet, twins Sam and Eli, both excellent artists, her oldest son B.J. Turner, an accomplished guitarist, and her "granddog" Abbey. Rabona can be reached by e-mail at *Rabona.Gordon@Respironics.com.*

Sheila Hammock Gosney writes Christian poetry and is a full-time housewife. Born and raised in Hannibal, Missouri, she now resides in Monroe City, Missouri. Contact her at *gosney@nemonet.com* for information about her Web site and free poetry. She dedicates the poem in this book to the memory of her friend, Marta English Davidson.

Kevin Hann is an award-winning writer and photographer who has been with the *Toronto Sun* for eleven years. He and wife Donna have two adorable children—Nicole, 6, and Alexandra, 5. In memory of Rachel, please consider becoming an organ donor and make relatives aware of your wishes.

Christie A. Hansen is a wife and mother of three young children. Sensing that parents wanted to hear from someone besides "experts," in October 1997 she began her self-syndicated column, "From the Trenches." Her weekly columns give readers a chance to laugh and reflect on ways to enjoy the challenge of raising children. Her column currently appears in eight papers across five states. Contact her by e-mail at *christiehansen@usa.net.*

C. J. Herrmann lives in the woods outside Los Angeles with his lovely wife of ten years and their magical three-year-old son. He's fascinated by stories about peak performance and the infinite reach of human potential, and has published numerous articles on an eclectic range of topics. He is currently working on his second novel. Contact him at 310-455-1843 or *Siege@ix.netcom.com.*

Mary Hiland is the director of volunteers at the Central Ohio Radio Reading Service. One of her other stories about being a blind parent appeared in the December 1974 issue of *Redbook*. In addition to running, she is also a cross-country skier, a long-distance tandem cyclist and a motivational speaker. She can be reached at *maryhila@cgfn.org.*

Margaret Hill writes articles, short stories and young adult books. Recent titles are *Coping with Family Expectations* (Rosen, 1990) and *So What Do I Do About Me?* (Teacher Ideas Press, Libraries Unlimited, Englewood, Colorado, 1993).

Bunny Hoest is one of the most widely read cartoonists today, reaching nearly 200 million diverse readers every week. She has produced *The Lockhorns, Agatha Crumm, What a Guy!* and *Hunny Bunny's Short Tale,* distributed internationally by King Features, as well as *Laugh Parade* featuring Howard Huge for *Parade.* Known as "The Cartoon Lady," this dynamic and versatile talent has twenty-five bestselling anthologies and a host of exciting projects in the works.

Bill Holton is a freelance writer living in Key West, Florida. He can be reached by e-mail at *bholton@reporters.net.*

Dawn and Tim Johnson have been married for twelve years and live in rural southwestern Alberta, Canada. Together they have five children, four on the earth plane and one in the spiritual realm. Dawn is primarily a homemaker and occasionally facilitates for the Hoffman Quadrinity Process—a seven-day residential personal development program.

Bil Keane draws the internationally syndicated cartoon *The Family Circus,* which appears in more than fifteen hundred newspapers. Created in 1960, it is based on Keane's own family: his wife, Thel, and their five children. Now nine grandchildren provide most of the inspiration.

Dan Keenan has worked as a sportswriter in the newspaper business since 1981. He's married, with two sons. Dan is thrilled to share the true version of his life story, which Hollywood made into a 1997 movie, *1,000 Men and a Baby.* He's excited to be working with Janet Matthews in producing the full-length book version of this incredible story called *The Navy's Baby.* Dan's father, a central character, was head surgeon at Walla Walla Veteran's Administrative Hospital and is now retired.

Cheryl Kierstead is a cook/supervisor, homemaker, foster parent and single mother raising Joey. She is now working on a book for Joey. Cheryl has dedicated herself to the caring and well-being of the children in her community, and now helps young mothers with new babies through her local child welfare agency. She can be reached by e-mail at *cheryl_kierstead@yahoo.ca.*

Douglas Kramp lives with his daughter in Dallas, Texas. He is coauthor of *Living with the End in Mind,* and speaks worldwide about it and related topics including "Parenting with the End in Mind" and spiritual discovery. Doug has appeared on many radio and TV shows including *Oprah* and *20/20.* Doug is Chief Executive Officer of *ZixMail.com* and Executive Vice President of ZixIt Corp. (Nasdaq: ZIXI). Contact Doug in his office at 214-370-2017 or *dkramp@zixit.com.*

Gary Lautens (1928–1992) was Canada's well-loved humorist and columnist for the *Toronto Star*. During his thirty-year career, his newspaper columns were syndicated throughout Canada, and briefly in the United States. His warm-hearted stories have been compiled into several books, mostly on the family theme. More information can be found at his son Stephen Lauten's Web site, *www.lautens.com*.

Josie Lauritsen is a graduate in Rhetoric and Composition from Arizona State University. She is the second of five children born to a poet (who practices clinical psychology on the side) and a mountain woman (who doubles as an English teacher). Her story is dedicated to Benny for inspiring the poem and Dad for treasuring it.

David Like resides in Orlando, Florida. The story, "Embassy of Hope," is dedicated to his grandmother, Opal Stayley Mathews; his two nieces, Jennifer and Jacqueline; his grandfather, Elzie Roy Mathews; his mother, Patty; and his friend, Chatta Denis Foster. David can be reached at *Beatleman-33@webtv.net*.

Chris Lloyd is a counselor at Crutcher's Serenity House and Manager of Double Rainbow, a clean and sober home for women who want to make a change in their lives. Both are located in beautiful Napa Valley, California. Chris is also a certified Domestic Violence counselor and advocate for Battered Women's Alternative and a loving mother of five. She can be reached at P.O. Box D, Deer Park, CA 94576. She would like to dedicate this story to Bob Crutcher, who is the wind beneath her wings.

Brian Locke lives in Ontario, Canada, with his wife and two teenage girls. He is a retail merchandising specialist with a twenty-six-year background in merchandising, management, operations and training. He is also a motivational speaker. He can be reached by e-mail at *blocke@cgo.wave.ca*.

Wendy Ann Lowden and her husband Steven have been married for twenty-two years and have two incredible teenagers, Kathleen and Michael. Her family is her first love and primary focus. Looking after children has always given back more than she could ever put into the job, so after several other careers, she now works as a full-time nanny. Wendy and her family live in Oakville, Ontario, Canada.

George Eyre Masters was born in Philadelphia, served in Vietnam with the U.S. Marine Corps and graduated from Georgetown University. Over the past twenty-five years his work has been seen in many publications, including *Reader's Digest*. He lives in Maine where he works in real estate, fishes for striped bass and continues to write. Contact him at P.O. Box 1081, Kennebunkport, ME 04046, 207-967-1927, or *gmasters@ispchannel.com*.

Paula Mathers is a full-time wife and mother, and a part-time independent kitchen consultant who sells quality kitchen tools. She, her husband Steve and their three boys have lived in Plano, Texas for nine years.

Janet Matthews is a freelance writer and editor. After twenty years in

Toronto's fast-paced fashion/photography industry, Janet was asked in 1997 by partner Raymond Aaron to help produce *Chicken Soup for the Parent's Soul* and *Chicken Soup for the Canadian Soul*. Additionally, Janet is working with Daniel Keenan to coauthor a book-sized version of "The Navy's Baby," which appears in this book. You can reach Janet at The Raymond Aaron Group at 905-881-8995 or *janet@aaron.com*.

Nancy McBee is a registered nurse and a single mother. She devotes her time to her fifteen-year-old daughter, Courtney, and to her mother, who has Alzheimer's. Nancy has always loved writing and gives credit to her Mom's encouragement as she was growing up. This story is dedicated to parents everywhere who know the joys and struggles of the "World's Greatest Job" . . . parenting. Contact Nancy at *beegirl@seark.net.*

Hanoch McCarty, Ed.D., is a professional speaker, trainer and consultant specializing in motivation, productivity and self-esteem enhancement. Hanoch is one of the most sought-after speakers in the nation because he combines humor and moving stories with practical skills that can be put to work immediately. His books and videotape programs include *Stress and Energy* and *Self-Esteem: The Bottom Line.* He can be reached at P.O. Box 66, Galt, CA 95632 or at 209-745-2212.

Louisa Godissart McQuillen publishes stories and poetry. She's a staff worker in the Kinesiology Department at Penn State University. Louisa lives in Philipsburg, Pennsylvania with an orange Somali cat named "Milo" and "Sharry," a slightly crabby Siamese. Contact her for poetry chapbooks at 525 Decatur Street, Philipsburg, PA 16866-2609. You can reach her by e-mail as well at *LZM4@psu.edu.*

Jan Meek has packed so much into her fifty-four years, her life reads like the plot of a book: from working in the film business with well-known stars; living and working in Saudi Arabia; being elected Mayor of her home town: learning Chinese while backpacking around China, to her *Guinness Book of World Records* Atlantic Rowing record. Now a professional speaker, she's authored the book *101 Atlantic Nights*, the full version of her Atlantic crossing with her son, Daniel. She also has a daughter, Becky, 27. Jan lives in Chipping Norton, England. Contact her at *JaniceMeed@aol.com.*

Anne Metikosh is a bookkeeper and part-time writer. She's an enthusiastic but tone-deaf singer who compensates for the racket with her skill in the kitchen. Chocolate chip cookies are her specialty. She lives in Calgary, Alberta, with her husband, their daughter, two dogs and a horse.

Darlene Montgomery is well known as a speaker and writer on dreams and spirituality. Her company Lifedreams Unlimited has sponsored hundreds of inspirational seminars designed to assist others in finding and living their true purpose. Darlene is the author of *Dream Yourself Awake*, an autobiographical journey through dreams and waking dreams. She can be reached at 416-696-1684 or by e-mail at *lifedreams@idirect.com.*

Beth Mullally is a columnist and senior reporter for the *Times Herald-Record* in Middletown, New York. She is also a regular contributor to *Reader's Digest* and author of the book the *Best of Beth,* a collection of her columns. She and her husband, Bob Quinn, have two sons, two dogs, two cars, two televisions and two mortgages. She can be reached at 914-346-3181 or by e-mail at *bquinn@th-record.com.*

Bob Mullen's three children are now twenty-two, nineteen and sixteen. In the fall of 1999, he retired and now lives with his wife Carol on a thirty-six-foot sailboat. In October 2000, they plan to leave Newport Beach, California, for an extended cruise to Mexico and the South Pacific. Those green with envy may contact him at *BobMullen@aol.com.*

Steve Nease is Art Director of the *Oakville Beaver,* Ontario, Canada, where he lives with his family. In addition to producing the family comic strip "Pud," Nease is a political cartoonist known across Canada. Winner of more than a dozen provincial and national awards, his works appear in over seventy weekly and daily newspapers, *Portfoolio,* an annual collection of Canada's best editorial cartoons, and *Best Editorial Cartoons of the Year,* a collection of the best editorial cartoons in the U.S.

Diane C. Nicholson is a freelance writer, as well as an internationally published, award-winning, professional photographer. Currently she holds the only national accreditation as an equine photographer from the Professional Photographers of Canada. She, her husband, Harry, and son, Ben, own and operate Twin Heart Photo Productions in B. C., Canada. She can be reached at 1-250-375-2528 or *www.twinheartphoto.com.*

Lou Ogston is an elementary school teacher. She was twenty-five when she adopted nine-week-old Darcie. For eight years she was a stay-at-home mom while Darcie and her brother were little. She and her second husband, Jim, live in Winnipeg, with one of her four children still at home. Today, her pride and joy is Darcie's son, Dawson.

Beryl Paintin is a freelance writer in Winnipeg, Manitoba, Canada. She is a columnist for *The Metro,* a local community newspaper. A former member and editor with the Winnipeg Club of Printing House Craftsmen, she has been involved with printing and newspapers for more than thirty years. She is a director with the Assiniboia Chamber of Commerce, Winnipeg. This story is dedicated to Phillip. Beryl can be reached at *bpconsul@escape.ca.*

Sharon Palmer is a freelance writer in Nashville, Tennessee, where most of her work is published locally. Her goal is to publish an inspirational book on living with a disabling medical condition, as she is learning to do. This story is dedicated to her father, Dr. Edward Johnson, for his help and encouragement with her writing, and to Bob Stamps for his unwavering, all-encompassing support. She can be reached at *sharon-palmer@mindless.com.*

Sharon Peerless has written many human interest articles over the years, but this is the first time that she has written for publication about her own family. She lives in Cleveland, Ohio, with her husband, Joel, twin sons, Elie and Benjy, and daughter, Ronit. Contact Sharon at *jsebr@aol.com*.

Bill Petch is a journalist, broadcaster, writer and actor. He lives in Belleville, Ontario, with his wife, Joy, and their children, Miriam and Joel. Bill recently returned to the stage after a fifteen-year absence, making his directorial debut shortly thereafter. "Miriam's Umbrella" is dedicated to his mother, Katherine, who died from breast cancer, and to all who have lost a loved one to the disease.

Debbie Rikley is a single parent working full time, raising two sons and taking courses at night. Writing keeps her focused. She writes from her heart as it helps her to express her feelings and thoughts about life's experiences.

Jewel Sanders and her husband have been Central Missouri farmers for forty-eight years. Jewel is a corn-husk doll artisan, and is assisted in her cottage industry by her children, Scott, Susie and Sherry. Her grandchildren, Kristen, Tracy, Hannah, Jesse and Luke, all help in the corn-husk business.

Andy Skidmore is a wife, mother, grandmother and freelance writer whose works have appeared in *Women's World, The Woman's Weekly, Christian Woman's Magazine, Chicken Soup for the Woman's Soul* and other publications. She is an award-winning amateur photographer, has taught children's and women's classes, and spoken at women's seminars, clubs and teas. She can be reached at *andyskid@aol.com*.

Nicole Smith lives in Colorado. She enjoys writing and loves the Rocky Mountains. She can be reached at P.O. Box 22963, Denver, CO 80222.

D. L. Stewart is a syndicated columnist based in Dayton, Ohio. His blended family includes a daughter, three sons, a stepson, two grandsons and a grandfather. He also has a closet filled with the world's largest collection of obsolete video games.

Marina Tennyson lives in Phoenix, Arizona, with Kenny, her husband of thirty-one years. Citing self-confidence gained from membership in the *TOUGHLOVE* Program, Marina successfully started a home-based business a year ago. She continues to work with *TOUGHLOVE* parents in Arizona on a part-time basis. For more information on the *TOUGHLOVE* program, please visit their Web site at *www.toughlove.org*.

Lori Thomas is the co-founder of the Moebius Syndrome Foundation. When Lori's daughter, Chelsey, was born in 1988 with this rare condition there was no accurate, easily-understood information available. This changed with the establishment of a network of parents and adults all working together to find answers, provide support and build a growing organization that has the respect of the medical community. Reach her at *lorit@netport.com*.

Diane Tullson is a writer in Delta, British Columbia, Canada. She collects stories about her children in a journal that she hopes one day will reveal to them the wonderful workings of their lives on hers. She has written a novel for young adults, and has contributed to *Canadian Living* magazine.

Joe Tye lives in Solon, Iowa, with his family. He is a founder of Never Fear, Never Quit International, and author of the book *Never Fear, Never Quit: A Story of Courage and Perseverance*. For more information about bringing the Never Fear, Never Quit program to your organization, call 800-644-3889, or contact him at *Joe@nfnq.com*.

Sarah J. Vogt, with help from her father, **Ron Vogt,** has written her second feature for the *Chicken Soup* series. Ron, father of three, was raised in Coshocton, Ohio. Retired from Cummins Engine Company, he lives in Columbus, Indiana, where he gave many years to his community. Sarah works as a systems analyst for a law firm in South Florida. Sarah or Ron can be reached at 80 Catalpa Way, Columbus, IN 47201.

Andrea Warren writes from her home in the suburbs of Kansas City, Missouri. She is the author of eight books, including *Orphan Train Rider: One Boy's True Story,* which won the Horn Book Award. Warren's articles have appeared in a long list of publications, ranging from *Reader's Digest* and *Ladies' Home Journal,* to the *Boston Globe* and the *Washington Post.* She can be reached at *AWKansas@aol.com.*

Joan Wiberg is a humorous artist living in the Virginia countryside. She is currently a public school art teacher, a mother and a wife. She has two cats, Nadjia and Juliet.

William G. Wood is a chemical engineer who has composed hundreds of verses over the past forty years. Topics have included love notes to his wife Mary, who died in 1996, and special occasion citations for friends, relatives and business associates. His family includes six daughters, three sons and numerous grandchildren. Mr. Wood can be reached at *wmgwood@aol.com.*

Noreen Wyper was raised in Northern Ontario, Canada. She remained there to teach and raise a family. She has two daughters and two grandchildren. She has a B.A., B. Ed. plus Specialists certificates in primary education and dramatic arts. Recently she graduated from the Children's Institute of Literature. She joyfully spends her retirement years writing.

Harriet Xanthakos is a storyteller, Unitarian chaplain and teacher. She helps couples create wedding ceremonies and services of union, and performs other rites of passage. Working in The Parent-Child Mother Goose Program in Toronto, Canada, she teaches rhymes and songs, and tells stories to caregivers and their young children. Harriet has two daughters and her grandson, David, is her most loyal listener. Contact her at 416-322-5000 or *dg200@freenet.toronto.on.ca.*

David Zinman writes for the *Horry (S.C.) Independent* and was a first-prize winner in the 1998 competition of the National Society of Newspaper Columnists. He was a former reporter for Long Island *Newsday* and the Associated Press bureau in New Orleans. Author of the books, *The Day Huey Long Was Shot* and *50 Classic Motion Pictures*, he is currently at work on a play based on the Long assassination and on a collection of short stories. He can be reached at Box 2030, Pt. Lookout, NY 11569.

Permissions *(continued from page iv)*

The Photograph Album. Reprinted by permission of Alvin Abram. ©1999 Alvin Abram.

The Spinner Plate. Reprinted by permission of Lori Broadfoot. ©1999 Lori Broadfoot.

Coffee Milk and Oreos. Excerpted from *Like Father, Like Son* by Hunter S. Fulghum, ©1996 by Hunter Samuel Fulghum. Used by permission of Putnam Berkley, a division of Penguin Putnam Inc.

Daddy. Reprinted by permission of Laurin Broadbent. ©1997 Laurin Broadbent.

Comic-Book Solomon. Reprinted by permission of Gary Lautens. ©1967 Gary Lautens.

Driving Me Crazy, It Takes a Special Man to Fill a Stepfather's Shoes and *Mapping Life's Journey on the Refrigerator Door.* Reprinted by permission of Beth Mullally. ©1999 Beth Mullally.

I'm Okay. Reprinted by permission of Rabona Gordon. ©1999 Rabona Gordon.

On Becoming a Stepmother and *I Live with an Alien.* Reprinted by permission of Janie Emaus. ©1999 Janie Emaus.

The Other Mother. Reprinted by permission of Jewel Sanders. ©1999 Jewel Sanders.

Daddy's Hair Is Red. As cited in *The Best of Bits & Pieces,* Arthur F. Lenehan, editor, ©1994 The Economics Press, Inc., 12 Daniel Road, Fairfield, NJ 07004-2565 USA; Phone: 800-526-2554 (US/Canada). Fax: 973-227-9742 (US/Canada). E-mail: *info@epinc.com;* Web site: *www.epinc.com.* Please contact The Economics Press, Inc., directly to purchase this book or for subscription information on (or a free sample copy of) the monthly magazine version of *Bits & Pieces.*

A Time for Love. Reprinted by permission of Noreen Wyper. ©1999 Noreen Wyper.

When He Sleeps. Reprinted by permission of Josie Lauritsen. ©1999 Josie Lauritsen.

Defining Love. Reprinted by permission of Eileen Goltz. ©1999 Eileen Goltz.

Housewife's Prayer. Reprinted by permission of Sheila Hammock Gosney. ©1999 Sheila Hammock Gosney.

My Wife Doesn't "Work." Excerpted from *No Sex Please, We're Married.* Reprinted by permission of Gary Lautens. ©1976 Gary Lautens.

The Gift of Life. Reprinted by permission of Beryl Paintin. ©1999 Beryl Paintin.

A Mother's Love Revealed. Reprinted by permission of Nicole Smith. ©1999 Nicole Smith.

Chicken Soup
for the Whole Family

Chicken Soup for the
Expectant Mother's Soul
Code #7966 • Quality Paperback • $12.95

Chicken Soup for Little Souls
Code #8121 • Quality Paperback • $12.95

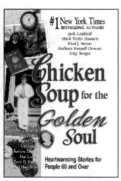

Chicken Soup for the
Golden Soul
Code #7257
Quality Paperback • $12.95

Chicken Soup for the Preteen Soul
Code #8008 • Quality Paperback • $12.95

Books for Living
Books for Life

TeenInk
Code #8164
Quality Paperback • $12.95

Chicken Soup for the Teenage Soul III
Code #7613
Quality Paperback • $12.95

Teen Love: On Friendship
Code #8156
Quality Paperback • $12.95

The 7 Best Things Smart Teens Do
Code #777X
Quality Paperback • $10.95

It's My Life
Code #8334
Quality Paperback • $11.95

Available wherever books are sold.
To order direct: Phone — **800.441.5569** • Online — **www.hci-online.com**
Prices do not include shipping and handling. Your response code is **BKS**.